Gender and Culture

at the Limit of Rights

PENNSYLVANIA STUDIES
IN HUMAN RIGHTS

Bert B. Lockwood, Jr, Series Editor

A complete list of books in the series
is available from the publisher

Gender and Culture at the Limit of Rights

Edited by

Dorothy L. Hodgson

PENN

UNIVERSITY OF PENNSYLVANIA PRESS

PHILADELPHIA

Published by
University of Pennsylvania Press
Philadelphia, Pennsylvania 19104-4112
www.upenn.edu/pennpress

Printed in the United States of America on acid-free paper
10 9 8 7 6 5 4 3 2 1

Library of Congress Cataloging-in-Publication Data
ISBN 978-0-8122-4328-4

Contents

Introduction

Gender and Culture at the Limit of Rights

Dorothy L. Hodgson

Since Charlotte Bunch (1990, 1995) and others first argued in the early 1990s for the need to reframe "human rights" to include, recognize, and support "women's rights," "women's rights are human rights" has become a global mantra, circulated and supported by a vast network of feminist activists, women's organizations, donors, multilateral institutions, and even nation-states.[1] As a result, women (and men) around the world have reframed their often long-standing demands and needs (for political power, economic security, reproductive freedom, and more) in the (seemingly) more powerful language of rights in order to expand the visibility (and thus recognition) of their issues in local, national, and global arenas and to demand accountability from states in ensuring and enforcing their legal rights.

By many accounts, the institutionalization and expansion of women's rights as human rights has been a success, providing an effective and potent way to challenge gender inequality, improve women's legal and political status, and protect women from acts of individual and collective violence (e.g., Hodgson 2002a; Agosín 2001; Merry 2006; Peters and Wolper 1995). Despite these successes, however, a growing number of scholars, policy-makers, and activists have become increasingly wary of the dominance of rights-based approaches to social justice and, increasingly, development. Some allege that human rights is merely a contemporary form of imperial intervention—yet another effort by the Global North to impose its values and views on the Global South (Basu 2000; Ackerly 2008; Oloka-Onyango 2002; Cornwall and Molyneux 2008; Nnaemeka 2005; Mutua 2002). Others claim that despite the seeming success of "women's rights are human rights," the human rights framework is still fundamentally androcentric in its assumptions, institutions, and manifestations (Charlesworth 1994, 1995). Finally, increasing numbers of scholars and activists within and outside the movement are concerned with how "culture" has been deployed and disparaged by some activists and institutions (Abu-Lughod 2002, 2009a; Merry 2006; Narayan 1997).

In contrast to those who easily celebrate or condemn the current ascendancy of the "women's rights are human rights" framework, the authors in the present volume are more circumspect, curious, and careful. Through nuanced historical and discursive analyses and grounded case studies, they seek to examine the very terms of the debate—gender, culture, and rights—and explore the centrality of gender to enduring tensions between "the culture of rights" and "the rights of culture." "Rights," whether environmental, human, indigenous, children's, or women's, are still too often perceived as global or transnational discourses that are produced and circulated by international institutions such as the United Nations, then imposed on "local" communities. Moreover, rights, especially those deemed "universal" or "human," are assumed to be ahistorical and acultural, despite the long histories of struggle over the definitions, meanings, and consequences of certain rights at many scales. In contrast, "cultures" are seen as fundamentally local, moored to specific places, people, and times. Culture (or at least so-called "third world" or "traditional" culture) is often attacked as the obstacle to rights, the impediment to human progress and prosperity. But such views of social progress are themselves predicated on static, ahistorical definitions of cultures.

By taking "gender" rather than "women" seriously as an analytical category and considering the local-global articulations of rights and cultures through a comparative gendered lens, the contributors probe the potential and limitation of the human rights framework as a strategy for gender justice. The chapters explore the specific social histories, political struggles, cultural assumptions, and gender ideologies that have produced certain rights or reframed long-standing debates in the language of rights. The contributors analyze the gender-specific ways that rights-based protocols have been analyzed, deployed, and legislated in the past and present, and the implications for women and men, adults and children, in various social and geographical locations. Questions addressed include, What are the gendered assumptions and effects of the dominance of rights-based discourses for claims to social justice? What kinds of opportunities and limitations does such a "culture of rights" provide to seekers of justice, whether individuals or collectivities, and how are these gendered? How and why do female bodies often become the site of contention in contexts pitting cultural against juridical perspectives?

Together, the chapters speak to central issues in current scholarly and policy debates about gender, culture, and human rights from comparative disciplinary, historical, and geographical perspectives. The authors are scholars, lawyers, and activists. They include five anthropologists, two sociologists, a historian, a linguist, a lawyer, and two lawyer/activists; they hail from the United States, Niger, Tanzania, the Philippines, and South Africa; and their articles explore situated engagements with human rights in Africa, Egypt, Palestine, Kenya, China, India, Mexico, Peru, Tanzania, Zanzibar, and the United States. Each contributor is positioned differently, but most of them have been involved with rights-based activism as activists, advocates, interlocutors, and critics. For example, Sally Goldfarb was an attorney working with the U.S.-based NOW Legal Defense and Education Fund to design and implement the Violence Against Women Act (VAWA) that she examines in her chapter. Similarly, Mary Jane Real, a Filipina lawyer and activist, was a founding member and coordinator of Women Human Rights Defenders International Coalition, the organization she discusses in her chapter. Salma Maoulidi, a Tanzanian activist, herself experienced many of the radical transformations she describes in the gendered legal culture of Zanzibar, as a Zanzibari resident. As an anthropologist, Dorothy Hodgson has worked with and studied Maasai activists for decades, most recently in terms of their involvement in the international indigenous rights movement. Robyn Rodriguez, a sociologist, has worked to document and improve the conditions of immigrant detainees in New Jersey. And the list goes on. All the contributors offer unique access and insight to the cases through either direct involvement or extended ethnographic and historical investigations.

Keywords: Gender, Culture, Rights

As the title of the volume suggests, the key terms of analysis are gender, culture, and rights. Although each of these concepts has its own complicated intellectual and political genealogy, our purpose is to examine their intersections and articulations in the formulation and circulation of rights-based discourses as a means for gender justice. In what follows, I briefly outline how each of these terms contributes to and complicates our analyses and suggest what some of the limits to a rights-based approach might be.

Although "gender" is often conflated with "women," the concept is analytically useful because it acknowledges that in order to understand the meanings and practices of being a "woman," we must also understand the meanings and practices of being a "man." Thus a gendered analysis includes but also moves beyond questions of whether women have rights, what rights they have, and whether they have gained or lost rights to explore the centrality of gendered ideas and assumptions to the formulation, promotion, and enforcement of human rights discourse, policy and practice, as well as how rights-based discourses presume, produce, reproduce, and transform gender ideologies and relations between and among men and women. Attention to "gender" signals and signifies how the fundamental terms of the debate—women, human, and rights—are dynamic cultural, historical, and political products with variable meanings and manifestations across time and space. For example, several chapters explore how women (and their bodies) variously serve as sites of ethnic pride, colonial intervention, and national reproduction. They describe how various collectivities, including colonizers, states, NGOs, and religious groups, justify their interventions in women's lives by claiming to "protect" their bodies from immoral appearances or unjust bodily practices (Scully, Maoulidi, Merry, Hodgson). Others examine how the implementation of rights not only rework (and legislate) dominant ideas of "proper" femininity (Maoulidi), but also masculinity (Yezer). Moreover, attention to gender can also illuminate other dimensions of rights that are often ignored or devalued—such as rights-claims framed in affective, emotional, or relational terms—like those of the male immigrant detainees in the United States discussed by Rodriguez. International and state laws at once reflect and produce prevailing gendered moral codes, including "approved" bodily practices, "proper" sexual relationships, and normative family formations. And as always, of course, gender relations are complicated and cross-cut by other forms of social distinction and difference such as age, sexual identity, ethnicity, and nationality.

Like gender, "rights," specifically "human rights," are also a cultural, political, and historical category, the product of selection, struggle, and consensus-building. Despite the existence of alternative modes of understanding, defining, and promoting justice, "human rights" have become the dominant model for making both positive (*for* free speech, for example) and negative (such as *against* bodily violence) claims against individuals and collectivities (primarily states) in the contemporary world. Rights-based frameworks have had significant success in advancing the claims of women and men for political representation and legal protection (so-called "first-generation" rights). Yet some scholars question whether such rights-based discourses, with their presumption of an individual, secular, gendered subject and their reliance on state-run legal systems as the mechanisms of implementation and enforcement, can ever be a truly emancipatory strategy for women. Can political strategies based on legal rights fully address the structural contexts and causes of gender-based injustice? Moreover, even for those who support rights-based strategies, significant concerns and questions persist about which claims get translated into rights, how and by whom these claims are translated, whose rights are protected and defended, and which rights become the priorities for advocacy and funding. In other words, when and how does a claim become a human rights issue, specifically a "women's human rights" issue? More fundamentally, what does a "rights frame" enable and what does it ignore, dismiss, or proscribe? Many of the chapters address these questions through tracing when, how, why and by whom rights are mobilized or contested—whether by Maasai women in Tanzania (Hodgson), nostalgic villagers in Peru (Yezer), Muslim women in Kenya (Alidou), indigenous women in Mexico (Stephen), or lesbian activists in India (Levitt and Merry). Others explore how some interventions in the name of women's human rights rely on long discredited but still powerful stereotypes about passive, powerless, "other" women—whether African (Scully) or Muslim (Abu-Lughod). Several chapters describe the persistence of overlapping (and sometimes contradictory) legal systems (including Shari'a courts, customary law, informal modes of dispute resolution, and access to international forums) and examine how everyday people, familiar with the possibilities and limitations of each system, go "forum-shopping" (Merry), that is, they strategically decide where to raise their complaints and issues to have the best chance at success (Abu-Lughod, Merry, Maoulidi).

The final concept that is central to the analytic frameworks of all of the chapters is "culture." Within discussions of human rights and women's human rights, the very definition of "culture" is controversial. Does culture refer to fixed, dated "traditional" practices and beliefs, which are often represented as obstacles to "progress," "enlightenment," and "emancipation" on the part of the "other"—especially poor women living in remote, rural areas—but not a feature of elite societies with their education, mobility, and cosmopolitanism? Or is culture merely performance—clothes, adornment, songs, and dances to be admired and photographed as colorful, nostalgic reminders of simpler times? If, like anthropologists, historians, and other scholars, we understand "culture" to refer to the assumptions, meanings, ideas, and practices that shape and are shaped by people's everyday interactions, then culture is instead a dynamic, historical, contested part of all of our lives and institutions. As such, cultural ideas and practices can be a source of strength as well as oppression, depending on the context and conditions. Moreover, every category of analysis and debate is profoundly cultural—law, rights, gender, human—and therefore open to alternative meanings, interpretations, deployments, and agendas. What does it mean, for example, to be human? Contemporary understandings of "human" in the Global North are histori- cal, cultural, and political products, predicated on certain assumptions about autonomy, personhood, and agency that contrast markedly with more collec- tive, relational, fluid ideas of personhood expressed in other times and places (see, for example, Strathern 1988; Van Wolputte 2004). Thus, for scholars, activists, and policy-makers involved in the women's human rights debates, the questions and concerns about "culture" are similar to those described above for "rights": Who is deploying the language of culture? States? Elites? Activists from the Global North or the Global South? How, why and in what context? Why, as Levitt and Merry ask in their chapter, does "culture" seem to emerge as an issue only in debates about women's rights, not in other do- mains of rights-talk, such as the right to food or the right to freedom from torture? All the chapters show how certain cultural assumptions, especially about appropriate gender ideologies and practices, shape the formulation, re- ception, circulation, implementation, and enforcement of rights, whether in terms of domestic violence law in the United States (Goldfarb); engagements with human rights discourses in Egypt, Palestine, Peru, India, China, and the United States (Abu-Lughod, Yezer, Levitt and Merry); or the challenges of transnational coalition building to protect activists who defend women's human rights (Real).

Engaging the Gendered Culture of Rights

The chapters are organized into three sections that probe different aspects of the tensions between and among gender, culture, and rights. The chapters in Part I, "Images and Interventions," examine the discursive power of certain gendered assumptions and ideologies in the formulation and implementa- tion of human rights and national law. Using a historical lens, Pamela Scully explores the charged interplay of racial and gender ideologies—specifically the image of the suffering African woman—in past and contemporary humanitarian campaigns. Through a gendered genealogical reading of the figure of the African woman in British anti-slavery campaigns, missionary and colonial interventions, and more recent human rights campaigns against gender violence, Scully shows the centrality of recurrent representations of African women as needing protection and "saving" to the elaboration and transnational success of human rights. According to Scully, claims about the supposed "neutrality" of human rights ignore the deeply gendered ideas about what it means to be a woman, the proper relations between men and women, and the hierarchal existence of a private and public sphere that shape the demands and expectations of rights.

Similarly, Salma Maoulidi analyzes how images of specific African women—in this case Muslim women in Zanzibar—inform and reflect their shifting legal rights in the colonial, post-revolutionary, and contemporary periods. Like Scully, Maoulidi investigates who was promoting particular images of women and why, and how these images shaped interventions into their lives. Thus, during the colonial period, British administrators colluded with male authorities to protect women, as the "custodians of culture," from the "modernizing" influences of secular education and "immodest" behavior. The revolutionary government of the 1960s, however, viewed women as "national subjects," to be emancipated from the "repressive" strictures of their male guardians, religious beliefs, and social and sexual regulations. Even in the current era of representative, multiparty democracy and ratification of human rights protocols, images and ideas of appropriate gender roles and relations continue to shape the introduction of new laws and thus the everyday realities of the lives of women and men.

Finally, Sally Goldfarb turns the critical discursive lens on domestic violence laws in the United States to examine how they, like the Zanzibari laws analyzed by Maoulidi, reflect prevailing cultural assumptions about women and gender. After outlining the cultural features of the American legal system, including its privileging of a male perspective, tendency to dichotomize (victims versus perpetrators, public versus private), and reliance on criminalization as the solution to social problems, Goldfarb analyzes how these cultural features, combined with certain cultural assumptions about battered women (especially that they are passive victims), have shaped the design, implementation, and limited effectiveness of domestic violence laws. In order to better meet the needs of battered women, Goldfarb calls for more attention to the diverse cultural and social contexts affecting battered women's lives, recognition of their complicated positions as both victims and agents, and a shift from criminal law to civil law and from negative rights to positive rights.

The chapters in Part II, "Travels and Translations," examine how the production and circulation of human rights discourses have been engaged, appropriated, challenged and reworked in different communities and contexts.[2] Drawing on findings from their collaborative, comparative research, Peggy Levitt and Sally Engle Merry explore the "vernacularization" of human rights by nongovernmental organizations (NGOs) in Peru, China, India, and the United States. According to Levitt and Merry, vernacularization is the process through which individuals and institutions appropriate and customize human rights discourses in ways that make sense in their own cultural space. Based on their findings, they argue that differences between how gender and justice are understood in human rights discourse and in local realities are handled by processes of negotiation and translation, rather than confrontation and conflict: "New ideas are typically adopted where there are areas of fit, resonance with preexisting ideas of justice and order, but they are also used to expand the boundaries of issues or develop new practices of intervention."

Similarly, through a comparative analysis of Egypt and Palestine, Lila Abu-Lughod traces how ideas and elaborations of "Muslim women's rights" travel through various world projects, circulate through debates and documents, organize women's activism in NGOs and transnational cyberspace, and mediate women's lives in rural villages and refugee camps. In Egypt, the three most significant shifts in the "social life" of rights in the last decade have been their governmentalization, their imbrications with Islamic institutions and religious discourses, and their commercialization. In contrast, in Palestine, the "social life" of women's rights can only be understood in the context of the ongoing war and occupation, and thus the consequent politicization and militarization of daily life. Finally, human rights discourses are experienced, mediated, and understood in multiple ways among rural "grassroots" Egyptian women, including through popular television programs, government-sponsored literacy classes, and religious study.

Caroline Yezer, in turn, examines how the proliferation of human rights discourses are experienced in a very different context—that of indigenous highland peasant communities in post-conflict Peru. Far-flung villages that were once militarized under the state of emergency have now become the focus of international aid organizations, human rights groups, and other post-conflict projects either funded by, or coming from, abroad. At the same time, the retreat of state troops and army bases has reduced the military presence in villages, leaving the former war zone with little state presence. Rather than welcoming the discourse of human rights and the demilitarization of the villages, however, some villagers experience the new implementations of human rights law anxiously, as a destabilizing force, and express nostalgia for the macho military discipline of the recent past. They understand the shift in governance in gendered terms that equate village leadership and solidarity with virility and military service and human rights with emasculation.

Finally, Dorothy Hodgson explores how the recent reframing of female genital modification (FGM) from a health issue to a human rights issue has intensified the pressure by international donors, transnational activists, the Tanzanian state, and even Tanzanian feminists on Maasai women activists to focus their energy and resources on its eradication. These groups continue to condemn and even criminalize Maasai for one specific cultural practice—FGM—and use its presence or absence as a measure of Maasai progress and "modernity." In contrast, although Maasai activists are concerned about FGM, they are far more alarmed by the increasing impoverishment, lack of legal rights, and political marginalization of Maasai women and have chosen to concentrate on the priorities of their constituencies—economic security and political empowerment. From their perspective, the conflict over FGM is not a "problem of culture" but a problem of power, "of the continued assumption by many Euro-American donors and activists, and, increasingly, by African elites, that they can speak for (rather than listen to) rural, poorly educated women or even well-educated African women who are deemed culturally 'other.'"

Chapters in Part III, "Mobilizations and Mediations," examine distinct gendered experiences, expressions, and mobilizations of rights, often in response to state interventions. Lynn Stephen analyzes a specific incident in Mexico—the takeover by hundreds of women of state and commercial radio stations in Oaxaca City in response to state repression—in order to examine how the women's appropriation of human rights discourse became gendered as they developed demands for the rights "to speak," "to be heard," and "to decide who governs." Through their experience running state television and radio stations and subsequently commercial stations, women who held the stations produced a gendered local vernacular of rights talk that then became accessible to many other women and men in the city. Women who were previously silenced and characterized themselves as "short, fat, and brown and the face of Oaxaca" allowed new voices to be heard, new faces to be seen, and permitted silenced models of governance and democratic participation to move into the cultural and political mainstream.

Ousseina Alidou's chapter also explores the potential power of the media and other information and communication technologies (ICTs) as vehicles for women to express and debate their perspectives on rights and justice. In Kenya, where Muslim women confront multiple marginalizations as Muslims and as women, the democratization movement of the 1990s, including the spread of private media outlets, has provided them with a new political space through which to advocate for their rights within their community of faith and multi-religious nation. Through a close reading of a discussion of the gendered and religious biases in a proposed national Sexual Offenses Bill during a Muslim women's radio talk show in Kenya, Alidou shows how these women (and female and male listeners) at once draw on and rework more patriarchal interpretations of the Qur'an and Shari'a law in their discourses.

Similarly, Robyn Rodriguez examines the gendered frames through which male immigrant detainees in the United States craft their claims to rights in their struggles against detention. Some immigrant rights groups frame immigrant detention, especially after 9/11, as a constitutional violation, while others insist on immigrants' economic contributions to the country in their struggles against the raids and other enforcement sweeps that put immigrants into detention. Many male immigrant detainees, however, frame their claims for the right to be released on the basis of their status as fathers and in relation to their families. Detainees with U.S.-born children argue that immigration authorities are violating their children's rights as citizens by detaining their parents. Others claim that increased enforcement contradicts the spirit of immigration law as it separates rather than unifies families and threatens family stability both financially and emotionally. In these claims, men often highlight their longings and desires to be with the ones they love. This analysis points to some of the limits of more conventional rights frameworks for immigrants in detention while perhaps identifying new affective and moral bases for immigrants' rights claims.

Finally, Mary Jane Real examines the complex challenges of transnational mobilizations to advance the cause of women's human rights. She focuses on the Women Human Rights Defenders International Coalition (WHRDIC), of which she is a founding member and currently coordinator. Her analysis reveals the power of coalition building, especially in terms of the leverage provided to defend women's human rights activists against state oppression. But she also explores the challenges—the fissures and fragile compromises—of coordinating decision-making, program-building, and even naming among diverse groups with different histories, agendas, and structures. For example, the issue of sexual rights—especially of LGBTI rights—has been central to the mission of the WHRDIC, but also to tensions among coalition members. As an activist immersed in the movement, Real provides a fascinating, grounded account of the gendered and cultural realities of political organizing.

Gender, Culture, and the Power of Rights

So what does the analysis of gender, culture, and rights in these chapters tell us about the potential and limits of a rights-based approach to gender justice? Intriguingly, the chapters suggest that the very sources of the power of human rights discourses, specifically "women's rights are human rights" discourses, to produce social change are also the sources of its limitations. Thus, for example, part of the broad appeal and power of rights-based protocols have been that they promote and reinforce the autonomy and self-determination of individuals, especially against violations by collective entities (or their representatives) such as states or religious institutions. But the gendered and culturally specific parameters of this liberal rights-bearing "individual" as an autonomous, male, free-agent obscure other modes of being, belonging and agency, including a person's various (and shifting) connections, obligations, affiliations, subjectivities, and positionings vis-à-vis overlapping collectivities such as their communities, political parties, families, friends, and co-workers. Women, for example, have often demanded collective self-determination, not individual rights, such as the right to speak and to be heard, the right to set priorities and be respected, and the right to land and livelihoods free from economic devastation produced by other agendas (Stephen, Hodgson). Male immigrant detainees in the United States invoke their membership in families and their relationships and commitments as fathers and husbands to frame their rights, emphasizing their interdependence and relationality with others, not their autonomy (Rodriguez). These and other examples suggest that there is perhaps no such thing as a neutral, generic, "individual" who exists outside culture, history, and relationships. Instead, we are all dynamic, complex beings with shifting alliances and allegiances, rights and responsibilities, as we age, love, marry, have children, learn, suffer, grieve, work, and more.

Another long-recognized limit of focusing on the individual as the site of rights is the inability of such paradigms to address larger structural inequalities such as the exploitative relations between states, classes, and communities. The demand of women (and men) in the global south for economic justice in the face of repeated efforts by states, elites and capital to alienate their land and undermine their livelihoods in the name of particular neoliberal visions of "progress" and "productivity" reveals the limits of legal frameworks for obtaining social justice. Part of the problem is that rights-based protocols empower states—the very entities most often accused of violating the rights of individuals and collectivities—with the power to implement and enforce laws to protect their rights. But nation-states are far more likely to selectively enforce the rights of privileged individuals than to guarantee collective rights for groups, whether indigenous, minority or women. Moreover, as the dramatic image of state repression (blowing up radio stations) documented by Stephen in response to the media takeover in Oaxaca suggests, states may also resort to violence and terror to maintain their power and sense of gendered order.

Another source of both the power and limits of rights-based protocols has been their secular foundation, which has conflicted with alternative modalities of morals and justice grounded in religious teachings and practices. This conflict has become most pronounced in debates over Islam and human rights, producing a complicated situation for Muslim women who wish to maintain (or even strengthen) their spiritual faith yet also seek changes in their relationships with men and the state (Maoulidi, Alidou, Abu-Lughod). Moreover, despite these secular pretensions, conservative Christians, among others, have been deeply involved in shaping the parameters and priorities of women's human rights, foregrounding marriage rights over sexual rights and the right to bodily integrity in their efforts to promote (and finance) the establishment of proper gender relationships and family formations.[3] The entanglement of women's human rights with Christian ideas of the politics of respectability echoes the concerns and interventions of Christian missionaries to promote particular kinds of nuclear, male-dominated families after the end of slavery in Africa (Scully).

Many of the chapters demonstrate the importance of a historical perspective to understanding the power and limits of rights, whether the "long view" taken by Scully and Maoulidi, or shorter time periods. History is often erased and ignored in debates about rights, thereby obscuring some of the non-western predecessors to human rights (such as Islam) as well as the struggles and processes behind the formulation and circulation of rights. Instead, policy-makers and activists often ignore the historical processes and focus on the outcomes. Taken together, however, the chapters reveal the shifting meanings, practices and assumptions of rights according to different historical and political-economic contexts. By historicizing such categories as gender, culture, rights, and personhood, they show the dynamism and contingency of these categories, and the implications and imbrications of power in their formations and reformations. Many of the contributors attend to the current contexts of debates over rights, in which several concurrent processes are shaping the contours and content of rights-talk. These processes include the rise of neoliberal policies and practices, NGO-ization of activism and advocacy, decreased presence and protectiveness of states, increased transnational activism and alliances, intensified impoverishment and class stratification, rising militarization and surveillance of everyday citizens, proliferation of resource-based conflicts, and growing presence and power of both Christian and Muslim religious fundamentalists. Another influential process is the rise of relatively inexpensive and accessible information and communication technologies. Several chapters highlight the importance of media as a space of political insight and action for women. The ability of radios, computers, and cell phones to transcend private spaces and connect individual users enabled disenfranchised women in Oaxaca to learn to speak and be heard (Stephen,) and Muslim women in Kenya to discuss and debate their rights and concerns, including long-taboo subjects like incest and pedophilia. Women also learned about their rights from the media, whether the internet in Kenya (Alidou) or televisions in rural Egypt (Abu-Lughod).

Similarly, all the chapters explore and analyze struggles over the naming, formation, and translation of categories and concepts. For example, the category "gender violence" currently includes a vast array of very different practices—from rape as a form of genocide to dowry deaths to FGM. Although clustering these dissimilar practices into one category enables certain kinds of visibility, recognition, and political action, it also elides important differences in the history, rationales, prevalence, and consequences of these practices. Thus, as Hodgson shows, the reframing of FGM from a health concern to a form of gender violence and thus a human rights violation empowered the Tanzanian state and transnational and national women's organizations to pressure Maasai women's organizations to conduct anti-FGM campaigns instead of focusing on their own development and empowerment priorities. Even the naming of women's rights organizations can be the subject of extended debate and deliberation as participants discuss who is included and excluded by different titles (Real).

In conclusion, all the chapters take a processual, situated approach to understanding the deployment, reception, and negotiation of rights that is attentive to the centrality of assumptions, images, ideologies, practices, and relations of gender, culture and power in these dynamics. They show that "women's human rights" is never a static category that an individual or collectivity either "has" or "does not have." Rather, the very terms of the category—women, human, and rights—are always in question, subject to alternative and sometimes competing interpretations, "vernacularizations," appropriations, and contestations. By tracing the "social life" (Abu-Lughod) of these concepts as they have circulated in different times and places, through specific media and institutions, the authors make visible how gender, culture, and power have shaped their images and interventions, their travels and translations, and their mobilizations and mediations.

PART I

Images and Interventions

Chapter 1

Gender, History, and Human Rights

Pamela Scully

Human rights has become a dominant ideological prism through which many activists at both the international and local level understand issues of justice and governance. In this context, the international order is finally taking violence against women seriously, particularly in the context of war, and in societies recovering from civil conflict.[1] Yet a long historical view of the humanitarian interventions in Africa suggests reasons to be very self-reflective about the methodologies and rhetoric of Human Rights work. As Sally Engle Merry has demonstrated, human rights itself is a form of "cultural practice" (2006: 228). This is particularly important with regard to discourses around rights, culture, and women.

A gendered historical analysis shows that human rights discourses about women's experiences of gender violence are more ambiguous and ambivalent than might appear. This chapter argues that we need to develop a more nuanced and critical understanding of the working of gender and racial ideologies within the history of Human Rights. We need to be alert to the ways in which discourses about gender-based violence and the suffering of women create particular cultural and political subjects, which often accompany and can come to subvert some of the other powerful enabling ideas of human rights. Human Rights positions itself as a neutral field of equality for all. Such a claim of neutrality, however, denies the myriad ways in which ideas about what it means to be a woman, about the proper relations between men and women, about the existence of a private and a public sphere, for example, structure the demands and expectations of rights.[2] In particular, I argue that human rights discourse has historically depended on a particular image of the suffering African woman to mobilize support and construct human rights interventions as necessary and morally secure.

A growing body of work has sought a rapprochement between the ideas of human rights contained in the original Universal Declaration of Human Rights of 1948, international legal frames, and local understandings of rights in Africa. In his survey of debates about whether notions of human rights existed before colonialism, Issa Shivji argues that human rights should be understood as an historically specific phenomenon arising out of the notions of Natural Law developed in Europe from the medieval through the Enlightenment period. Despite seeing human rights as part of what he calls an imperialist agenda of the USA after World War II, Shivji believes that human rights is a viable agenda for Africa, especially the rights to self-determination and development (Shivji 1989). More recently, with different degrees of success, scholars have sought to develop a theory of universal human rights which acknowledges and seeks to move beyond an imperialist agenda (Baxi 2006; Ackerly 2008; Ibhawoh 2007; Nussbaum 2000).

Since the late 1990s, international feminist activists have increasingly invoked human rights language in a bid to end male violence against women, particularly in the context of civil war and post-conflict situations (Stiglmeyer 1994; Meintjes et al. 2002; Scully 2009b). Activists across Africa continue to invoke the language of rights to push for democratic reforms and an end to cultures of corruption (Maathai 2006; Risse et al. 1999). International nongovernmental organizations such as UNIFEM and the International Rescue Committee, as well as Médicins sans Frontières, in a new move, have started numerous programs focusing on the elimination of gender-based violence especially in countries emerging from conflict (Redfield 2006). In the first decade of the new millennium, the UN Security Council also passed two landmark resolutions focusing on women. Security Council Resolution 1325 in 2000 focused on the impact of war on women, and the contributions women make to peace-building. SCR 1820 in 2008 focused more specifically on sexual violence in wartime. SCR 1820, which makes sexual violence "particularly against women and girls" in wartime a matter of international security, arose very much out of the context of sexual violence in African countries such as Sierra Leone and the DRC (Scully 2009a).[3] In recent years, groups such as the African Union have also sought to affirm their commitment to women's rights and scholars in Africa and elsewhere have focused on ways in which indigenous women's rights movements can embrace and transform human rights (Hodgson 2002a).[4]

Yet, despite the spread of human rights ideologies and structures across

Africa, actual implementation and securing of rights for all, particularly for women, remains an ongoing challenge. The international human rights community tends to see the challenges as arising from within indigenous cultures. Merry argues that the "practice of human rights is burdened by a colonialist understanding of culture that smuggles nineteenth-century ideas of backwardness and savagery into the process, along with ideas of racial inferiority" (2006: 226). In addition, human rights tends to register this backwardness through gender: dominant human rights frames have tended to see gender practices in these so-called traditional settings as posing supreme ongoing challenges to the expansion of human rights beyond the urban setting.

In recent years, scholars and practitioners have delivered powerful critiques of human rights. An influential body of feminist legal scholarship disputes whether an international human rights framework can address women's needs. Feminist scholars have long charged that international human rights law has an inherent gender bias because it privileges the public over the private sphere. The statism in international law poses great challenges for realizing women's human rights. State actors such as police are often the perpetrators of violence against women, and women often experience the most violence in the home and in intimate relations (Lacey 2004; Knop 1994).[5] Central criticisms of rights include the arguments that rights-based law and international interventions focus on the rights of the individual rather than that of community, in part because the idea of rights is embedded in culturally specific contexts of the Enlightenment West and neoliberalism (Baxi 2006; Harvey 2005). In addition, critics argue that, at least as practiced in the post Cold War era, human rights advocates tend to focus on the rule of law rather than on issues of social and economic justice such as labor relations and struggles against capitalist accumulation (Englund 2006). Indigenous rights groups and nongovernmental groups from the Global South have been largely responsible for bringing some of these critiques to the platforms of the United Nations (Minde 1996; Martin and Wilme 2006). We are currently witnessing the extension of rights, or "generations of rights," moving from civil and political, to social and economic, and finally to communal rights (Charlesworth 1994).[6]

Yet the critiques of human rights have generally ignored the significance that a historical perspective might bring to bear on our understanding of present practice. The transnational culture of rights is part of a long history of European interventions. As many scholars of Africa know, seemingly separate histories are often much intertwined: colonialism and humanitarianism, missionaries, and development are enmeshed in African history. I argue that one can see the campaigns to end the trans-Atlantic slave trade as the first major international humanitarian intervention. Precisely because of the place of Africa as the source of slaves, rhetoric about Africa and Africans figured prominently in these campaigns.

However, works that deal with the history of human rights tend either to analyze the growth of human rights in the second half of the twentieth century, or, when they go back to the Enlightenment, to be celebratory in tone (Peters and Wolper 1995; Fraser 1999; Zinsser 2002; Hunt 2007). Starting with one of the first transnational human rights campaigns, the ending of the trans-Atlantic slave trade, provides us with compelling cautions about a purely celebratory history of human rights, particularly with regard to the very aspect that is being touted as its central mission: to "empower women" and give them equality and respect.

In her book *Inventing Human Rights* (2007), Lynn Hunt traces the idea of human rights back to the American and French Revolutions of the late eighteenth century. She argues that the eighteenth century witnessed the rise of an empathetic sensibility as well as one of natural rights, which all helped create the context in which the notion of human rights took hold. Hunt's book also attends to the many contradictions and complexities that allowed politicians and philosophers to invoke natural rights as they denied them to women and to Africans or people of African descent.[7] The emergence of human rights lies precisely at that juncture: in the rise of empathy, the capacity to imagine people from far away as somehow connected to one through shared humanity, and the rise of democratic political and religious formulations that gave structural roots to the humanitarian sentiment. Despite caveats, Hunt celebrates the notion of rights as a concept and practice, as being unencumbered by ambiguities and situations in a broader historical and contemporary political economy.[8] Hunt's book is premised on a kind of teleological expectation that human rights itself is free from ambiguity, that it needs only to be extended to every person—women, minorities, colonized people—to fulfill its potential.

In contrast, I suggest that we need to recognize the structural ambivalence and ambiguity of early human rights ideologies and anti-slavery sentiment, as well as of contemporary human rights culture in the sense used by Merry. Numerous scholars have explored how slavery and racism in the Americas represented black women as hypersexualized figures, or as Mammy figures to white children (Bush 1990; Morgan 2004; Wallace-Sanders 2008). Here, I want to consider a different figure that has a very long history. I argue that the success of the humanitarian sentiment with regard to the ending of the slave trade, and then the missionary endeavor in Africa, related precisely to the appeal of a particular subject, the African woman needing protection,[9] and it focused specifically on bodily rights. Woman as a category, particularly the African Woman as a category, has been and remains crucial to emancipatory/human rights discourse. While the figure of the abject African woman requiring liberation and protection is a recognizable one, the purposes to which that figure has been used have been different over time. Paying attention to the centrality of this image in humanitarian discourses, as well as to the transformations of that idea in history, helps develop a more nuanced idea of the challenges and opportunities created by the discourses of human rights.

A genealogical reading of gender and human rights illustrates the historical transformations and sinews binding human rights over time. This genealogy also shows that the figure of the African woman has been central to the elaboration of human rights and the success of its adoption transnationally. Ironically, the figure of the indigenous woman also remains, as Merry suggests, the ground on which human rights flails. I propose that precisely humanitarian movements' historical invocation of the African woman or woman of African descent as needing rescue helps create the continued morass at the local level.

The Abolition of Slavery and the Figure of the Abject African Woman

The ideology of human rights is constituted in both domination and emancipation. A fuller examination of this complex history would entail charting the history of slave emancipation, through the imperial moment, as exemplified by Frederick Lugard in Nigeria, to the creation of the League of Nations and the final Declaration of the Rights of Man.[10] This chapter concentrates on what one might call the pre-histories of European human rights' engagement with Africa. From as early as the publication of Aphra Behn's *Oroonoko* (1688), the figure of the black woman vulnerable to terrible depredations on the plantations of the Caribbean became something of a staple in abolitionist literature and political tracts. The private sphere of the slave family was the terrain for much abolitionist writing. Up to the 1770s, "protests zigzagged from sentimental pleas for improved conditions in slaves' lives and condemnation of atrocities to moral contempt for the fracture of families induced by slavery and limited advocacy of rebellion" (Ferguson 1992: 3; Wiseman 2004).[11] By 1807, such a revolution had occurred in the sentiments of the British public regarding the horrors of the trade that the parliament was able, finally, to pass a law ending the British trans-Atlantic slave trade, despite the continued economic success of plantation slavery.

With the loss of the American colonies and the ending of one of the key pillars of British economic greatness, the British in the nineteenth century created a new national image founded on the notion that to be British was to mean rescuing the Atlantic world from the slave trade, and, from the 1820s, slavery itself (Brown 2006). The nineteenth century ushered in the period of Britain's great moral authority, founded on abolition of the slave trade, rise of more democratic religious practices in the form of Methodism, great naval strength, and commitment to searching out both sources of raw materials and markets for the goods of the newly industrializing economy. By the 1820s, some communities in Britain began to see the whole institution of slavery as inimical to British identity. Thus was born one of the greatest community activist campaigns in the history of Britain. British women were central to the organization, spread, and success of that campaign.

Women wrote thousands of petitions to parliament demanding the ending of slavery; they spoke out in village halls, in meetings, through letters (Midgley 1992: chap. 2). Moreover, the figure they invoked to convince the British public of the evils of slavery was that of the black woman enslaved on a Caribbean plantation, vulnerable to sexual abuse, working in degrading physical labor, without the lawful and moral protection of a husband. The autobiography of Mary Prince, published in 1831, is a good example of this trend. *The History of Mary Prince* contributed to an emerging picture of British slavery populated with figures of abject women bound to stocks, beaten, and abused, separated from their children and husbands, and under the power of illegitimate male authority: the slaveholder and the plantation overseer (Ferguson 1992).

Many antislavery activists in Britain, as well as many enslaved women and men themselves, saw freedom as entailing a new relationship between husbands and wives, parents and children. Emancipation was to usher in the great Age of the Family. Emancipators envisaged this family as a nuclear family with a father at the head, properly in charge of a newly created private sphere. The contradictions inherent in this model with regard to former slaveholders' access to the labor of women and children soon became clear, but at least at the level of ideology, emancipation inaugurated the public emphasis on the nuclear male-headed family in former British slaveholding colonies. Freed people imagined different forms of family depending on the colonial context, involvement with mission stations, and so on, but in general evidence suggests a more capacious view of family, which included adopted children and multiple generations, and accommodated various forms of labor inside and outside the household (Scully 1997; Paton and Scully 2005). The specific attention to women under slavery referenced the emergence of the female laborer as a political subject of wide debate in Britain as well as the colonies about the rights of women under the new regime of the factory. Thus, I argue, the rise of Britain's prominence as a world power of moral suasion coincided with the emergence of concerns, debates, and resolutions about the place of women in industrial society: in the labor market, in the home, in relation to children and to men. By the early 1830s, the campaigns to end slavery had been sufficiently successful that most British slaveholding colonies had passed ordinances to give slaves some rights. Importantly, many of these newly configured rights extended to slaves focused precisely on the family, constituted as part of a private sphere. For example, ordinances permitted slaves to marry and forbade selling young children away from their mothers. The black female body also became a focus of concern (Scully 1997). Many colonies ended the flogging of women slaves. As Diana Paton has suggested, abolitionists found the public exposure of women's bodies as unacceptable as the violence visited on those bodies (Paton 2004: 6). Abolitionists rallied to save the enslaved black woman from the depredations of the male slaveholder.

They saw the private sphere, one they identified with the nuclear family, as the place of male authority. Slavery, abolitionists felt, was illegitimate precisely because it did not separate the private and the public; it thus denied women the protection of their husbands and slave men the rights of masculinity. This had ambiguous results for women in post-emancipation society. Emancipation would liberate the slave woman into the correct form of family, the nuclear family under the authority of her newly liberated husband. In this moment of great political upheaval, women entered the world of freedom as subjects needing protection. Emancipation freed all slaves into a qualified citizenship: the vote was limited to men of property and precluded women entering fully into political rights. It also launched a particular kind of political landscape premised on ideas of public and private, and on the notion of respectability (Scully 1997). As Darlene Clark Hine has argued for the United States, African American women developed a politics of dissemblance in which they refrained from discussing sexual abuse at the hands of slaveholders, and created new ways of being in the world that stressed invisibility as a form of protection (Hine 1989; Sklar and Stewart 2007). Abolitionist tracts affirmed the politics of dissemblance as a marker of freedom. The linkage of women's emancipation to claims to respectability created constraints upon women within rights discourses; a legacy I think requires far more attention. The sexually desiring woman, as Merry has pointed out, was a far more difficult figure than the respectable woman (whose sexuality was either contained and hidden in marriage, or denied) for abolitionists and freed people to accommodate in the wake of slavery,[12] and, one might add, a difficult one to represent in contemporary gender-based violence campaigns.

In making the nuclear family headed by the husband the marker of true free status, abolitionist rhetoric also marked the heterosexual relationship between a woman and her husband as the defining relationship of modernity. This emphasis on the spousal relationship downplayed the role of elders, extended family, and other relationships in sustaining people's emotional lives.[13] As we shall see, this emphasis on heterosexual relationships continues to mark contemporary movements regarding women's rights.

The long nineteenth century witnessed the rise of European nationalism as outlined by Lynn Hunt (2007). It also witnessed the ending of slavery in the British Caribbean and African colonies (1834), and then the expansion of slavery in Africa itself. Particularly in the West African coast, economies formally tied to the Atlantic slave trade now used slave labor to grow the crops for the legitimate commerce in cotton and palm oil for example, with which the British sought to replace the trade in human beings (Law 1995). As slavery slowly ended across the Americas, and finally in 1888 in Brazil, Europeans became ever more convinced that Africa remained a barbarous continent, and indeed had become evil through the expansion of slavery. The rise of legitimate trade from about the 1830s coincided with devout and earnest missionary activity on the subcontinent.

African Women's Activism and Colonialism's Abject African Woman

The image of the African woman requiring protection from patriarchy, now of a different sort, returned. Particularly in Southern Africa, missionaries such as Livingstone and Moffat documented in reports and public letters what they saw as the terrible status of African women. Women were "beasts of burden" doing agricultural labor while the men, sat around doing nothing (see, for example, Deane 1880).[14] In the rebuilding of the relationship between

Britain and Africa, the figure of the African woman again emerged, this time in a more minor key, as a justification for greater colonial interventions at the end of the century. With the scramble for Africa from the 1880s, European powers justified their colonization of most of Africa through a discourse of bringing civilization and ending slavery.

In fact, slavery continued to exist far into the colonial period in many parts of Africa formerly connected to international slave trades. In West Africa, in all periods, women made up the majority of the enslaved. Being a slave in the African setting did not necessarily equate with enslavement in the plantations of the Americas. Many slave women married their owners and became farmers. The degree of freedom of slave women varied across the continent, depending on the form of slavery, religion of the master, and other factors. For example, Islamic law freed women on the death of their master if they had borne his child. Women enslaved by wealthy owners had more opportunities for social advancement than women enslaved in domestic servitude (Robertson and Klein 1983; Klein and Roberts 2005). The expansion of slavery and the coming of colonialism in French West Africa in the late nineteenth century created a newly dependent and expanded class for enslaved women, often married to their slaveholders and bearing children by them. This situation helped resurrect in some ways the image of women as needing aid from the West to free them from terrible patriarchy.

Far from being abject, however, women sought freedom. They took masters and often husbands to court, they deserted in great numbers, and they sought to return to their natal families. The litany of court records of the early twentieth century shows not passive women requiring intervention, but vigorous activity to avoid sexual violence and pursue different kinds of freedoms (Burrill and Roberts 2010; Cooper 1997; Klein and Roberts 2005; Roberts 2005). Cati Coe (2010) has shown that in the early years of colonialism in the Gold Coast, young women who had previously been victims of sexual assault by employers or foster parents used new laws to challenge the status quo.

In the colonial era, the fact of activism on the part of so many women did little to reshape European perspectives on gender relations on the continent. Coming from societies that were newly emphasizing women's proper place as being in the private sphere, European administrators and missionaries were appalled at women's involvement in agricultural labor and their role as traders, the latter particularly the case in West Africa. The colonial era witnessed a consolidation of the sociological portrait of the African woman as a beast of burden who had to be rescued from the patriarchal grip of her husband

and family (Beoku-Betts 2005). Moreover, far from being liberators, colonial states were often complicit in trying to return women to their masters and husbands (Klein and Roberts 2005).

Colonial states also sought in often very contradictory and ambivalent ways to inculcate femininity according to gender norms in Europe, which often rested on unspoken assumptions about the significance of marriage as the key relationship in the life of an individual. Across British colonial Africa, for example, and even in the post-independence era in countries such as Tanzania and Zambia, governments and missionaries enacted programs to educate women for domestic service (both for their husbands and settlers) even as women continued to engage in agricultural and other labor (Walker 1990; Hansen 1992; Schmidt 1992). The focus on married women's duties to their spouses and children again reproduced the notion that the spousal relationship was the only key arena of meaning for women and men.

The neat binary/dyad of husband/wife fits very uneasily with the variety of marriage and affiliations in the continent. In fact, such an emphasis on the spousal relationship and a putative private sphere flattened very complex social relations involving same sex associations, age grades, the dual sex system in West Africa, and the widespread practice of polygamy (Oyewumi 2003). For many people in Africa, the relationship between individuals tied by marriage was just one of a variety of important social and economic relationships, including for women relationships to other wives and women's groups. In matrilineal and acephalous (stateless) societies, women had access to power and status by controlling cults associated with ancestors (Mikell 1997: 14). Women's societies that controlled puberty rites and other forms of gender identity provided important power bases for women (Amadiume 1987; McCormack 1980). As we shall see, this continues to this day.

The ideology of the nuclear family also of course assumed the existence of separate public and private spheres, with the family in the private sphere. In many colonial settings the family was never a private realm in quite the way the rhetoric of the nuclear family suggested. As we know from the history of colonialism in Africa, the African family was subject to great public scrutiny, particularly in colonies such as South Africa and Kenya, where labor for white settler minorities was a central pillar of the colonial regime (Cooper 1989). In South Africa, state policies sought to ensure the geographical separation of African families. From the era of segregation in the 1920s through to Apartheid and Separate Development in the second half of the twentieth century, the South African state cleaved the African family: men working on the mines and in towns, and childbearing women and the elderly forced to stay in the rural homelands. The worlds women and men created in the interstices of Apartheid by navigating pass laws, labor laws, and housing rules show both the resilience of African families and the degree to which the private sphere, at least in a legal sense, was always subject to state intervention (Bozzoli 1991; Cock 1980).

Another feature of continuity between the campaigns to end the trans-Atlantic slave trade and the focus on women under colonialism was the emphasis on African women's bodies as a site of public rhetoric and legislation. As we see perhaps most clearly in Kenya, the British focused on the female body as a way of articulating a vision of colonial rule as concerned with the rights of women. Representations of gender, the African female body, and the creation of colonial rule were tightly knitted. In the late 1920s and into the 1930s, British officials and missionaries campaigned against female circumcision, a practice associated with puberty rites in Kikuyu society. After hostile campaigning by protestant missionaries, the Kikuyu Central Association defended the practice. Soon the right to circumcision became linked to anti-colonial resistance. Lynn Thomas's observation of why clitoridectomy (and abortion) became so central to the landscape of colonial rule has resonance for today. Contemporary international campaigns against female genital cutting also demonize culture as the place that sustains patriarchy (Merry 2006; Obiora 1997). Thomas argues, with reference to colonial Kenya, that "while Africans understood these practices as sustaining two pillars of political order, gendered personhood and generational authority, Europeans claimed that they threatened 'tribal' and imperial health, perpetuated the subjugation of African women, and confounded colonial rule" (Thomas 1998: 145, 2003).

The figure of the African woman has long been the terrain on which the West has sought to establish their credentials relating to Africa and in sub-Saharan Africa itself (Oyewumi 2003; Okome 2003). It behooves us to pay attention to the ways humanitarian discourses of emancipation and liberation, as well as more specifically colonial rhetoric (although often calling on similar political philosophies of rights) helped construct a gendered field of justification for intervention.

The New Humanitarianism

Transnational activism around women's rights continues in the twenty-first century. The UN and other agencies and international NGOs direct many resources to ending sexual violence against women, creating opportunities for women to be engaged in peace-building, and reconstruction of post-conflict societies. The New Humanitarianism embraces action and ongoing intervention as means to eradicate the root causes of violence in societies ravaged by war (Schumer 2008). Addressing women's experience of gender-based violence, sexual and otherwise, has become a leading focus of UN work in Liberia, Sierra Leone, and elsewhere. Efforts include giving women political voice in truth and reconciliation processes, preventing gender-based violence, and rethinking the meanings of security for women so that they can contribute to establishing just post-conflict societies.[5]

As activists, NGOs, and the UN call for women to be involved in post-conflict reconstruction, they also operate in a discursive gendered field in which protection of women is again becoming part of the rhetoric. A new ethic of female protection is being elaborated in various Security Council resolutions and in documents on how to work to end gender-based violence in post-conflict societies (Scully 2009a,b). The willingness of men on the Security Council to pass resolutions that speak to the special violation of women and girls in times of war (SCR 1820) suggests that men can easily affirm a vision of women requiring protection. Not only men share such a vision: women's organizations labored long and hard to write the texts of the resolutions, and internal debate in international forums large and small preceded the final draft (Cook 2008). The new language of protection also is part of an admirable and complex history based on feminine empathy and international organizing, which as we have seen dates back at least to the women's campaigns to end slavery in the 1830s.

It seems counterintuitive to raise a voice that queries the contemporary focus on women's experiences of sexual violence in so much international and local organizing. So many women at so many meetings and levels have fought so very hard to have violence against women taken seriously. It is thanks to all this work that we have had major developments in international law. For example, the 1998 Akayesu decision found a mayor in Rwanda guilty of rape as a crime of genocide, and the International Criminal Tribunal for Yugoslavia put rape as a weapon of war on the agenda of international law (Russell-Brown 2003). Yet the adoption by the international human rights world of the figure of the raped African woman as a trope around which everyone can organize around is worrisome.

The contemporary campaigns against violence against women, now traveling under the sign of gender-based violence, like their colonial predecessors, attempt to create the "modern woman" by seeking to bring women under the aegis of the state (Scully 2009b). Human rights campaigns seek to create this new figure in part by instigating a break of the young woman from the extended family so that she becomes an individual, the proper subject who can thus enjoy human rights. What is not often examined is that campaigns against gender-based violence not only are campaigns to end violence by men against women, as is often represented, but involve severing generational ties between older and younger women.[16] As such, the contemporary campaigns to end violence against women are involved in complicated realignments of authority within African societies that belie the apparent simplicity of intervening to rescue African women from African men.

A look back to the campaigns to end the slave trade and slavery suggests that we inherit a political figure created in that important juncture of humanitarianism and international organizing. In the late eighteenth and early nineteenth centuries, this figure did not have the vote, and did not appear as a political agent, but nonetheless provided the bedrock for a new kind of international politics. The figure of the vulnerable African woman or the woman of African descent provided anti-slave trade, and later anti-slavery activists in Britain and the USA with an almost unassailable moral claim to intervention. As we have seen, particularly in the early nineteenth century, when domesticity and women's place in the home became central to a variety of political discourses, the view of the sexually vulnerable African woman proved a powerful trope to organize around. The rhetoric of the anti-slave trade and anti-slavery movements constituted women of African descent as vulnerable subjects needing protection from sexual depredations and containment within the nuclear family.

In the early twenty-first century, after some centuries of feminist organizing, and with women in positions of political power in African and elsewhere, it is perhaps strange to encounter the figure of the abject African woman once again. It is somewhat ironic that we encounter her in the world of what Halley calls Governance Feminism, where feminists have managed to put rape and domestic violence on the agenda (Halley 2006). That this is so requires a different paper. However, this chapter has considered how gendered discourses can also help establish racial discourses of disempowerment, and the disempowerment of particular women. Awareness of such histories might help women to support one another in more fruitful ways within international human rights work.

The figure of the abject African woman still holds sway in international

humanitarian work, although of course the contours of that supposed abject-
ness have changed over the centuries of engagement. Now, I would argue,
the African woman is seen as requiring the intervention of the human rights
community in order to liberate her from her patriarchal family and into the
arms of a supposedly caring and dispassionate state. What does such a figure
enable the world to ignore? The focus on women in an exclusive way frames
the issue of rights primarily within the field of governance and encounters
with culture. It seems more difficult to bring discussions of sexual violence
within the field of economic and social justice. How might we meld a discussion of multinational interests with a focus on rape in the DRC? How does
the violence done to women become complicit and part of a much wider history of violence (Hunt 2008)?

Much contemporary internationally funded programming on sexual and
gender-based violence in post-conflict societies such as Liberia reproduces
the focus on the nuclear family and heterosexual relationships as the key
sites of identity for African women. Little respect is shown to sites where
women find solidarity and make meaning about womanhood and gender.
For example, in Liberia, a woman might be married to a man, but she also
derives social status and power from her identity in a host of other groupings. As Caroline Bledsoe has outlined for Kpelle society, women are tied to
people through kinship, marriage, affiliation, and clientship. Women's membership in the Sande society and their status within it affect their life beyond
the society. Elder women play an important role in Sande, teaching what are
considered appropriate gender roles for women, including by continuing the
practice of female genital cutting (Bledsoe 1980, 1984). Yet these important
realms of female interaction are often the very areas targeted as unacceptable by international organizations. For example, a report on Liberia by the
UN High Commissioner for Refugees identified the Sande (female) and Poro
(male) societies as contributing to gender violence in post-conflict Liberia.[17]
As Mary Moran has shown, however, the strength of West African women
to organize collectively against injustice and war could in fact be seen to de-
rive from these social structures, which international human rights circles
attack as being bastions of cultures hostile to women's rights (Moran 1989:
443; Merry 2006).

As we work with human rights in the twenty-first century, the inscription
of new forms of domination is easy to miss if one does not pay attention to
the gendered language of rights and responsibilities invoked in the history of
humanitarian interventions. How to acknowledge the grip of history while

moving forward is of course the central challenge for any post-conflict society; being aware of such challenges is also important for theorists and activists involved in trying to chart new landscapes of justice.

Part of the framing of the various human rights campaigns against gender-based violence that are taking place in Liberia, the DRC, and elsewhere achieve their sense of purpose and ethics through the figure of the abject and violated woman who needs the intervention of non-governmental organizations.[18] History suggests that we invoke such a figure with caution. Economics, male and female bodies and the different and similar uses to which they are put in different contexts, and histories of intervention must be connected analytically. Otherwise, there is in a danger in thinking that a brave new world is being made when in fact people are participating at the very same time in much older discourses tied to histories of disempowerment as much as to rights.

Chapter 2

Between Law and Culture: Contemplating Rights for Women in Zanzibar

Salma Maoulidi

Culture, as embodying the personality of a society, constitutes the interplay between human relations and gender boundaries. It is an expression of historical phenomena defined in place and time, in which experience and expression is deeply gendered. In colonial and post-colonial Africa, the defense of culture mollified a people's sense of domination and violation against that which was viewed as foreign, alien. Great effort was thus made to present culture as entrenched, immutable, and static, exacting loyalty to preserve what was perceived as authentic against encroaching elements or influences personified by colonialism and recent migrations.

The defense of the cultural assumed particular significance in societies identifying strongly with Islam. Muslim populations used the sanctity of Islam to delineate the extent of the colonial incursion. Cultural preservation became a way to assert resistance against missionary incursion and to counter a discourse that attempted to justify missionary and colonial aggression and domination on the basis of the cultural inferiority of colonial subjects. One area where this negotiation is evident is law where Muslims insisted on a separate (or exclusive) legal scheme based on the Shari'a, or Islamic law, to govern the most intimate aspects of their lives (that is, personal law matters).

Women became the ultimate cultural icons through which a society would resist cultural intrusion and assimilation. In a Muslim context, women are revered as "the centre of sacred and ordinary Muslim life and culture—the pivots that hold together the family, the core of the social group" (El Guindi

2005: 262). Thus, according to El Guindi, any intervention involving women becomes a key concern of those in power. Similarly, Deniz Kandiyoti (1997: 7) sees a close association between the (changing) status of women and cultural imperialism in the minds of many Muslims sparking countervailing attempts to maintain and reinforce "authentic" relations and roles for women to resist such imperialism. By and large, therefore, formerly colonized communities continue to insist on a disparate treatment for women, often against what is considered the universal norm, to preserve their peculiarity and thus their personality as a people. The preoccupation with a defense of local mores and ways of being has tremendous implications for women. Chiefly, it brings about simplistic and often rigid interpretations of cultural and societal norms. Similarly, it leaves women with the singular burden of epitomizing cultural representations. Whereas culture is dynamic and evidences a progression of reciprocal interactions and accommodations, biased interpretations and application of the "cultural" leaves women in abeyance, frozen in time, legally and socially.

Zanzibar, an influential seat of Swahili culture in modern times, presents a formidable phenomenon for analysis in that the island was not totally subordinate to the will of the colonizer but retained some influence over key aspects of its political, social, and cultural fabric. Furthermore, Zanzibar's cultural legacy is greatly influenced by an Islamic history that stretches over a millennium. The oldest standing mosque in Zanzibar was built in 1107. This legacy has informed the outlook of the law in the islands.

Women's status in Zanzibar is influenced greatly by the interplay between law and culture. The legal regime is used to construct not just legal but also cultural subjects. Specifically, constructions of the female subject are motivated and shaped by political forces interested in either preserving or changing the social and moral order. Women have been targeted not only as the principal objects for social transformation by colonizing forces but also by nationalist forces and reformists who view women as objects for intervention and change (Hajjar 2001).

Literary works like the poetry of Mwanakupona and anthropological studies like Margaret Strobel's *Muslim Women in Mombasa* (1979) and *Three Swahili Women* (1989) gave us a glimpse into the lives of Swahili women in the past. Building on feminist legal theory, I propose to go farther and examine how law was/is used to assert prevailing cultural notions about women and consequently how the law shaped societal and gender expectations in specific political contexts of the island's history.[1] My discussion is set in three distinct periods in Zanzibar's history: colonial or pre-revolution; post-revolution; and at the advent of the new constitutional order. Moving away from past trends in examining women's social status in Swahili society, I use law as a tool to unearth the underlying cultural discourses constructed by different social interests and groupings.

Why use law? I do so for the simple reason that law forms the basis for social and public policy through which individual and citizens' entitlements are defined. The process of policy-making and legislating essentially preserves a distinct social and moral order whereby culture is constantly being negotiated, revised, and reproduced by different forces.

Zanzibar's Modern History in Context

Zanzibar, a semi-autonomous island state within the United Republic of Tanzania, is made up of Unguja and Pemba Islands and several islets.[2] Zanzibar unified with Tanganyika in April 1964, some argue to secure the bloody January 1964 Revolution, which took place only a month after the island gained independence from Britain in December 1963 (Fairooz 1995; Clayton 1981; Juma 2007). Zanzibar's local people are a mixture of diverse ethnicities indicative of her colorful history and intermarriages. Islam is the dominant religion (99 percent of the population). Zanzibar's high level of religious tolerance is captured in the 1948 census, which registered 21 different religious categories in the isles (ZNA AB 33/7).[3] Kiswahili and its dialects are widely spoken and comprise the distinguishing features of the island's Swahili identity.

Although Zanzibar is only a few miles from the East African coast, it has been associated with long periods of non-African rule, a reality that is at the heart of ongoing political and identity contestations. Indeed, beginning in the eighteenth century, Zanzibar was ruled by the Alawi Dynasty of Persian (Shirazi) descent, and from 1832 to 1963 it formed part of the Omani Sultanate. The Omani takeover was legitimated by their successful late seventeenth-century expulsion of the Portuguese from key parts of the east African coast, following which Zanzibar accepted the supremacy of the Muscat ruler. The decision of the Omani ruler to move his capital to Zanzibar in 1840 supplanted the local ruler of Shirazi descent, the Mwinyi Mkuu, who died in 1873 without an heir (Pearce 1967; Juma 2007; Loimeier 2009).

The Omani ascent in Zanzibar marked a period of great transition and modernization. The move of Sultan Said bin Sultan, patriarch of the Bu-Said royal family, to Zanzibar reinforced the island's position as the paramount political and economical center of the east African coast. The economy blossomed, benefiting from extensive maritime trade and associated tolls, the introduction of the clove industry, and the highly lucrative trade in slaves. By end of the eighteenth century Zanzibar and Pemba produced nearly 90 percent of the world supply of cloves (Middleton 1961; Liebst 1992; Aley 1994; Al-Ismaily 1999).

Sayeed Bargash (1870–88) and his older brother Majid (1856–70), the former well traveled and educated in India, are credited with much of Zanzibar's infrastructural development (Aley 1994; Fairooz 1995; Al-Ismaily 1999). Their progressive attitudes in international diplomacy and commerce were in sharp contrast to their feudal predisposition and strong nationalistic tendencies. Moreover, the Bu-Said belonged to the conservative Ibadhi sect in Sunni Islam, which meant that they applied strict interpretations of Islamic law in daily life and politics.

British contact with Zanzibar was a period of extensive missionary incursion in the island. The influence of the sultans waned considerably with greater British influence in local politics and the unusually short successive regimes (Aley 1994; Al-Ismaily 1999; Juma 2007). In 1878 Zanzibar signed a Protection Treaty with Great Britain, putting it under the administration of the Foreign Office. Following the German annexation of the Mainland territories in 1888 soon after the Berlin partition of Africa, Zanzibar was placed under British Protection to avert war. It was proclaimed a British protectorate in November 1890 and continued as such until granted independence in December 1963. The agreement between the British government and Sultan Hemed bin Thuwein in 1895 placed all administrative matters in the hands of the British government with the sultan acting as local ruler. In 1914, Zanzibar's administration moved to the Colonial Office (Middleton 1961; Pearce 1967; Liebst 1992; Mvungi 2005: 63; Juma 2007).

Zanzibar's economic fortunes changed drastically with the advent of British rule. Slavery, one of the main features of the local economy until this period, was officially abolished in 1897, severely limiting available labor power. Clove exports suffered as the clove plantations were struck by sudden death disease, and huge debts were incurred by land owners (Middleton 1961; Bader 1985).

A distinctive feature of British administration that polarized the local population was the concept of a natural hierarchy of races. Coupled with the creed of indirect rule, it changed the islands' social patterns, creating racial identities whose dynamics touched both private and public lives and had lasting and devastating effects on pro-independence policies as well as the revolution of 1964 and beyond (Clayton 1981; Glassman 2000; Loimeier 2009: 23). The local population was now stratified not along social criteria but according to three distinct races: Arab, often associated with the aristocracy; British Indian communities, mostly the commercial class; and Swahili of Afro descent, 90 percent of the population, the indigenes of the islands.

The Swahili, hitherto considered a cultural category, was converted to a tribal or racial category albeit a degree above the Mainland African, who was not seen to be an authentic islander having come to the island either via the slave trade or as laborers in coconut and clove plantations. This classification was complicated by the fact that the Swahili and other ethnicities often classified themselves as Arab to benefit from racial hierarchies, a practice that pro-independence Africans, especially from the Mainland, interpreted as a rejection of their African identity in favor of Arab cultural vestiges (Clayton 1981; Loimeier 2009). The 1964 Revolution attempted to put to rest the question of Zanzibar's African identity, justifying the ousting of the sultan along racial lines.

The British Colonial Phase 1885–1963: Protecting the Custodians of Culture from Modernizing Influences

As already noted, the ruling dynasty's grip on political affairs was gradually weakened by the British, who systematically embarked on a process that encroached on local governance, redefining political, legal, and social structures (Al-Ismaily 1999; Juma 2007). The retention of the sultan at the helm of government provided some balance between prevailing cultural mores and laws introduced to facilitate British governance. The longest serving sultan in this period, Sayeed Khalifa bin Haroub (1911–60), is credited with bringing Zanzibar in line with modern political and social norms (Aley 1994).

During this era, women's status was negotiated at two levels: as cultural and religious subjects under the sultan and as colonial subjects under the British crown. Despite ardent attempts to preserve the Zanzibari Swahili identity under the British colonial assault, the islands were not immune from developments in different parts of the world, especially given their geographical and political position at the gateway to the Indian Ocean. In particular, the introduction of western education highlighted how Zanzibari society increasingly found itself torn between modernization and a desire to maintain cultural authenticity, commonly expressed in religious terms. Between 1830 and 1850 prominent *madrasas* (Islamic religious schools) were established in the island enabling Zanzibar to become a center of Islamic education (Loimeier 2009).

Western schooling, introduced in the 1880s by missionaries and faith societies, was segregated by race, class, and gender. At its inception western education competed with an influential system of *madrasa* education which many considered a more effective method of ensuring continuity of the Swahili and Islamic cultural legacy. In 1905, the Department of Education was created and public education was instituted. As elsewhere, formal schooling was initially only for boys, but some prominent families managed to enroll their daughters in private schools qualifying for government education grants as early as 1907.

This enlightenment project was fiercely opposed by influential sections of Zanzibari society who objected to its modernizing influence. They considered Muslim children's exposure to western influences "dangerous." The opposition grew more vocal and also physical when women's education was officially introduced in 1927, as captured by the accounts of Bi. Zaynab Himid Muhammed, one of the first women to be enrolled in public school.[4] People usually considered taking girls to institutions that did not necessarily reflect an Islamic religious character as being beyond the limits of Swahili respectability.

The education project overcame initial opposition by accommodating local mores about women's modesty. Education was not only segregated by sex but also tailored to social expectations. The superintendent of education at the time, Mrs. G. R. Johnson, who unfailingly advocated for girls' education, nevertheless reinforced social expectations for educated women. For example, during a Prize Giving Speech in 1934, she decried the practice of pulling girls out of school as hampering their ability to become "good Mohammedan wives and mothers" (ZNA File 7AD 21).

Whereas in the rest of sub-Saharan Africa the colonial project was tainted with Christian morality, in Zanzibar a mix of Victorian values and Islamic traditions dictated policy and legislative measures during this period. The adoption of the notion of Qawamah (male protection as per Qur'an 4:34) in local law and practice relegated a woman to the status of "weaker sex," unable to make decisions or fend for herself. Men were considered the main providers and protectors of women and the family, an attitude that also had social and economic consequences.

The economic fortunes of Zanzibar changed considerably after the British assumed power. The ban on the slave trade meant that Zanzibar was no longer the commercial gateway to the region. The substantial drop in (human) cargo considerably reduced maritime traffic. The false economic boom of 1920 from rising clove prices and expanding clove markets did not bring prosperity, as most plantation owners were deep in debt and had mortgaged their land during hard times (Bader 1985: 71).

Zanzibar's economic decline was compounded by the war effort in the colonies and the economic slump of 1929. Two world wars left many women without male assistance in the form of husbands or sons. They also had to contend with a sharp rise in the cost of living. The welfare of women who had no protectors or means of income became a state priority.

Additionally, the number of dependents among the surviving members of the Royal Household—the Aulad Imam—which included their offspring, children they fostered, wives as well as *suriyas* (concubines), and in some cases long-time servants and emancipated slaves, was increasing. To care for their needs the government introduced a law on pensions in 1921.[5] Entitlement to pensions was race-based, effectively maintaining class privilege.[6] According to a letter of one Chief Secretary, R. Sheridan, two categories of pensions were provided: (1) annuities to the relatives of his Royal Highness; and (2) allowances to the families of the ex-sultans (ZNA File 10/128/134/135). The bulk of correspondence on file is mostly from female members of the Royal Household, showing how they used their status to benefit from this scheme. In their letters, they invoked their special status to negotiate revisions of their maintenance allowance, secure alternative accommodation befitting their status, or obtain loans and other contributions.

The aunts of Sultan Khalifa, Fatma Mohammed binti Said and Alia Mohamed binti Said, for example, in a 1935 communication use their age as the "oldest, most senior members of the Aulad Imam whose brother and son had assumed the throne," to protest their eviction from a house they had lived in for thirty-two years, and also to request an exemption from paying the water tax (ZNA File AB 10/89). The suriyas of Sayeed Ali bin Said (1890–93), Sayara binti Yussuf, Fatma binti Yussuf, Nurain binti Abdullah, and Rasha binti Abdullah, who identified themselves as concubines, bed companions, and handmaidens, on different occasions from 1923 to 1929 asked for revisions of pensions due to a rise in the cost of living (ZNA File AB 10/116).

Faced with financial difficulties of its own, the colonial government tried to impose restrictions on who could qualify for the state pension. For women, these restrictions included that they be without male guardianship and behave themselves "properly" according to their status. Thus, when an ex-concubine of Sultan Ali bin Humoud (1902–11), Bi. Rozuna binti Jamim, applied in 1923 for a review of her pension, the government tried to deny her claim by alleging that she had conceived a child out of wedlock. But since they could not prove the existence of the child, they failed (ZNA file AB/10/108). A similar condition was placed on Taj Chakras, a suriya of Sultan Ali bin Said, when she claimed her allowance. In a letter dated 16 October 1932, the Chief Secretary approved her request for an allowance as long as she remained unmarried.

The concern with and regulation of women's bodies during this period is evident in the introduction of offenses against morality in the Penal Decree of 1934. About 31 provisions in the law detailed various forms of carnal crimes against women's chastity. The prevailing sense of morality in colonial Zanzibar was conveyed by what was prohibited or permitted in the law. Any sex outside marriage, whether incest, adultery, or any act that suggested that a girl was involved in illegal sexual activity (for example, abortion), was criminalized. The moral integrity of unmarried women between sixteen and twenty-one was left not to themselves or their parents but to the state, despite the fact that the women were technically considered adults.

Apparent in the law were the divergent outlooks with respect to the suitable age for coitus for girls. For instance, Section 7 of Chapter 91 of the Marriage and Divorce (Muslim) Registration Act required a wife to be above the age of puberty without qualifying this age. The Penal Code offered a compromise position with local norms in permitting what are today termed child marriages, but prohibited female children under thirteen or before reaching puberty, even if married, from engaging in sex. Meanwhile, Chapter 53 of the Laws of Zanzibar put the age of majority at eighteen, twenty-one for purposes of property. If a girl was governed by Islamic law, a male relative would be expected to manage her property even if she was an adult. Of course, women's limited mobility socially narrowed their options to exercise greater autonomy over their affairs, relegating them to perpetual dependence.

Additional examples of how the female subject was controlled by the state concern the Royal Marriage Decree Chapter 31 of 1940. This law regulated the future marriages of female members of the royal family. The Decree forbade a woman, as well as her legal guardian, from contracting her marriage without the consent of the sultan, whose consent was evidenced by his seal. Furthermore, Section 3 prohibited marriage registrars, mostly religious officials who were Kadhis (Muslim judges), from registering marriages if the sultan had not agreed to it. The Act made it an offense to solemnize or assist in the solemnization of such a marriage, punishable by imprisonment or a fine of 1000 shillings (a considerable amount at the time).

This law marked a major departure in criminal justice, since criminal law tended to be of universal application. Moreover, the insistence on the sultan's authority over royal marriages challenged the very mandate of appointed officials in overseeing religious and personal law matters. However, the sultan was also conferred the title Imam, granting him not just worldly leadership but also religious leadership of the Muslim community, the *umma*.[7] By so legislating over his female subjects, the sultan strongly communicated the limits of colonial intrusion in the social fabric of the isle, particularly his "house."

Importantly, this law shows the ongoing tension between a modernizing society and the need to control its cultural symbols—the women. Unlike their foremothers who largely led a secluded and pampered lifestyle, women from the Royal Household at the peak of the British colonial regime were not immune to the changes going on in the islands: they received an education in public institutions and joined a work force that was mostly mixed. Thus, the possibility of "respectable" women meeting men from other social classes and straying was great. Possibly, in fear of the rebellious female spirit that almost a century before had led one of the daughters of the first sultan, Sayeeda Salme, to elope and marry a non-Muslim German officer, the Royal House did not want to take chances and moved to rein in their women.[8]

Consider, for example, the experiences of Mariam Abbass (b.1933), granddaughter of Taj Chakras. Her father worked for the Health Department at Prison Island, and by her own account gave her a western lifestyle. She studied at a convent school, rode a bicycle, swam, played netball, and read poetry. Most of her friends were Goan and Parsees, thus not Muslim. The patricians of Zanzibar objected to her upbringing, criticizing her father for giving her "an open rope." As she grew older they increasingly called on him to "tighten the rope" and rein her in as was socially expected for a girl of her stature.[9]

Female commoners were not subject to such overt regulation and led lives that were relatively free. As subjects of the empire they could travel the breadth of the empire for work, study, or leisure. While the government recognized women's increased participation in the labor force, it also sought to reflect the social expectations associated with their reproductive work. Therefore, women could not engage in jobs that in any way interfered with their status as homemakers. Restrictions applicable to working women were outlined in the Employment of Women (Restriction) Decree No. 62 of 1953. These restrictions, however, did not apply to women holding responsible positions of a managerial or technical character, or working in health or welfare services (Section 5). And while women may have constituted a minority among professionals, already social hierarchies were being formed in the law on the basis of qualification and position.

Nevertheless, on the whole, professions were still viewed along gender lines. For example, the law relating to the registration of midwives, Chapter 71, still viewed it as an exclusively female profession. A midwife was only allowed to employ another woman to assist her. Likewise, a number of laws like the Evidence Decree or Chapter 91 of the Marriage and Divorce (Muslim) Registration Act precluded women who were *hijabiyya* (women who observed purdah) from appearing in public if they (the women) objected, despite the fact that the Islamic Rules of Evidence had no bearing in Zanzibar courts pursuant to the Evidence Decree Chapter 5 of 1917. This is another example of the negotiation that took place between the two contrasting legal regimes in operation in the isles.

Despite the advances women made in public life during this period, laws were still influenced by what was considered acceptable social practice. The Marriage and Divorce Act, for instance, did not require a woman to personally register a marriage (or a death, for that matter); it was the duty of her male guardian. However, a mother was required to register a birth, since this was seen as an exclusively female function. In the case of Bibi Rozuna binti Jamim cited earlier, the colonial administration attempted to prosecute her for not registering the birth of her illegitimate child as required under Section 5 of Decree No. 13 of 1909. Of course, had she done so, she would have admitted the birth and would have been forced to face the legal consequences of having a child out of wedlock.

Section 7(1) of the Nationality Decree Chapter 39 of 1952 granted women married to Zanzibar subjects, whether or not of full age and capacity, citizenship through their husbands, not on their own. Thus, men in Zanzibar had an automatic right to confer citizenship status to their wives, but female subjects did not have similar rights. Sayeeda Salme contended with this bias following the death of her husband, when she tried to reclaim her status not only as a subject of Zanzibar but also as a member of royalty. Furthermore, her adoption of the Christian faith was considered an automatic renunciation of her right to citizenship, leading her brother Bargash to sever her from her inheritance share of numerous family members (Reute 1998).[10]

Nowhere was the modernizing influence in Zanzibari society as obvious as under the Regency Decree (Chapter 30), which created a new role for the wife of the sultan: the law required her evidence to certify if the sultan was incapacitated (Section 4). This move is significant in two main respects. Sultan Khalifa bin Haroub had already nominated his son Sayeed Abdullah to the throne in 1929. The "natural" expectation was that the crown prince and perhaps the British consul would ascertain the same. Also, Zanzibar had had a history of female rulers before the advent of the Omani rulers. In contrast, the Bu Said had a paternalistic attitude toward women, and their religious ideology could not entertain women at the helm. It is therefore not surprising that on the abdication of Sayeed Ali Humoud in 1911, it was his brother-in-law,[11] the husband of one of his sisters, Sayeeda Matuka bint Humoud Al-Busaid, who was chosen to become sultan, not the daughter of a sultan. Probably at that time Arab sensibilities could not accept an Arab woman coming into direct contact with colonial officials and agents.

Second, the Regency Decree brought into prominence Bibi Nunu, the sultan's second wife. Unlike Sayeeda Matuka, she was a commoner.[12] In many ways, she epitomized Zanzibar's flirtations with modernity, since unlike Sayeeda Matuka she wore western dress and was a public personality who accompanied her husband in most state-related functions inside and outside the country. She was a comparatively young wife, married to a sultan whose reign was relatively stable and lengthy—it lasted almost fifty years. Her public image was in sharp contrast to that of Sayeeda Matuka, who rarely appeared in public, let alone in mixed company, nor bared herself by removing her *barakoa*, a covering that hides the face.

Largely, the legal measures introduced during the British colonial period resulted in some shifts in cultural attitudes toward women. Although powerful social forces in the society initially resisted policy and legal measures granting women rights, they were won over by colonial assurances against upsetting the patriarchal order. Therefore, women's full agency as subjects was limited by the prevailing social norms and expectations and justified through a legally sanctioned cultural and religious framework dictated by the sultan and the colonial administration.

The Revolutionary Years 1964–1984:
Molding a Novel National Subject

The relative stability of Sultan Khalifa's rule came to an abrupt end soon after his death in 1960.[13] At this time, political forces in Zanzibar were agitating for self-rule and parity in racial representation. Until 1957, members from the different racial groups were appointed to the Legislative Council, with the first Shirazi appointed in 1946.[14] In 1957, reforms introduced an electoral system to replace the system of appointments. Although the reforms also granted women the right to vote, women could not immediately stand for public office.

Following the constitutional reforms of 1957, Zanzibar held four intensely contested multiparty elections, in March 1957, January and July 1961, and July 1963.[15] Racial politics were used to delay and even sabotage the process toward self rule (Fairooz 1995; Lofchie and Payne 1999; Al-Ismaily 1999; Juma 2007). Since the only permissible forms of organizing among local populations during the colonial era were through racial/ethnic community and sports and professional associations, the emerging political organizations in the isles had a strong racial/ethnic identity.

Accordingly, the African Party was comprised mainly of members of immigrant African communities, most of who came to Zanzibar as farm laborers, while the Shirazi Party was comprised of native Zanzibaris described as Watumbatu, Wahadimu, and Wapemba.[16] Shiraz has a political connotation, serving as a distinction from the Arab and African mainland (Middleton 1961: 7, 9). This distinction was heightened when the Shirazi Party split and a faction joined the African Party to form the Afro-Shirazi Party (ASP), and another faction formed the Zanzibar and Pemba's People's Party (ZPPP), a party that would tilt the political balance during the political transition of this period.

The Zanzibar Nationalist Party (ZNP), or Hizbul al Wattan, was commonly associated with the Arab Party because of prominent Arab personalities in the party's leadership. Although this has since been disproved by many writers it served to stoke already inflamed racial sensitivities (Clayton 1981; Fairooz 1995 Juma 2007). In July 1963 youth members of ZNP, mostly young leftists, formed a splinter group, the Umma. Influenced by Marxism, they denounced religious influence in public life arguing that religion facilitated ongoing class dynamics and retarded progress. Of course their anti-God stance provided ammunition to elders to oppose their candidacy. In many ways, these political parties represented the array of political ideologies in Zanzibar at the time, ideologies that would later find expression in the isles' policy and legal framework (Clayton 1981; Fairooz 1995; Juma 2007).

The Revolution of January 12, 1964, put an abrupt end to the independence Zanzibar had attained in December 1963. Those who carried out the revolution justified their actions on two main grounds. They claimed they were putting an end to racial and economic domination by a minority Arab population against a majority African population. They also sought to put to rest the question of Zanzibar's identity as an African, not an Arab or Persian dominion. The question of Zanzibar's and more specifically Zanzibaris' identity continues to be at the heart of the islands' politics. To discredit the revolutionaries, loyalists argue that the Revolution was neither conceived nor led by indigenous Zanzibaris but was run by foreigners from the African mainland, thereby upsetting the local social and moral order.[17]

Nevertheless, under the electoral system in place, it was difficult for one party to win the elections outright and to form a government. An alliance of any two parties could tilt the balance against the party, with the most seats enabling it to form a government. In two decisive elections the ZNP and the Shirazi-dominated ZPPP party merged to form a ruling coalition, an affiliation that was read to signify the indigenous population's rejection of immigrant Africans from the Mainland. Aggrieved by the electoral system, African Mainlanders and their Shirazi sympathizers saw no option but to take power by force.

The search for political and cultural legitimacy was therefore key to the laws that were passed after the revolution and before the resumption of multiparty democracy. Indeed, immediately after the revolution, the new leaders suspended most democratic institutions, including the Constitution, because they were believed to aid minority domination and uphold the status quo. The judicial system was replaced by People's Courts composed of ordinary citizens (People's Court Decree of 1969). The legal system was presided over by the Revolutionary Council, led by the president. Multipartyism was abandoned, and in May 1965 Zanzibar was declared a single-party state, governed by the Afro-Shirazi Party (ASP), which purported to represent the interests of the majority: the Africans. Available literature and narrated accounts by those who lived through this tumultuous period make it abundantly clear that Zanzibar's political demons were played out (and settled) on the bodies of women (Clayton 1981; Fairooz 1995; Napoli 2005).

On assuming power the Revolutionary Government (RG) set out to implement a policy of racial integration, one that would allow African men access to non-African women. Among the first notable actions of the RG was the passage of the Equality, Reconciliation of Zanzibar Peoples Decree (No. 6 of 1964), which sought to abolish the racial and class system in Zanzibar, but in effect it put into process the RG's major racial strategy acted out on the bodies of women—forced marriages. The expectation was that the integrationalist policy would tear down existing social and class barriers by allowing those in love who faced unreasonable opposition from their families the possibility to get married by the state without the approval of the legal guardian. Effectively, it gave young people, especially young women, a façade of freedom in that they could marry without parental consent and the union would have legal recognition, contrary to the prevailing Islamic School of Law, which required the presence and consent of a legal guardian, the *wali*, for a marriage to take effect.[18]

Alas, in practice, the exercise became an avenue through which older men, most of whom were already married, preyed on young "virgins" to satisfy their sexual appetites or settle old scores. Members of the Revolutionary Council led by example, many forcibly marrying women previously denied to them, especially Arab and Indian girls and some women from prominent Shirazi families.[19] In response, many girls who were still in school were hurriedly (and ironically forcibly) married off by their parents to protect them from undesirable suitors. However, this did not deter determined figures who used their positions of power to dispose of their rivals in the most expedient manner—death or imprisonment—to fulfill their desire.

In this way, many arranged (and nonconsensual) marriages took place in the islands at this time. Yet few historians allude to the violations against women as a class, choosing instead to treat them as violations against a particular race, social class, or family. Arranged marriages were also instigated by financial need, as many families were rendered insolvent after their businesses and properties were seized or redistributed by the government (which had a leftist Marxist orientation) with the passage of the Confiscation of Immovable Property Decree of 1964 and the Land (Distribution) Decree of 1966. Other families resorted to this option as an escape mechanism to leave the island, which had become inhospitable for those who were seen to be representatives or supporters of the old order. Young women were therefore married off to relatives or men from their communities living on the Mainland or in neighboring states. To curb this route of escape, travel restrictions were imposed and fines set for parents who smuggled their daughters out of Zanzibar (Clayton 1981: 121).

Perhaps to curb the excesses and diffuse the unpopularity of the practice, the Marriage Solemnization and Registration (Amendment) Decree (Decree No. 6 of 1966) was passed indicating that a marriage could be denied if a suitor was a convict; had a venereal disease, TB, or leprosy; or was mentally ill (Section 17a). Although these qualifications were deemed reasonable they proved futile. In addition to the sheer terror paralyzing families from action, the prospect of women and their families seeking to enforce their rights in

People's Courts was small. How could a matter that was deemed *aibu* (shameful) be publicized in a hostile and populous court?

And while men in power passed legislation to facilitate their access to a diverse pool of women, they sought moral vindication by further regulating women's bodies. In 1970, the government passed the Spinsters Protection Decree (No. 5 of 1970). Under the law, spinsters were women between ages eighteen and twenty-one who were unmarried. Although the motivation behind the law was not clear, it was possibly an attempt to diffuse the influence of the global youth cultural revolution of the 1960s and 1970s on young women who increasingly transitioned from school to work before marriage. Under the law certain behaviors were criminalized, including having a child out of wedlock, a crime that carried a prison term.

Likewise, the state imposed strict dress codes consonant with local mores and modesty, a task previously confined to religious quarters. The National Cultural Protection Act of 1973 banned miniskirts, *booga* (bell bottoms), and the Afro hairstyle.[20] Women, including tourists, wearing certain types of clothing like backless dresses or shorts could be arrested and taken to a correctional facility. Foreign women entering Zanzibar were often issued with dress advisories or given a *khanga* cloth to cover their exposed skin. Because this law was not motivated by religion per se but by the preservation of Zanzibari culture, at no time were women compelled to cover themselves completely.

The political tension of the time resulted in undue political and social repressions. Local notions of respect were tested and directly undermined by the violent practices of the Revolutionary Government. For instance, killing men in front of their women, marrying girls without their family's consent, public humiliation of elders, and deliberate severing of social ties between neighbors or acquaintances were contrary to Swahili social mores of *muhali* (consideration) and *insafu* (generosity). As their "protectors" were killed, imprisoned, or neutralized, women became vulnerable and in many instances had to negotiate sex for their own or their families' survival, as typified in Adam Shafi's novel *Haini*. The situation was rendered more complex by the unavailability of contraception, which was illegal, even for married couples, resulting in unwanted pregnancies.

Certainly, the revolution and its aftermath remain a traumatic episode in Island history, especially for its women. Yet it also marked a period of great progress for women, especially in the realm of education and employment. If a girl was married while still in school, the husband was required to sign a pledge at the local party branch promising he would not interfere with her scholastic and extracurricular activities.[21] Marital relations were not just about what the husband or what the parents wanted, but also about upholding the vision of a revolutionary state.

Female subjects acquired a new status after the Revolution. The Registration of Citizens and Residents Decree of 1966 ascertained women's citizenship status. Women were enrolled in the National Military Service (Youth Camp Decree of 1971). They were also active in the ruling party, as well as in women's societies. As a result of the Africanization policy, affirmative action measures were implemented in the civil service aimed at increasing educational and professional opportunities especially for African women.

The RG's policies toward women were also communicated in symbolic terms. Whereas during the colonial era women were dissuaded from joining the public space, after the revolution their participation was expected and accepted. During the 1965 Revolutionary Day celebrations, women were compelled to attend the parade without any covering or *baibui* (a Swahili type of outer cloak), to signal a break with the past and the emergence of the "new woman." This scene was, however, never repeated, indicating the limits beyond which even a revolutionary authoritarian government could not transgress.

Clearly, the policy associated with racial and social integration produced contradictory results for women, but it also set new cultural standards. The first president set the example of his vision for women. In contrast to custom under the sultan and even on the Mainland, the president's wife was a public figure in her own right, accompanying the president at various events and leading the women's wing of the ruling party, even after her divorce. A number of women were appointed to public office. Some women even became directors and ministers, opening up leadership possibilities for women beyond the traditional female professions of teaching and nursing. Various development projects initiated during this period employed women in nontraditional sectors such as construction, factories, and agriculture. Religious influence, though present, was peripheral and did not determine women's legal rights. Rather, women were key subjects of the revolution whose reconfigured status validated it.

From 1985 to Date: Recognizing a Constitutional Subject

Shivji (1990) postulates that Zanzibar's union with Tanganyika is based on a shaky foundation. Indeed, the relationship has been anything but easy, especially after 1977, when Chama cha Mapinduzi (CCM) became the only and supreme political party in Tanzania, replacing the two political parties closely associated with the liberation movements in both Zanzibar and the Mainland. A constitutional crisis over the position of Zanzibar in the union saw the resignation of the second president of Zanzibar, Sheikh Aboud Jumbe Mwinyi, in 1984. This event was a precursor to a new climate of political dispensation, facilitated by the adoption of a new constitution containing a Bill of Rights.

By 1979 Zanzibar had reinstituted a representative body, the House of Representatives. Members were initially appointed by the Party and later elected directly. Multiparty democracy was formerly reintroduced in 1992, but increased liberalization has not rid Zanzibar of its volatile political disposition. Since 1995 the island has experienced three hotly contested elections reminiscent of the 1957, 1961, and 1963 elections, where, in addition to civilian deaths, countless women, especially from the opposition, have been raped or sexually abused to settle political scores.

Racial politics continue to dominate competing political discourses, where one's origin (whether of Mainland, Arab, or native extraction) and allegiances (to the ruling party, Oman, or Zanzibar) legitimize one's claim to political leadership. Lately, political divisions of the past have been relived with the association of the sister island Pemba, the opposition stronghold, with pro-Arabism and the main island Unguja with Africanism. It must not be forgotten that the Shirazi African leadership from the ZPPP, which allied itself with the ZNP during the transition to independence, originated in Pemba, while those who affiliated themselves with the African Party mostly came from Unguja.

Amid the recriminations, women have been able to make significant imprints in the political transition. For instance, in 1995 Naila Jidawi, a businesswoman and prominent member of the opposition, became the first woman to vie for the Zanzibar presidency.[22] This achievement prompted women from the ruling party such as Amina Salum Ali, the first female minister of finance, to contest the presidential seat in 2000 resulting in an open political campaign process within the ruling party. Women have also contested local elections with some success.

Women's increased agency in civic matters is evident in Zanzibar's political arena. Women's cloth, the khanga, is effectively used as a campaign tool and attests to women's increased presence in the political space. The strength of political rallies, for example, is often measured by the intensity of the khanga colors either worn by female and male members or used as banners.

Political actors no longer see women as marginal supporters of political parties, but recognize their role in defining local politics. For example, during the Treason Trials of the late 1990s against members of the main opposition party in Zanzibar, the Civil United Front (CUF), two women were among those charged and detained.[23]

A new human rights discourse is also taking shape in Zanzibar. The legal framework in the islands is visibly informed by international human rights standards, not partisan or class interests. And unlike the situation in other countries in the region, where civil society has played a pivotal role in ushering in favorable legal codes for women, in Zanzibar the state has been strongly involved. In particular, the creation of a department (presently a full Ministry) responsible for women's affairs[24] in the late 1980s has played a mediating role, reconciling community expectations with public policy.

Also, the participation of key government figures in important international forums involving women's human rights resulted in some concrete measures on the ground. For example, the enactment of the Sexual Offenses (Special Provisions) Act (SOSPA) is a testament to the implementation of CEDAW and the Vienna Declaration. The law, passed amid intense public outcry over egregious incidences of "immoral acts" and sexual crimes against women and children, aims to safeguard the personal integrity, dignity, and liberty of women and children.

In addition to adopting human rights language to define women's rights, SOSPA is significant in that it fundamentally amends the Penal Decree with regard to sexual crimes. Chiefly, the Act reflects development in international human rights law and advocacy for women's human rights. For example, it includes emerging forms of crimes committed against women such as trafficking for sexual and labor exploitation[25] and female genital mutilation (FGM) which is not common in the islands; it raises the age of consensual sex to eighteen years; and adopts gender sensitive language in all provisions related to sexual crimes. Moreover, SOSPA requires a lower standard to prove grave sexual assault or rape.[26] It does away with most of the old evidentiary requirements to prove rape such as ejaculation and corroboration. In 2004, SOSPA was further amended and included directly into the Penal Code.[27]

The Penal Act of 2004 shows great strides in redefining intimate relationships, at least legally even if offenses are still viewed as against morality. The Act introduces new crimes like "marital rape" and "sexual harassment," recognizing a woman as not just a passive recipient of male sexual advances but as someone with choice over the sexual act. Notably, the new legislation has empowered more women and parents to break the silence against crimes previously considered *aibu* (shameful) and thus not worthy of public display. However, procedural aspects of the law make it ineffective.

Although gender neutral and gender inclusive language is used in the 2004 law, it still demonstrates a bias toward the male sexual norm. Under the Act, sexual crimes committed against males attract higher sentences than those committed against women and other marginal groups. For instance, indecent assault against women, upon conviction, carries prison terms of three to fourteen years, while similar assaults on young boys attract a jail term of not less than twenty-five years. One can only assume that though the sexual act may be committed unlawfully against women and girls, it is less grave because it appears more "natural," whereas carnally knowing a man is "unnatural" in a society where sexual roles are defined in deeply heteronormative ways.

In this period of Zanzibar's history, we see a growing preoccupation with male sexuality. Homosexuality is criminalized and hefty prison terms and fines are imposed more severely on men than on women.[28] This criminalization occurred in response to extensive advocacy by the Lesbian, Gay, Bisexual, Transsexual and Intersexed (LGBTI) community globally against homophobic tendencies. Reacting to religious opinion and probably pushed by a desire to maintain some measure of moral leadership, amid fierce political opposition, the government inserted the provision against same sex relationships.[29]

Another significant milestone for women in recent times is the Spinster and Single Parent Children Protection Act of 2005. This Act replaced the much-decried Spinsters, Widows, and Female Divorcee Protection Act of 1985, a mutation of the 1970 Spinsters Protection Decree (No. 5 of 1970). Amendment to this law resulted from the concerted advocacy of the Zanzibar chapter of the Tanzania Media Women Association (TAMWA), which exposed the plight of girls under the law and worked with the relevant Ministry for women to see that the law was changed.

The 1985 law was loaded with moral connotations about what was considered "acceptable" sexual behavior involving girls or young women under twenty-one. The Act reflected legal (and perhaps social) attitudes against extramarital sex involving female students or spinsters, especially if it resulted in pregnancy.[30] Under the law, young women who became pregnant out of wedlock were incarcerated for two years (either while still pregnant or after delivery), while men responsible for the pregnancy, if found guilty, were sent to a correctional facility or reform school for a few months. Clearly, such provisions demonstrate strict attitudes toward extramarital sex. Ironically, while moral alarm persists over the sexual activity of older but unmarried women, there is renewed tolerance of sexual activity for girls who are minors, as long as they are married. In their case, chastity is no longer a social concern.

This disparity in treatment and sentencing outraged women's rights activists, prompting them to action. Often a pregnant girl would languish in jail while the culprit roamed free since absent DNA evidence he could always deny parentage. Activists argued that different moral standards were applied to women and men with dire legal consequences for women. They also invoked rights-based arguments based on the Convention on the Rights of the Child and the National Health Policy to question whether prison was the best place to house a pregnant woman or a newborn child.

Formerly, most parents had supported the 1985 law, arguing that pregnant girls were a bad influence on well-behaved girls. They reasoned that if pregnant girls were expelled from school they would be able to fully concentrate on their primary role as wife and mother. Other parents marry off their school-going daughters for fear that once enlightened they would become too liberated and promiscuous.[31] Although the government has been reluctant to take action against parents who marry their daughters who are still in school, to its credit the government has resisted pressure by purist religious elements to segregate girls from studying with male pupils or being taught by male teachers. Faced with a critical shortage of schools and teachers, the government can hardly afford to compromise women by conceding to these demands.

The 1985 law was changed in 2005 to require pregnant women to do community service for six months after delivery (Section 3(6)). While the amendments are hailed as a legislative victory, they do not go far enough in extricating women from "socially acceptable behavior." A sexual faux pas on her part has consequences beyond public scorn; it affects a child's social legitimacy. Under the law, male parents are absolved from any responsibility, moral or otherwise, toward a child born out of wedlock, the burden falling squarely on the mother. Nor can the child inherit from his or her father even if paternity is ascertained (Section 5(3)).

Some in the Muslim community have criticized the 2005 law as too lenient on girls and encouraging them to engage in premarital sexual activity. These accusations have not swayed the government to rescind it. The minister of health and social welfare defended the government's position, arguing that it brought the legal code up to international standards (AFP 2005). The minister of education, culture and sports defended the move in rights terms, arguing that "Thousands of girls are currently being denied their right to education regardless of the circumstances that led to their getting pregnant. This is what we want to change" ("Zanzibar Minister to Press for Repeal" 2003).

Perhaps for the first time the government defended its action to strike down a draconian law as necessary to reach a balance between its obligation to protect vulnerable groups under the constitution and international human rights norms. This departure represents a shift insofar as how the legal status of women is being negotiated in contemporary Zanzibar, which increasingly considers itself as being part of a wider global culture, one guided by human rights norms, not just cultural traditions or religious edicts.

Conclusion

In this chapter, I have argued that the legal framework provides insights into cultural discourses in Zanzibari society at different times in the islands her-story. Certainly, the cultural fabric has been influenced by its rich cultural crossroads. The legal system forms part of this legacy. Analyzing the content and context of laws reveals the prevailing attitudes and debates in the community about a desired order and future for human and gender relationships. Indeed, diverse political and social forces in Zanzibari society have claimed or deployed and continue to claim or to deploy existing or new understandings of culture, to construct novel cultural subjects to fulfill either social or political objectives. And in this process, culture is not just confined to the past, but is also something that is or could become.

During the colonial era, the concern of the state was to ensure that new laws conformed to local notions of propriety to achieve legitimacy in a patriarchal semi feudal setting. Islamic conceptions of "protection" and "seclusion" of the female body defined not only gender boundaries but also political boundaries, where the sexual and cultural body was out of bounds to colonial and foreign intrusion.

The 1964 Revolution boldly challenged segregationist policies that perpetrated class boundaries among the island communities via the implementation of a policy of social and racial integration that essentially facilitated access to the female body. These policies seriously compromised women's bodily integrity, but they nevertheless brought women out of seclusion and into the public sphere, calling for the renegotiation of cultural and gender subjects. It was through the physical and sexual access to the bodies of the custodians of culture that the revolutionaries managed to forge a new vision of Zanzibar, more aligned to national identities than to cultural or subcultural categories. Ultimately, the basis of the revolution redefined a new, more universal construction of Zanzibari society whose shared culture was national, warranting equal treatment of her subjects.

These developments are being seriously tested at present as Zanzibar engages with a new constitutional order and democratization. The country is keen to return to the world stage following a period of relative isolation, compelling the government to meet international standards in various aspects of governance. During this period, the legal framework demonstrates an ongoing negotiation between the particular and the universal in defining women's rights. However, the lack of an effective political opposition has propelled religion to act as the unifying force for today's Zanzibari identity, one that is not just insular but very global. At this moment in time women's experience in Zanzibar can perhaps be best understood in this light—on the one hand their status is defined by international human rights standards, but on the other their lived realities are a negotiation between those standards and a more transnational understanding of Islam, an increasingly political Islam that has a universal appeal, relevance, and impact.

The rise of political Islam in the island's landscape raises new challenges for the evolving legal culture and its conception of the female subject. While women's citizenship status has been enhanced in the democratic transition, religion is gradually being deployed to regulate women's personal and political choices. In the larger community women's rights are increasingly conceptualized and legitimized in an Islamic framework. In political literature the Zanzibari identity is affirmed by the image of the Muslim woman's dress, the distinguishing feature between women from the islands and those from the Mainland. This new identity is so strong that girls and women in Zanzibar have adopted the head covering as an integral part of the school uniform for both government and private schools as well as in public and private sectors. Female members from the opposition have also adopted a conservative mode of dressing perhaps to appeal to public opinion against the Ruling Party, which they accuse of representing the interests of mainland Tanzania not Zanzibaris. More than ever, women continue to define Zanzibar's political trajectory and her quintessential identity.

Zanzibar Laws and Statutes

Judicature and Application of Laws Act

Marriage and Divorce (Muslim) Registration Chapter 91

Regency Decree Chapter 30

Majority Decree No. 5 of 1917 Chapter 53 of the Laws of Zanzibar

Widows and Orphans Pensions (Amendment) Decree No. 43 of 1921

Asiatic Widows and Orphans Pensions Decree No. 48 of 1931

Penal Decree of 1934

Royal Marriage Decree No. 31 of 1940

Nationality Decree Chapter 39 of 1952

Employment of Women (Restriction) Decree No. 62 of 1953

Widows and Orphans Pensions (Amendment) Decree No. 1 of 1963

Presidential Decree No. 8 of 1964

Presidential Decree No. 13 of 1965

Presidential Decree No. 5 of 1966

Equality, Reconciliation of Zanzibar Peoples Decree No. 6 of 1964

Confiscation of Immovable Property Decree of 1964

Marriage (Solemnization and Registration) Amendment Decree
    No. 6 of 1966

Land (Distribution) Decree of 1966

Registration of Citizens and Residents Decree of 1966

The People's Court Decree of 1969

Spinsters Protection Decree No. 5 of 1970

Youth Camp Decree of 1971

National Cultural Protection Act of 1973

Education Act No. 6 of 1982

Constitution of Zanzibar, 1984

Sexual Offenses Special Provisions Act of 1998

Penal Act of 2004

Spinster and Single Parent Children Protection Act of 2005

Chapter 3

A Clash of Cultures: Women, Domestic Violence, and Law in the United States

Sally F. Goldfarb

For centuries, the American legal system condoned or ignored violence committed against women by their intimate partners. One of the major accomplishments of the American feminist movement during the past forty years has been the enactment of ambitious legal reforms designed to prevent and redress domestic violence. Yet it is widely acknowledged that these reforms have fallen short of achieving their goals. Although rates of domestic violence have declined in recent years, battering continues at epidemic levels. Moreover, many battered women choose not to utilize available legal remedies.[1] Examining battered women's legal rights through the lens of culture is one way of gaining insight into the inadequacy of current domestic violence laws. As the following discussion will show, domestic violence laws are too deeply immersed in mainstream legal culture and in prevailing cultural assumptions about women, while at the same time they are insufficiently attentive to the diverse cultural influences affecting battered women. Focusing on this "clash of cultures" will help to suggest promising directions for the next generation of domestic violence law reform in the United States.

Domestic Violence and the Culture of Law

Culture has been described as "a flexible repertoire of practices and discourses created through historical processes of contestation over signs and meanings" (Merry 1998: 577). American law itself can be viewed as a culture—one that, like any other culture, is fluid, contested, and porous, not static, monolithic, or bounded (Mezey 2001; Post 2003). It is experienced differently in different contexts and by members of different groups (Sarat 2000; Silbey 1992). The formal apparatus of American law includes a vast and varied network of federal and state constitutions; federal, state, and local legislation and administrative regulations; and judge-made case law. Despite this complexity, it is possible to identify certain distinctive characteristics of law in the United States that reflect and reinforce qualities of the society in which the law is embedded (Rosen 2006). Domestic violence law in particular provides a window into evolving conceptions of marriage, family, and gender.

Although legislation forbidding wife abuse was enacted in the Massachusetts Bay Colony as early as 1641, civil and criminal penalties for domestic violence remained rare until recent decades (Bartlett and Rhode 2006: 490). Initially, the law's refusal to intervene in cases of domestic violence was an outgrowth of the English common law rule of coverture. According to this rule, when a woman marries, her legal identity is incorporated into that of her husband and she ceases to have a separate legal existence. Since "the husband and wife are one person in law," a legal action by one against the other is a logical impossibility. These principles shaped the development of American legal doctrines such as interspousal tort immunity, which forbids civil suits by one spouse against the other, and the marital rape exemption, which dictates that a man's rape of his wife is not a crime (S. Goldfarb 2000b). Furthermore, because marital unity made the husband legally responsible for his wife's actions, coverture was deemed to confer on him the power of "domestic chastisement"—the right to use physical force to punish his wife and control her behavior (Siegel 1996). This legal approach, which prevailed from the colonial period until the mid-nineteenth century, expressed and perpetuated married women's subordination to their husbands.

During the mid-nineteenth century, with the emergence of the ideal of affectionate companionship in marriage and the image of woman as the "angel of the house," the common law rule permitting husbands to inflict corporal punishment on their wives came to seem both antiquated and indefensible. Judges consequently became less willing to rely on the right of chastisement. However, a new rationale arose for the laissez-faire approach to domestic violence: the concept of family privacy (Siegel 1996). This concept was predicated on the separate spheres ideology, with its vision of a split between the public sphere of government, law, and commerce and the private sphere of home and family (Kerber 1988). Privacy soon became a guiding principle for domestic violence law. In a typical case, refusing to allow a wife to sue her husband for assault, the Maine Supreme Judicial Court stated in 1877 that "'it is better to draw the curtain, shut out the public gaze, and leave the parties to forget and forgive'" (*Abbott v. Abbott*: 307, quoting *State v. Oliver*: 61–62). Similarly, in 1864, the North Carolina Supreme Court explained that "unless some permanent injury be inflicted, or there be an excess of violence . . . the law will not invade the domestic forum" (*State v. Black*: 263).[2]

The early and middle twentieth century brought some changes, such as the establishment of family courts that relied on social workers and took a therapeutic approach to family violence (Siegel 1996). But it was not until the 1970s, as a result of feminist advocacy casting domestic violence as a form of systemic gender oppression rather than an intrafamily conflict, that the legal response to domestic violence began its dramatic transformation. In striking contrast to previous eras, battered women over the following decades gained access to a host of vigorous legal remedies, ranging from mandatory arrest of batterers to civil protection orders to tort actions for damages.

One notable achievement of this period was the enactment of the federal Violence Against Women Act of 1994 (VAWA). Previously, legislation concerning domestic violence had been adopted almost exclusively at the state level.[3] As the federal government's first attempt at a comprehensive response to violence against women, VAWA contained dozens of provisions and authorized a then-record amount of $1.62 billion in federal funding to improve prevention, protection, victim services, law enforcement, and data collection.[4] VAWA also contained a civil rights provision, which declared for the first time that there is a federal civil right to be free from violent crimes motivated by the victim's gender. As discussed further below, the U.S. Supreme Court issued a controversial decision invalidating the civil rights provision six years after it was enacted (*United States v. Morrison* 2000).[5] However, the rest of VAWA remains in force, and since 1994 it has twice been reauthorized and expanded (Violence Against Women Act of 2000; Violence Against Women and Department of Justice Reauthorization Act of 2005).[6]

In comparison to notions like coverture and separate spheres, the cultural underpinnings of contemporary domestic violence law may not initially appear obvious. Yet it is possible to identify a number of cultural features of the American legal system that help explain current legal rules concerning domestic violence.

Patriarchy

When examining how law reflects the surrounding culture, it is always necessary to ask whose culture is being reflected. The answer is usually that law promotes the dominant culture while maintaining a guise of cultural neutrality. In general, American law openly acknowledges the influence of culture only when discussing disempowered groups that are perceived as "the other," such as in cases raising a "cultural defense" for crimes committed by immigrants (Volpp 2003). In comparison to these discussions of minority cultures, the influence of the dominant culture on law is both more hidden and more pervasive (Roberts 1999).

One aspect of the dominant American culture that is salient in American law is patriarchy. Patriarchy, which has been defined as the historically produced institutionalization of men's domination over women (Marshall 1997: 102), has continued to shape legal rules and their interpretation long after overtly discriminatory doctrines like coverture were officially discarded. Even when it is prohibiting domestic violence, the law is often unable to avoid privileging a male perspective. For example, the definition of domestic violence in state and federal laws typically emphasizes individual episodes of physical assault, with the severity of the assault determining the severity of the crime. This definition is consistent with the way men generally experience violence. However, it fails to capture many of the features that make domestic violence damaging to women, including the devastating harm inflicted by emotional abuse, the cumulative terrorizing impact of multiple "minor" assaults, and the function of domestic violence as both cause and effect of men's control over their female partners (Stark 2007).

The implementation of domestic violence laws by individual judges also reveals the influence of patriarchy. In one notorious case, a Maryland judge said that he did not believe a petitioner's testimony that her husband had held a gun to her head "because I don't believe that anything like this could happen to me" (Schafran 1990: 30). A Massachusetts judge denied a woman's request that her abusive husband be temporarily evicted from their home, despite the fact that the police confirmed that he had beaten her. The judge stated, "I don't believe she was beaten. I didn't see any bruises; most women bruise pretty easily. . . . My wife tells me I hate women. . . . I don't hate women.

I just hate what they do sometimes" (Ptacek 1999: 55). Studies of gender bias in the courts conducted during the 1980s and 1990s found that judges commonly trivialized or excused domestic violence despite major statutory reforms granting rights to battered women (Schafran 1995).

The Tendency to Dichotomize

Although categorization is basic to human thought (Krieger 1995), categories are not necessarily dichotomous. Dichotomous reasoning is extremely prevalent in Western cultures, and not surprisingly, American law is full of dualities. A number of these dualities have proven especially problematic when applied to domestic violence.

The concept of adversarialism is fundamental to the American legal system. In any legal action, there are assumed to be two parties whose interests are diametrically opposed. This assumption is ill-suited to the situation of a battered woman whose assailant is also her lover, her source of financial support, and the father of her children. Frequently, the only remedies offered by the legal system are incompatible with the emotional and practical entanglements that connect many battered women to their batterers. Battered women often say that they want to end the violence and keep the relationship, but there is typically no room to articulate this position within the law's adversarial framework. If a woman expresses sympathy for her abusive partner or is hesitant to end the relationship, some police, prosecutors, and judges will conclude that she does not deserve legal assistance. Conceiving of batterers and battered women as if they were pure antagonists is inaccurate and leads to distorted results. Although mediation and other restorative justice models have been proposed as alternatives to adversarial litigation, those models present problems of their own, which will be explored further below.

Similarly, the law's rigid distinction between victims and perpetrators creates an untenable situation for many battered women. Inadequate police protection and other factors lead many battered women to fight back against their abusers (Goodmark 2008). But when a battered woman fights back, she may lose her status as a victim and face harsh legal consequences. She may be subject to laws mandating arrest of domestic violence offenders (even though she was not the primary aggressor), she may be denied a protection order (even though her safety is at risk), and she may be prosecuted for injuring or killing the abuser (even though she was acting in self-defense).

Another example of a dichotomy that runs through American law is the distinction between public and private. As discussed above, this distinction was used to justify legal nonintervention in domestic violence beginning in the mid-nineteenth century. The principle of family privacy dominated domestic violence law into the 1970s, and its vestiges are still evident in the unwillingness of some police, prosecutors, and judges to interfere in cases of violence within the family. Moreover, the public-private split actually has two faces. In addition to the division between the market and the family, the law also recognizes a division between the state and civil society. Consequently, many federal constitutional and civil rights are not applicable to domestic violence because they are enforceable only against the state and state actors, not against private individuals (S. Goldfarb 2000b). In the words of Catharine MacKinnon, "For women, this has meant that civil society, the domain in which women are distinctively subordinated and deprived of power, has been placed beyond reach of legal guarantees" (1989: 164–65).

When Congress passed the civil rights provision of the Violence Against Women Act of 1994, opponents of the legislation relied heavily on arguments derived from both forms of the public-private split (S. Goldfarb 2000b). Ultimately, they succeeded in having the Supreme Court invalidate the civil rights provision on the ground that Congress lacked constitutional authority to enact it, despite extensive evidence that the provision was a legitimate exercise of congressional power under both the Commerce Clause and the Equal Protection Clause of the Constitution (*United States v. Morrison* 2000). The Supreme Court decision, reached by a five-to-four vote, was strongly criticized by the dissenting justices, legal scholars, and others (S. Goldfarb 2000a; Goldscheid 2000; MacKinnon 2000). The outcome in this case demonstrates the continuing power of the public-private distinction in American law.

Criminalization

The American legal system, like American society generally, relies heavily on criminalization as a putative solution to social problems. This has caused significant challenges for the effort to create appropriate legal remedies for domestic violence.

At its inception, the battered women's movement aimed to empower women and achieve social change through grassroots collaborative measures like safe homes, shelters, and consciousness raising groups. Many in the movement intentionally avoided entanglement with the state, which they viewed as male-dominated and untrustworthy (Schechter 1982). Even when battered women's advocates increasingly sought government funding and pushed for legal reforms during the 1970s and '80s, their focus remained largely on attaining social and economic equality for women. Recognizing that a woman's ability to avoid and escape violence is tied to her financial independence, their agenda included issues like employment, welfare, child support, child care, and housing. Although advocates called for the criminal justice system to treat domestic violence as seriously as other crimes, this was not their primary demand (Miccio 2005). However, given the underlying cultural bias toward criminalization, this was the demand that the legal system was most prepared to hear and embrace. As a result, since the 1980s, aggressive criminal justice approaches toward domestic violence have been widely adopted throughout the United States. These include mandatory arrest policies, which require police to arrest anyone who they have probable cause to believe has committed domestic violence, and "no-drop" prosecution policies, which prevent prosecutors from complying with a victim's request to drop charges against the abuser (Hanna 1996).

Along with critiques that have been leveled at criminalization generally—for example, that it is ineffective, diverts resources from needed social programs, and is an instrument of racism (Incite-Critical Resistance and Sudbury 2005)—the criminalization of domestic violence raises additional questions because domestic violence is in many ways different from other crimes. Unlike most crimes, domestic violence takes place within intimate relationships, in a context that often includes love, dependency, ambivalence, and other complicating factors. While some battered women want the abuser subjected to criminal punishment, many do not. Thus, it is not surprising that legal reform based on a model of treating domestic violence like other crimes has engendered a host of unforeseen problems.

Law and the Possibility of Cultural Change

Among the scholars and advocates who have critiqued current domestic violence law, some have concluded that legal remedies are of little use and that the surrounding culture must change before meaningful legal reform will be possible (Dasgupta and Eng 2003; Mills 2003). However, this approach fails to recognize that law is part of the larger culture, and that just as culture can change law, law can cause a change in broader cultural norms. Law both produces and is produced by social relations and cultural practices (Mezey

2001). The law's symbolic function in distinguishing right from wrong, as well as its ability to impose punishment and allocate resources, contribute to its power to create standards and categories that come to seem normal and inevitable (Geertz 1983; Sarat 2000). Seen in this light, the legal arena is a crucial site for initiatives to improve society's response to domestic violence.

The dramatic changes in domestic violence law achieved through feminist advocacy demonstrate that legal culture is not impervious to the pressures created by new discourses and power relationships. Furthermore, there is evidence that changes in law have affected the larger society, both by causing a drop in the rate of domestic violence (Dugan 2003; Farmer and Tiefenthaler 2003) and by serving a public education function that has persuaded many people that domestic violence is unacceptable. Indeed, the instrumental and cultural effects of legal reform are intertwined; one reason for the decline in the rate of domestic violence is the fact that legal prohibitions set a cultural tone that condemns domestic violence as wrongful.

Yet, as indicated above, the success of domestic violence law reform has been limited by deeply entrenched cultural factors. What does this tell us about the role of law in the battle against domestic violence?

First, it is clear that legal reform can never be successful in isolation. Legal strategies must be integrated with complementary social and political analysis and advocacy (Schneider 2000). At the same time, because of the unique power of law and legal institutions in American society, legal measures can play a valuable and distinctive role in the movement to secure women's freedom from domestic violence.

Legal rights claims are intrinsically assertive and constitute a demand to be heard (Minow 1987). They thus provide a potent source of empowerment for battered women. Patricia Williams wrote, "For the historically disempowered, the conferring of rights is symbolic of all the denied aspects of their humanity: rights imply a respect that places one in the referential range of self and others, that elevates one's status from human body to social being" (1991: 153). In the words of Elizabeth Schneider, "Rights claims assert women's selfhood collectively, thereby giving them a sense of group identity and pride; they make manifest the fact that women can act and claim their place in history" (2000: 40). For a battered woman to realize that she has rights is often deeply transformative.

As one example of this process, studies have shown that applying for a protection order often leads to profound changes in a woman's perception of herself and her situation. One woman who obtained an order said, "After so long of just taking it and taking it I needed to be able to show myself as much as show him that I was tired of being a victim. . . . [T]hat feeling, of fighting back and speaking out, will never leave me" (Fischer and Rose 1995: 424). Another woman said that by obtaining a protection order "I proved something to him and proved something to myself" (Ptacek 1999: 165). "[Protection orders] tell women that their pain is taken seriously and they tell men their behavior is wrong, that violence must cease, and that women are the aggrieved party, not the criminals" (Schechter 1982: 317). By breaking the silence about the abuse and demanding public redress for injustices that have been hidden in private, battered women can regain a sense of control, which in turn enables them to take further steps toward improving their lives (Fischer and Rose 1995).

Together with their ability to change individual women, rights claims also have the capacity to bring about a cultural shift (Minow 1987; Schneider 2000). The very existence of legal remedies for domestic violence counteracts the traditional view that domestic violence is a personal, private problem that is the victim's fault. In her study of a family court domestic violence program in Hawaii, Sally Engle Merry described the way that "the discourse of the court denaturalized domestic violence. As judges, attorneys, and advocates talk about domestic violence, it slips from the unseen to the seen. . . . Actions that were part of the 'normal' order of family relationships acquire new names, such as abuse. And abuse, unlike the violence embedded in patriarchal authority, is reconstituted as a crime" (Merry 1995: 19). Thus, law can promote a new vocabulary, a new perspective, and a new cultural understanding of domestic violence. The impact of this change is not limited to men and women directly involved in legal proceedings.

The Violence Against Women Act illustrates the potential for cultural transformation through law. Its civil rights provision changed the terms of the national debate by framing domestic violence and rape as forms of discrimination.[7] Numerous congressional hearings and reports, along with extensive press coverage, helped publicize this perspective to the general public. Even though the Supreme Court invalidated the civil rights provision, the legislation has had a positive and lasting effect on the evolution of social and legal responses to violence against women. The idea that women have a civil right to be free from violence directed at them because of their gender, which was once considered a radical notion, has become a familiar, mainstream concept, despite the fact that it is no longer enforceable under federal law. VAWA's civil rights provision has continued to inspire legislative activity on the federal, state, and local levels to expand legal protections against gender-motivated violence and its effects (Goldscheid 2005).

However, any law has intrinsic limitations. Foremost among them is the fact that claiming rights does not necessarily mean that one will obtain them. "The law provides a place to contest relations of power, but it also determines the terms of the contest" (Merry 1995: 20). Although law can help change discriminatory attitudes, those attitudes do not disappear overnight and can hamper the enforcement of even the most revolutionary statutes (Kahan 2000; Römkens 2001). Legal reforms in favor of historically disadvantaged groups often trigger resistance, as dominant groups seek to reestablish prior norms that operated in their favor (Siegel 1996). There is an implicit paradox in attempting to use the law to overcome gender inequality, since the application and interpretation of the law rest largely in the hands of non-feminist officials. The Supreme Court decision invalidating the VAWA civil rights provision certainly demonstrated the limits of the law's ability to alter patterns of unequal power between men and women.

Even when a law is not struck down as unconstitutional, there is no guarantee that it will be properly implemented. Although enforcement of domestic violence laws has improved dramatically in recent years, gaps remain. The case of Jessica Gonzales provides a tragic example. In June 1999, Gonzales's estranged husband violated a protection order by kidnapping their three daughters. The police took no action in response to Gonzales's repeated pleas for assistance, despite a state statute that instructed police to arrest or seek a warrant for the arrest of an offender who has violated a protection order. The three girls were later found dead in their father's truck (*Town of Castle Rock v. Gonzales* 2005).[8]

Just as the law's refusal to provide redress supports cultural trends permitting domestic violence, laws that vigorously forbid domestic violence undercut the cultural tolerance for such violence. Engaging with the legal system poses risks, but given the centrality of law in American society, feminist advocates can't afford not to include legal measures among their strategies for combating domestic violence. The question that remains is how to do so most effectively. Feminists must dwell in "the murky middle ground between total rejection and total endorsement of working with the state" (Schneider 2000: 196). Law, like the state generally, "is a site of active contestation over the construction of gender inequalities and power. Legislative decisions and institutional practices are made in historically specific social, political, and economic contexts that shape, by either perpetuating or altering, particular social formations of gender" (Reinelt 1995: 87, quoted in Schneider 2000: 196). Thus, feminist legal advocacy on domestic violence must be grounded in a critical analysis that focuses on advancing gender equality.

Cultural Assumptions About Battered Women

Feminist legal theorists have consistently maintained that legal doctrines should grow out of and reflect women's actual experiences (Bartlett 1990; MacKinnon 1989). Yet the law often relies on stereotypes about women in general and battered women in particular. A case in point is the widespread assumption that all battered women are passive victims. This assumption has colored a number of legal doctrines, to women's detriment.

Mandatory arrest laws, designed to ensure that police arrest anyone they have probable cause to believe has committed domestic violence, have had an unexpected consequence: a major increase in the number of women arrested (Coker 2001). Contrary to popular belief, many battered women do fight back. Policies grounded on the premise of female passivity can backfire against women who do not fit the stereotype.

Similarly, the "battered woman syndrome" defense has done harm as well as good. The battered woman syndrome was originated by psychologist Lenore Walker (1979, 1984), who described domestic violence as a cycle consisting of a tension-building phase, an acute battering incident, and a honeymoon phase. Walker also drew on the research of experimental psychologist Martin Seligman, who showed that dogs subjected to random electrical shocks would eventually stop trying to escape; she concluded that battered women, like the dogs in Seligman's experiment, suffer from "learned helplessness" that renders them incapable of acting in their own self-interest (Walker 1979: 45–51). Walker's theories gained rapid acceptance. Media depictions of domestic violence, such as the book and movie *The Burning Bed*, reinforced the image of battered women as pitiful and submissive (Mahoney 1991). As a result, courts began to admit expert testimony supporting the battered woman syndrome defense in cases of a woman accused of killing or attacking her abuser.

Critics have pointed out that the cyclical pattern described by Walker does not occur in all abusive relationships and that no single psychological profile describes all battered women (Dutton 1993). In contrast to the learned helplessness theory, there is ample evidence that battered women actively seek assistance, but that the people and institutions that they approach typically fail to help them (Gondolf and Fisher 1988).

Although the battered woman syndrome defense has been helpful to some defendants, its portrayal of all battered women as weak and helpless can lead judges and juries to conclude that a woman who struck back forcefully against her partner must not really have been abused. As a result, her claim that she was acting in self-defense may be rejected (Goodmark 2008). African American women, who are often stereotyped as strong and aggressive, are particularly unlikely to benefit from the battered woman syndrome (Allard 1996; Ammons 1995). So too, a battered lesbian who kills or attacks her abusive female partner does not fit the image conveyed by the battered woman syndrome (P. Goldfarb 1996).

Furthermore, by describing battered women as psychologically impaired, the battered woman syndrome has negative implications for domestic violence survivors in other types of legal proceedings. To the extent that a battered woman is perceived as passive or helpless, courts are likely to count this against her when deciding a case in which she is seeking child custody or defending herself against charges of child abuse or neglect (Mahoney 1991).

Ironically, the cultural message that labels all battered women helpless victims coexists with exactly the opposite message: that women are just as violent as men and therefore need no special legal protection. In fact, empirical studies consistently demonstrate that most domestic violence is committed by men against women, and that the gender disparity grows as the risk of physical injury increases (S. Goldfarb 2008: 1491). Moreover, women are far less likely than men to act as primary aggressors or to engage in a pattern of coercive control of their partners (Stark 2007). Like the stereotype that women are purely victims, the stereotype that women are as violent as men is reductive, inaccurate, and fails to provide a valid basis for law and public policy.

The way out of this impasse lies in recognizing that battered women are both victims and agents. On one hand, the range of choices and actions open to battered women is sharply circumscribed not only by the abuse itself, but also frequently by other forces such as poverty and racism. On the other hand, contrary to Walker's learned helplessness theory, battered women are often remarkably resourceful in their efforts to stop the violence and seek outside assistance. For battered women, victimhood and agency are inextricably intertwined; they exercise agency under conditions of constraint (Abrams 1999; Mahoney 1991). Forging an appropriate legal response to domestic violence requires a rejection of the false dichotomy between victim-hood and agency.

Battered Women's Cultures

The law tends to assume that all battered women fit a single mold and that the same legal measures will work for all cases. This tendency can be seen in the recent adoption of uniform policies, such as mandatory arrest, no-drop pros-ecution, automatic issuance of protection orders in criminal cases (Suk 2006), and requiring all civil protection orders to prohibit contact between the parties (S. Goldfarb 2008). In fact, women's multiple identities demand a more nu-anced approach.

One hallmark of current legal remedies for domestic violence is that they usually require the victim to separate from the abuser. Examples include di-vorce, arrest and prosecution of offenders, and protection orders prohibiting contact between the parties.[9] The law's emphasis on separation is one of the principal reasons for women's reluctance to utilize available legal remedies for domestic violence (S. Goldfarb 2008). By requiring women to separate from their partners as the price of receiving legal assistance, the law ignores several types of cultural influences on women.

Most women are acculturated to place a high value on establishing and maintaining interpersonal relationships, including relationships with a spouse or other intimate partner (Friedman 2003: 99, 136). Abusive relation-ships are often multidimensional, with episodes of abuse interspersed among positive experiences characterized by mutual emotional commitment, com-panionship, intimacy, and sharing. While many battered women want to sever their ties with the abuser, many others do not. They want the law to re-habilitate the relationship, not end it. This aspiration should not be dismissed as naive or misguided. Contrary to the usual expectation that battering will inevitably escalate over time, studies show that many women have succeeded in remaining in their relationships and putting an end to violence; with the assistance of the legal system, many more might be able to do so.[10]

By requiring the victim to separate from the abuser, the most common remedies for domestic violence are consistent with the values of individual autonomy and protection of the self. These values are deeply rooted in the legal system and, not coincidentally, they are culturally associated with men. However, it is possible to reconceive both autonomy and self-protection in ways that are more compatible with women's commitment to maintaining relationships. Although autonomy is often considered synonymous with atomistic individualism, some feminists have advanced an alternative view, which emphasizes that an important component of autonomy is the ability to express and constitute oneself through relationships with others (Friedman 2003; McClain 2006: 18; Nedelsky 1989). If the power of law could be directed at improving relationships rather than ending them, women's opportunities for developing autonomy through relationships would be enhanced. With regard to self-protection, it is by no means clear that forcing a battered woman to separate from the abuser actually advances her safety. On the contrary, leaving the abuser often places her at greater danger because of the prevalence of "separation assault"—that is, an intensification of violence triggered by the woman's attempt to end the relationship (Mahoney 1991).

Aside from cultural forces that lead women to place a priority on intimate relationships, some women's cultural circumstances discourage separation for additional reasons. A woman in a minority or immigrant community who is linguistically and culturally isolated from the majority culture will find it difficult to leave her partner, particularly if doing so would entail rejecting her community. Cultures in the United States differ in the extent to which a woman's choice to leave an abusive relationship is viewed as an acceptable option. While the dominant culture is relatively supportive of a battered woman who chooses to leave her relationship, live as a single parent, and work outside the home to support herself and her children, there are cultures in which many people would see any of those actions as selfish or immoral (Yoshioka and Choi 2005).

In general, the law needs to develop more awareness of and sensitivity to cultural diversity among battered women (Sokoloff and Pratt 2005). In particular, aggressive criminalization of domestic violence has different impacts on members of different communities. Women of color are often reluctant to embroil their partners in the criminal justice system, which has historically engaged in rampant racial and ethnic discrimination (Crenshaw 1991). Women living in cultures that emphasize community honor face significant obstacles to pressing criminal charges against their partners. For immigrant women and partners of immigrant men, the threat of deportation is an additional deterrent to bringing criminal charges. For victims of violence in lesbian relationships, the prospect of outing oneself and one's partner in a homophobic society, the likelihood of facing disbelief and hostility from the legal system, pressure from the lesbian community to present a positive image to outsiders, and the scarcity of shelters and other service agencies that are receptive to lesbians combine to make calling the police an unattractive option (Kanuha 2005).

Criminalizing domestic violence can be particularly burdensome for low-income women. Poor women are at high risk of experiencing violence, and experiencing violence is one of the factors that make and keep women poor (Raphael 2003). Women with limited financial resources may be unwilling to have their partners arrested and incarcerated because of the losses they would suffer as a result. These might include loss of access to the abuser's income, loss of his child care assistance leading to the survivor's inability to keep a job, and loss of support from his extended family.

Along with gender, many other factors affect the situation of battered women, including race, ethnicity, religion, class, disability, sexual orientation, and immigration status. An essentialist approach that treats battered women as a homogeneous group is doomed to failure. As Kimberlé Crenshaw has pointed out (1991), gender intersects with other aspects of women's identities to shape their experiences of oppression. In keeping with Crenshaw's theory of intersectionality, all the cultural influences that affect battered women must be considered in order to devise suitable legal responses.

Currently, when the law does take note of culture in domestic violence cases, it often does so in harmful ways. The "cultural defense" offered in some domestic violence cases attempts to excuse the defendant's behavior on the ground that as an immigrant from a non-Western country, he was merely following the dictates of his inherently misogynistic culture. This reflects a broader pattern whereby Americans tend to see domestic violence in "foreign" or "primitive" cultures as culturally determined, while looking to other factors like individual psychology or interpersonal conflict to explain domestic violence in their own group (Narayan 1997). This approach ignores both the support for women's rights in other cultures and the presence of misogyny in the mainstream culture of the United States. The law must recognize that culture influences domestic violence in every community, but that the specific circumstances of each case mediate the impact of culture (Volpp 2001).

Future Directions in Domestic Violence Law Reform

The preceding critique of contemporary domestic violence law points to a number of directions for future reform efforts. Although further work is needed to develop each of the following proposals, they suggest promising areas for research, analysis, and advocacy.

Diversity

Because of the diversity of domestic violence survivors, the law must provide diverse resources and remedies. Uniform legal interventions are problematic because of their failure to provide different choices for different women. Access to the legal system must be available through varied channels, including culturally sensitive legal assistance programs. A number of grassroots organizations have appeared throughout the country that specialize in serving battered women belonging to specific racial, ethnic, religious, immigrant, and sexual orientation minority groups. Mainstream domestic violence organizations—as well as judges and other actors in the legal system—must develop "cultural competence," which requires awareness of one's own perspective and preconceptions, openness to accurate information about other cultures, and the ability to treat people as individuals rather than as representatives of cultures (Goodman and Epstein 2008: 104; Ramos and Runner 1999: 1–41–1–47).

Listening to Women's Voices

Listening to battered women is a source of empowerment for them and a source of information for people and institutions that seek to meet their needs (Goodman and Epstein 2008). Accordingly, women's voices must be given primacy in the development and application of legal remedies. This can take place simultaneously on many levels and in many settings. Research on domestic violence and the legal system should incorporate women's own narratives (Fischer and Rose 1995; Goodmark 2005). In legislative advocacy, coalitions must not merely include diverse members but must allow those members to set priorities and decide on strategy (Rivera 1998). In attorneys' representation of individual clients, the "woman-defined advocacy" approach provides a helpful model. Woman-defined advocacy

> means advocacy that starts from the woman's perspective, integrates the advocate's knowledge and resources into the woman's framework, and ultimately values . . . [the survivor as] the decision maker, the one who knows best, the one with the power. . . . [I]t seeks to

craft the alternatives that will enhance women's safety, given the realities facing each battered woman. (Davies, Lyon, and Monti-Catania 1998: 3–4)

This approach stands in sharp contrast to the "service-defined advocacy" approach used by many lawyers, which focuses on what the law can do rather than what the woman needs.

Enabling women's authentic voices to be heard in court is particularly challenging. First, more time will need to be allocated simply to give women the opportunity to speak. Studies show that the average protection order hearing lasts less than fifteen minutes.[11] Second, lawyers often pressure clients to present their stories in a way that coincides with cultural stereotypes about battered women. Lawyers fear that allowing a woman to deviate from the "stock narrative" of domestic violence victims (for example, by revealing that she fought back, or that she does not want to end the relationship, or that she is angry rather than frightened) will alienate judges and juries. However, if battered women began to tell a greater variety of stories in court, judges and juries might become increasingly able to recognize and respect the differences among battered women (Goodmark 2008).

Shifting the Emphasis from Criminal to Civil Remedies

Criminal penalties serve an important purpose by signifying society's condemnation of domestic violence and holding batterers accountable for their acts. If a woman wants her abuser arrested and punished, criminal laws are an indispensable resource. However, as indicated above, excessive reliance on criminalization has undermined the effectiveness of the legal system's response to domestic violence and has created particular problems for women of color, immigrants, lesbians, and poor women.

In comparison to the criminal justice system, the civil justice system is better suited to recognizing the diversity and agency of battered women. Unlike criminal actions, which are controlled by a prosecutor, civil cases are brought by an individual woman to serve her own purposes, permit the woman to seek various forms of relief including financial compensation, and are governed by a more favorable burden of proof. While civil actions are not a panacea (Goldscheid 2007), they have significant potential to advance the interests of battered women.

Examples of civil proceedings include civil protection orders, tort actions for personal injury, and lawsuits for violation of the victim's civil rights. Access to these types of claims should be expanded. For instance, in some states, protection orders are unavailable to same-sex couples, victims in dating relationships, or minors (Little 2008; Saperstein 2005).

Legal Remedies That Do Not Require Separation

Since many women want to end the abuse without ending the relationship, and since separation often triggers intensified violence, legal remedies should be available that do not require the survivor to sever her ties with the abuser.

As one illustration of this approach, battered women should have the option of obtaining a protection order that permits ongoing contact but forbids future abuse. Although such orders are not unprecedented, they are currently prohibited in some jurisdictions, rarely used in others, and virtually unknown to the general public as well as many lawyers, judges, and scholars. Through the use of careful screening mechanisms and enforcement procedures, this system can protect a woman's safety while putting the force of law behind her personal choices. While protection orders permitting ongoing contact are not suitable for all cases, they are a valuable alternative to conventional "stay-away" orders (S. Goldfarb 2008).

Positive Rights and Material Support

In general, the U.S. legal system is more oriented toward guaranteeing negative rights (such as the right to be free from government interference with certain freedoms) than positive rights (such as a government obligation to fulfill basic socioeconomic needs). Domestic violence law is no exception.

The law has been relatively ineffective in addressing what many battered women consider their single most pressing need: material support. Employment, financial assistance, housing, and child care are among the material goods women desperately need to overcome the impact of violence and attain independence and security for themselves and their children.

Legal reform has made some progress toward meeting women's material needs. Civil protection orders and tort claims offer the possibility of monetary recovery, particularly if the abuser or other defendant has financial resources or insurance coverage (Sussman 2006; Wriggins 2001). Some federal, state, and local laws protect victims' rights to housing and employment, but these protections are limited in scope (Goldscheid 2005). Under federal welfare law, the Family Violence Option permits states to exempt domestic violence victims from certain restrictions on receiving public assistance. However, implementation of this program by the states has been inadequate, and the 1996 federal welfare overhaul has been extremely detrimental to battered women (Casey et al. 2009). Domestic violence survivors may be eligible for government-funded victim compensation programs, but the amounts awarded tend to be low (Goldscheid 2004).

Although piecemeal reforms have provided some material resources for victims of domestic violence, a far more ambitious framework is needed. A positive right to material welfare has not always been foreign to the American legal landscape. Such an approach dominated American law during the New Deal of the 1930s and briefly thereafter (Harvey 2004). However, that approach was eclipsed in subsequent decades. To recapture this perspective would require either looking to the example of other countries such as South Africa, which has enshrined a right to certain material goods in its constitution (Christiansen 2007), or effectuating the standards established in international law instruments like the Universal Declaration of Human Rights (Columbia Law School Human Rights Institute et al. 2008). Either step would represent an ambitious transformation of American law.

In the absence of a wholesale shift to positive rights, a useful fallback position would be to apply the "material resources test" formulated by Donna Coker (2000). Under this test, "priority should be given to those laws and policies which improve women's access to material resources." Furthermore, "the standard for determining the impact on material resources should be the situation of women in the greatest need who are most dramatically affected by inequalities of gender, race, and class" (1009). This method would help identify the legal reforms that could best serve the neediest battered women.

Using Law to Change Legal Culture

One way to improve legal culture is by harnessing the power of law itself to change legal actors and institutions.

The Violence Against Women Act of 1994 exemplifies this approach. Many of the Act's dozens of provisions were designed to effect change in the legal system. The statute authorized federal funds to educate police, prosecutors, and judges about violence against women. It required government agencies applying for certain grants to show that they were collaborating with nongovernmental domestic violence and sexual assault programs, and to document the "demographic characteristics of the populations to be served, including . . . disability, race, ethnicity and language background." Grants were made available to law enforcement and prosecution agencies specifically for the purpose of "developing or improving delivery of victim services to racial, cultural, ethnic, and language minorities." In distributing the grant funds, the statute required that state governments recognize and address the needs of underserved populations, based on factors such as rural isolation, racial or ethnic identity, language barriers, or physical disabilities (VAWA, subtitles A, B, D).

In addition to the grant programs, the enactment of the statute as a whole triggered a change in norms within the legal system. VAWA was the first major federal legislation addressing violence against women. As such, it signaled a new level of governmental commitment to combating violence against women and put actors at every level of the justice system on notice that this issue should be treated with the utmost seriousness.

Involving Community

The effectiveness of law depends in large part on informal community norms. For example, domestic violence rates are higher in areas with higher rates of social disorganization (Hampton et al. 2005), and some research suggests that arresting domestic violence offenders has a stronger deterrent effect in neighborhoods with lower crime and unemployment rates (Schmidt and Sherman 1996). In addition to whatever consequences a batterer incurs from the legal system, he might also pay a social cost as a result of community disapproval. Because prevailing cultural norms determine the existence and amount of that cost, they can encourage or discourage domestic violence.

Community-based education and advocacy can play an important role in the fight against domestic violence. A number of models exist for community involvement, including grassroots community organizing, peer leaders drawn from the local community, and community-based counseling programs (Rivera 1998; Yoshioka and Choi 2005). All these approaches deserve further consideration and study.

However, problems arise when community-based programs are considered as a substitute for legal intervention in domestic violence cases. Some commentators have proposed that therapeutic or restorative justice approaches, such as victim-offender mediation, sentencing circles, and group conferences, should take the place of legal sanctions. These models typically provide a non-adversarial forum that draws on extended family and community members to assist in resolving the parties' dispute (Coker 1999; Mills 2003). Although these alternatives reflect a well-intentioned attempt to avoid the pitfalls of the legal system, they do not sufficiently safeguard the interests of battered women, have not been demonstrated to be effective, and run the risk of deemphasizing the wrongfulness of domestic violence (Fiore and O'Shea 2007; Herman 2005). Furthermore, they lack the resources and the actual and symbolic power of law. Similar criticisms apply to batterer intervention programs. Although well-designed programs seem to help some men change their abusive attitudes and behavior, empirical research has failed to demonstrate their effectiveness at preventing recidivism (Feder and Wilson 2005; Jackson et al. 2003).

When contemplating the role of the community in the fight against domestic violence, it is important to remember that the community is potentially part of the problem as well as part of the solution. Community members may explicitly or implicitly support gender inequality and the use of violence. Therefore, educating and mobilizing the community against domestic violence must precede any attempt to rely on the community to promote an anti-violence message.

Nonadversarial dispute resolution methods that have been developed in other cultural contexts, such as the Navajo peacemaking process or South Africa's Truth and Reconciliation Commission, have not been consistently successful in dealing with violence against women (Andrews 2007; Coker 1999). Even if these methods were entirely effective, it is not clear that they could maintain their effectiveness when transplanted into a different cultural setting.

In short, community-based programs should be regarded as complements to, and not substitutes for, the legal system. Ideally, formal legal norms and informal community norms can be mutually reinforcing and achieve a level of influence together that neither could achieve alone.

International Human Rights Law

New insights can be gained by placing American domestic violence law in a global perspective. International human rights sources, such as CEDAW General Recommendation No. 19 on Violence Against Women (1992), the Vienna Declaration and Programme of Action (1993), and the Declaration on the Elimination of Violence Against Women (1993), provide a clear, unequivocal statement that violence against women is a human rights violation.[12] With the demise of VAWA's civil rights provision, no such statement exists in federal law in the United States, and only a small minority of American states and localities have adopted similar legislation (Goldscheid 2006).

Although American legislators and courts have often been unreceptive to international human rights law (indeed, the United States is one of the few countries that have not ratified the Convention on the Elimination of All Forms of Discrimination against Women), there are signs that this resistance may be weakening. Feminist lawyers in the United States have begun to incorporate arguments based on international human rights law in cases involving domestic violence (Schneider 2004). Reports have been compiled in at least three states that chronicle the family courts' treatment of battered women in the form of a human rights investigation, complete with first-person narratives of victims and an analysis of international human rights norms that have been violated (Arizona Coalition Against Domestic Violence 2003; Cuthbert et al. 2002; Voices of Women Organizing Project and Human Rights Project 2008).

In addition to bringing international law to the United States, another strategy is to bring the United States to international law. In 2007, the Inter-American Commission on Human Rights agreed to decide a human rights claim brought by Jessica Gonzales, the domestic violence survivor whose three children were killed after the police failed to enforce her protection order against her estranged husband (Bettinger-López 2008).[13] This is the first international human rights complaint brought by a domestic violence survivor against the United States. At this writing, the Commission has not yet issued its decision on the merits of the case. Although the Commission has no enforcement authority, a decision adverse to the United States would be politically embarrassing and would put pressure on the government to strengthen enforcement of domestic violence laws.

Invoking international human rights norms changes the frame of reference.

The human rights framework, which concentrates on governmental accountability for state acts and omissions that violate basic notions of dignity, civility, and citizenship, offers a different approach [from U.S. law]. Because the government has an affirmative obligation under international law to exercise due diligence and protect individuals known to be at risk, human rights can be a powerful mechanism for highlighting the state's role in perpetuating violence against women when it fails to respond appropriately to victims. (Bettinger-López 2008: 188)

Thus, international human rights claims are one way of shifting cultural norms within and outside the legal system toward greater recognition of the rights of battered women.

In conclusion, despite significant progress on improving domestic violence law in the United States, much work remains to be done. An awareness of the role of culture in shaping the legal response to domestic violence can help point the way to effective future reforms.

PART II

Travels and Translations

Chapter 4

Making Women's Human Rights in the Vernacular: Navigating the Culture/Rights Divide

Peggy Levitt and Sally Engle Merry

Culture and rights usually seem at war with each other. They are portrayed as opposites, such that the advance of one means the retreat of the other. Anthropologists have criticized this opposition for some time, yet it persists in popular culture (e.g., Wilson 1996; Cowen, Dembour, and Wilson 2001). Both popular discussions and human rights debates end up juxtaposing these two ideas. Cultural practices undermine and diminish rights. Rights concepts disrupt and weaken culture and social order. The two seem irreconcilable. One of the most vivid illustrations of this opposition is the portrayal of the Taliban political movement in Afghanistan in the late 1990s with its depictions of fully veiled women, exclusion from schools, and oppressive punishments for alleged sexual misbehavior. Such images proved that the culture of Afghanistan was so unjust that U.S. intervention in Afghanistan was necessary to protect women's human rights. And of course, female genital cutting is seen as a classic example of the oppression of culture, with its depictions of the pain and suffering of women forced to endure the surgery by fathers, husband, and "cutters," who are portrayed as embedded in a "traditional" culture.

These stories insist that there is an inevitable opposition between rights and culture, and that rights are weapons that push against intractable culture. Many of the stories about the opposition of culture and rights have a gen-

dered subtext. They typically zero in on women as the quintessential innocent victims of culture. Many of the examples where human rights challenge
what are defined as oppressive cultural practices concern women: female
genital cutting, honor killings, sex selection, sex trafficking by parents or
relatives who sell their daughters, child marriage, dowry murders, *devadasi*
(women dedicated to serve a deity in a temple who sometimes become pros-
titutes) arrangements, and sometimes veiling. The response to critiques of
these forms of injury is often that these are parts of culture and must be
preserved, although such arguments are often made by political leaders or
lineage heads rather than the women themselves. As passive and vulnerable
persons, women need to be rescued by a muscular human rights or humanitarianism or even by a masculinist state such as the Bush regime in the U.S.

Human rights interventions in nongendered domains, such as torture or
the right to food, rarely portray such a stark opposition between an emancipatory rights discourse and an oppressive culture. Intriguingly, there are
few reports of objections to installing traffic lights or licensing regimes because they will disrupt culture, although such systems clearly do alter practices of governance. Conducting a census does not seem to challenge culture,
although making statistical measurements of populations is a particular
historically and culturally specific practice that emerged with the rise of the
modern nation-state in Europe and the U.S. in the early nineteenth century.
The census was an important technology for the emerging nationalism of
nineteenth-century Europe and its focus on political economy. The effort to
map and tally a nation's population along with its size and capacities was premised on the idea that a state's population is the basis of its wealth. Assessing
its characteristics facilitates managing this wealth.

Moreover, even the questions asked in a census are cultural products,
expressing established social categories and prevailing social concerns. The
decision to measure the distance to work or the presence of indoor toilets in
a census cannot be understood outside culture. Despite the culturally embedded nature of a census, there are rarely international debates about the way
a census disrupts or undermines culture. In my visits to meetings of the UN
Statistical Commission, I (Merry) heard virtually no discussion of the way
these new technologies of knowledge might threaten cultural understandings, social order, or subjectivity.

The international human rights system is also deeply cultural in its procedures, ideas, and work. Rights are a cultural phenomenon, expressing a
particular way of talking about the individual and the state, validating the

forms of respect for difference, and articulating how individuals should re-late to each other in order to behave justly. The system has its own historical trajectory that builds on Western political theory, its distinct procedures for handling problems, making judgments, and carrying out its work. These pro-cedures, along with their assumptions about how to handle conflict and dif-ferences, are replicated in various international venues where human rights work is carried out.

Nevertheless, in UN meetings culture is "out there" in remote villages and jungles. It is what other people have, while the cosmopolitans who feel at home in New York, Geneva, Vienna, and other world capitals see themselves as outside culture. Yet their world is also a cultural system, one premised on ideas of human rights and universality. As a social system, this is what an-thropologists used to call a nonlocalized quasigroup, consisting of pockets of social interaction and shared meaning through which individuals circulate. The social world is coherent, but exists in various locations. The cosmopoli-tan world of government diplomats, UN and NGO experts, and donor offi-cers, such as those working in transitional justice or development projects is a world of frequent mobility around the globe in sites that they do not have time to get to know in detail or, necessarily, think it is important to know. In these settings, culture refers to the way of life of the "other."

Thus, our understanding of the inevitable conflict between culture and rights is premised on a particular set of images of culture opposed to rights, even though rights are a cultural phenomenon. We argue that these images are fundamentally those of women oppressed by their culture, and that this framing, in which rights are the heroic weapon that frees women from an oppressive "traditional" culture into a world of freedom and choice, underlies human rights work. However, this image misrepresents the intersections be-tween rights ideas and cultural practice that actually take place. It misunder-stands how rights and culture work and instead builds on imperial narratives of the civilizing process and the transformation of "backward" society.

Female Genital Cutting and the Opposition
Between Culture and Rights

Female genital cutting (FGC) is a classic example of a human rights violation in which culture and rights appear opposed. After discussing the meanings of culture and rights embedded in this debate, we offer another way of thinking about culture/rights intersections that is far more realistic: one that considers the process of vernacularization of human rights. One of the intriguing questions about FGC is its enduring importance as a human rights violation. Why this rather than other forms of injury or suffering? There are many forms of suffering in the world, but only a few are singled out, raising the question of what converts some forms of suffering but not others into human rights violations. We do not dispute that FGC can be harmful to women, but we query the selection of some forms of harm for global attention while others are ignored. What are the narratives about culture and rights that the chosen violations provide? They seem to replicate the colonial narratives of civilization and savagery along with the victimized woman and the rescuing male hero.

Human rights emerge over time from social movements that name and describe a violation, gather information about the nature of the violation and its prevalence, develop media presentations that generate public outrage, gather supporters, raise funds, build organizations, and consequently are able to press the human rights system to include it as a violation. It becomes attached to a particular institution such as a treaty, is expressed in general comments, and/or becomes the mandate of a designated investigator, a special rapporteur. Ultimately an issue will produce nonbinding declarations and, in a few cases, a new human rights treaty. The issue is, in a sense, a commodity: it is built through activism and representation, serves to generate attention, membership, and funds, and gradually becomes formalized as a legally recognized right or violation.

Violence against women followed this path over a period of thirty years (Merry 2006). It became a human rights violation after the issue inspired a strong social movement. The conversion of women's right to a life without violence into human rights in the early 1990s was a product of extensive 1980s global feminist organizing and the international spread of the battered women's movement. Because the human rights push built on this global movement, the issue had traction and could collect members, media, and money. In this case, as more generally, the social movement defined the problem by means of the cultural categories that have power at the time. In the 1970s, the battered women's movement was concerned with women's subordination more broadly and fixed on violence as a primary mechanism maintaining subordination. In contrast, the 1970s concern with FGC grew out of both concerns about the neglected role of women in development and women's right to sexual pleasure. Both issues pointed toward more attention to FGC.

Eliminating this practice has been a concern of missionaries and British colonial officials since the late nineteenth century (Kenyatta 1962: 125; Boddy 2007) and of feminists and human rights activists since the 1950s (see Daly 1978; Boyle 2002) . It is often labeled a "harmful traditional practice" as well as a form of violence against women and a violation of human rights. The human rights framework does not see consent as diminishing the violation. Even if a woman chooses to have this surgery, it is still a human rights violation. The critique of FGC incorporates concerns about health consequences, loss of sexual pleasure, violence against women, and gender oppression (Daly 1978; Hosken 1982; Boyle 2002).

Other forms of surgical bodily modification receive no similar critique. The rampant use of plastic surgery in the U.S., for example, from breast implants to liposuction to face lifts, has never been considered a human rights problem. There have been recent reports of vaginal surgeries similar to FGC in the U.S., but designed to enhance sexual pleasure rather than reduce it. The Special Rapporteur on Violence against Women did raise these forms of beauty practice as a form of human rights violation in her 2002 report (Coomaraswamy 2002) on cultural practices in the family harmful to women, but they have not been accepted as forms of human rights violation, particularly in countries like the U.S. where these practices are common. Yet the bodily consequences of various cosmetic surgeries can be quite debilitating.

Male circumcision has similarly escaped global critique. Typically performed on infants in the U.S., this surgical practice is clearly done without the individual's consent although generally with parental consent (see Darby 2005). In many parts of the world, circumcision is part of adolescent initiation, so its "victims" are typically below the age considered capable of consenting. Yet male circumcision, subincision, and other forms of penile surgery are very widespread in the United States, Africa, Australia, and many other parts of the world. They are often practiced on adolescents where the trauma, pain, and risk of scarring and injury are substantial (Miller 2002; Darby 2005). Intriguingly, it was virtually absent in the U.S. except for those who practiced it for religious reasons until the late nineteenth century. At that time, it became a health issue and a way to stamp out the "disease" of masturbation (Gollaher 2000; Goldman 1997). By the mid-twentieth century in the U.S., the practice of infant male circumcision was very common, but since the mid-1990s it has been in decline. In the U.S., the situation is likely to return to the pre-Victorian situation in which male circumcision is morally neutral but acceptable as a religious practice. There is a small anti-circumcision movement in the U.S. and other countries, but it has little if any traction as a human rights issue. Feminists have resisted joining forces on the basis of similarities in the surgeries. Internationally, UNICEF has mobilized against FGC but not male circumcision, as have the World Health Organization, UN Fund for Population Activities, Amnesty International, and other human rights organizations.

The common explanation for these differences is that some, such as cosmetic surgery, are chosen while FGC is not. However, many of these sexual operations are performed on infants and children with the consent of parents and other relatives who may or may not understand that they have choices. There are more serious consequences for resisting FGC than plastic surgery, in the form of exclusion, inability to marry and assume adult status, and even violence. Nevertheless, there are also pressures for cosmetic surgery with its assumptions about beauty, ideal body types, and appropriately sized breasts. Those whose bodies do not conform face exclusion and negative social responses. People who choose plastic surgery seek a more positive response and greater acceptance and recognition. Physical appearance seems to affect access to jobs and mates. The consequences of not engaging in the practice are far less severe than for FGC, but in both cases there are significant social pressures that induce women to change body shape to satisfy the expectations of others.

How can we explain these differences? The narrative of the oppression of FGC is the familiar colonial trope of the backward traditional society coercing the innocent young woman. As Michelle McKinley demonstrates, the idea that culture is the culprit in the persistence of this practice has a long history (2009). In contrast, male circumcision is performed on young men and children not typically understood as victims, and it is widespread in societies understood as modern and governed by choice, such as the U.S. Despite the enormous pressure to have a particular body shape in modern society, cosmetic surgery is again understood as a product of choice. Thus, the form of sexual bodily modification that has earned enduring status as a human rights violation is that in which the perpetrator is custom and tradition. The civilizing process means freeing innocent women from custom. The construction of the passive female victim oppressed by "traditional culture" makes FGC appealing as a human rights violation while neither cosmetic surgery nor male circumcision posits this source of oppression. The limited concern about the pain and suffering of males undergoing circumcision, widely practiced in "modern" as well as traditional societies, supports this hypothesis. We are not suggesting that these practices are not harmful to women, nor that trying to change them might not be a good thing for women, but that there is a selection taking place in which other practices harmful to women are ignored, such as overly long work hours or neglect, and that there is an odd boundary drawn around those that warrant attention as human rights violations and those that do not. Those singled out for attention as rights violations are those where the offender is an oppressive traditional culture and the victim is female, young, passive, and without agency. Thus, imbedded in these human rights campaigns is an idea of culture reminiscent of the concept Malinowski was critiquing in 1926—the "iron hand of custom"—almost a century ago. This idea has proved a very durable idea. It was well established in the imperial era and by constituting the category of "tradition" is fundamental to modernity. Culture is the other against which the modern is defined. Its antecedents are French and British ideas of the civilizing process and the battle against backward customs in the name of civilization. This familiar trope sells to media and donors in the global north and is more appealing than attributing responsibility to global capitalism or military expansionism.

Vernacularization: Another Way to Understand the Culture/Rights Divide

Escape from this conundrum requires recognizing that culture and rights are part of same social world: that rights are a cultural category for justice talk but only one of many. The human rights ideology was created out of a set of national and local social movements and forms of activism. Particular national issues coalesce into the global movement. For example, the list of forms of violence against women includes many regional and local issues—sex selection, dowry murders, honor killing, beauty practices, female genital cutting, child marriage—as well as more generic ones such as rape and domestic violence. Through the human rights system, these specific issues are transformed into a set of ideas and standards that claim universality and the legitimacy of global consensus, although they are neither universal in fact nor accepted by all countries.

Out of this field of international human rights law, values, and philosophy that circulates transnationally, ideas and practices are seized within particular sites and translated into a language and form that makes sense in that cultural space. We call this process vernacularization, analogous to the creation of vernacular languages out of Latin in the context of the rise of nationalism in Europe. This is a process of appropriation and customization. Vernacularization translates globally produced ideas into myriad specific social settings in ways that are often indirect, fragmented, and diffuse. The term describes a range of ways that human rights ideas and words are communicated to diverse communities. This is a not only a linguistic process, with new terms and words, but also one involving new practices and theories. It brings new ways of doing things, new ideas about role of the state and its responsibilities, and new ways of defining social justice. Vernacular human rights move into a space already rich with ideas of justice, law, and the state. New ideas are typically adopted where there are areas of fit, resonance with preexisting ideas of justice or order, but they are also used to expand the boundaries of issues or develop new practices of intervention.

This analysis of the process by which women's human rights are localized is based on a study of the work of women's human rights NGOs in four countries: India, China, Peru, and the United States. It focuses on the way women's organizations used the international human rights system in their everyday work to help women cope with issues such as violence, divorce, and inheritance. Most of the organizations also developed programs to spread new messages about the position of women. Each organization translated the global set of ideas about women's human rights into local frameworks and practices in some way. The research was a collaborative effort among scholars in Peru, China, India, and the United States. In each site, we compared two or three nongovernmental organizations (NGOs) working to implement women's human rights to see how they translated global concepts into local terms. All the organizations were selected because they expressed some form of commitment to women's human rights.

Each university collaborator hired and supervised one or more graduate students to carry out intensive ethnographic research on two to three organizations over a two-year period: Mercedes Crisóstomo in Peru; Vaishali Zararia in India; M. Liu, Y. H. Hu, and M. L. Liao in China; and Diana Yoon and Mihaela Serban in the United States. Each team carried out interviews with the leaders of each organization, its trustees, and its staff members. They observed staff/client interactions, determined caseload information, and traced the history of the organization. As far as possible, the researchers spent considerable time in each organization engaging in participant observation, including training sessions, celebrations, rallies, and festivals. There are clear differences in how each team carried out this process, despite the collective development of shared sets of questions and issues for investigation. Each team spent about one year on the data collection process and then analyzed and wrote an article on the case, published in a special issue of *Global Networks* (Levitt and Merry 2009).

We developed the overarching research questions and raised the funds for the project from the National Science Foundation, but the detailed research strategies and questions for each site emerged through collaborative discussions. We traveled twice to each study site and organized two conferences that were attended by all the research team members, ensuring an active intellectual exchange among all our colleagues. Thus, this research is itself an international collaboration in which we all learned from one another. We worked to translate ideas about research, about the questions we asked, and about the meanings of our results from one national context to another. Each team, however, wrote its own analysis (see Levitt and Merry 2009a).

Our research revealed that several kinds of *global values packages* are critical to the spread of ideas about women's rights. Their emergence depends on much more than the work of individual activists. Instead, it is shaped by the broader historical context, influenced by events like the end of the Cold War, the decline of socialism and communism, and the rise of the Washington Consensus. A neoliberal package, promoting democracy, capitalism, human rights, the rule of law, transparency and accountability, and gender equity through institutions like the World Bank and the Ford Foundation, is perhaps most familiar. A fundamentalist religious package based on gender complementarity, tradition, conservatism, and authority, spread by religious networks like Tablighi Jamaat, is a second example. (Tablighi Jamaat is a transnational religious movement present in Muslim communities around the world. Its members actively spread an interpretation and practice of Islam that they see as closer to the ways of the Prophet.) A third, "anti-globalization" package revolves around anti-consumerism and materialism, environmentalism, fair trade, and living locally and simply.

In the case of global feminism, we see a core values package based on the notion of woman as a homogeneous subject, consisting of ideas about women's rights, equality, selfhood, and freedom from violence (see Basu 1995; Grewel 1998, 2008). It includes the idea that women should own property, be able to divorce, inherit money and land, earn income, and express their views. It stresses a woman's right to protection from domestic violence and discrimination and to enjoy reproductive autonomy and the right to sexual choice. It views women as participating equally in the public and private sphere and embracing a particular kind of agentic self that is self-interested, secular, and rational rather than religious, affective, and communitarian. This women's rights package embraces gender equality rather than gender complementarity. In other words, it stresses improving women's position by making them the same as men, at least in opportunity. The global women's rights package is expressed in a set of national and international laws and practices such as CEDAW, international women's conferences, International Women's Day, and the theoretical work of many Women's and Feminist Studies Programs that have proliferated at universities over the past thirty years.

We understand the circulation of a set of ideas and practices such as the core values package as an inherently transnational process. The individuals and organizations we studied are embedded in the social fields where circulation occurs. These fields are influenced by multiple sets of laws, cultural repertoires, and institutions. Their daily rhythms and activities respond not only to more than one state but also to social institutions and networks, such as religious communities, that operate within and across borders. While ideas and practices circulate globally, nationally, and regionally, the boundaries between these layers of social experience are extremely porous. Because they are nested and mutually constitutive, circulation between and across different scales is just as important as the exchanges within them (Swyngedouw 1997; Khagram and Levitt 2007).

By following the trajectory of ideas from global documents, theoretical writings, and international conference discussions through the talk of national leaders and NGO heads to discussions with staff members and clients, we link grassroots discussions of women's rights with global ideas of women's human rights. The organizational channels and networks through which values packages circulate strongly influence where they are appropriated and by whom. Moreover, in each site these values packages encounter local social justice ideologies, gender norms, and an organizational ecology that strongly influences how and where they land, what they combine with, and how and by whom they are appropriated. In some cases, the connections to the global were quite tenuous; in others, the international reference and substance remained strong. Of course, the global values package and other global understandings are a pastiche of local and national ideas, practices, and issues that have crossed national borders and connected with other local and national ideas. The flow goes both ways, although not equally and not without bottlenecks, forms of resistance, and obstacles.

One of the striking findings from this research was the diversity of meanings and uses of human rights in these organizations. Even though all the organizations we studied claimed to use a human rights framework to improve the position of women, they did so in very different ways. Although all drew on the global values package, the specific meanings they drew from it, the way they defined women's human rights, and the practices they appropriated from the human rights system were quite different. Human rights served as an open discourse subject to many different interpretations and meanings as activists applied them to particular problems in specific situations. Instead of simply transferring human rights ideas as articulated in conventions to local situations, the leaders and staff in the organizations we studied typically sought to redefine and adapt the ideas to facilitate understanding and assimilation. They modified aspects of women's human rights in an effort to make them comprehensible and appropriate in a particular context.

Vernacularization is somewhat different from the simple transfer of ideas or practices to a new location. Vernacularizers not only transfer ideas, but also modify or alter them so that they are more acceptable. They reinterpret and reframe issues and ideas with an eye toward assimilation and acceptance. They strategically combine elements of the existing cultural repertoire with specific pieces of the package that is being introduced. Vernacularization is a process of creating meaning by connecting, in a variety of ways, the discourse of human rights law and that of particular organizations working in specific contexts using other discourses of social justice as well.

Three Forms of Vernacularization

Our fieldwork revealed three types of vernacularization. The first relied on the imaginative space created by women's human rights rather than on the discourse of rights itself. It drew on the aspirational possibilities created by the words. Staff did not talk about rights directly in their work but used the momentum and power provided by the backdrop of global discourses about rights to advance their cause. It connected particular local struggles to global ideas of justice and gender equality.

The second type of vernacularization stretched the boundary of issues considered by women's groups by using the language of human rights to tackle new issues. In this type, staff used English words to describe local narratives and symbols and made explicit reference to human rights. The organization using this type of vernacularization worked on sexuality rights as a form of human rights. They appealed to the grounding of these ideas in the

West combined with a strong claim that these same ideas had deep Indian roots.

The third type of vernacularization took the core concepts of women's human rights and translated them into locally appropriate ideas and practices in a newly created institutional setting. Thus, the meanings of women's human rights not only were influential in shaping issues but were also put into practice in a new context. As women took their problems to a local women's court, for example, they discovered how the human rights framework redefined the way they could think about and handle their problems. Like the second type, the third type of vernacularization expands the range of issues organizations consider, but also puts these new meanings into practice by adopting some of the strategies and techniques of human rights activism.

In all three types of vernacularization, the ideas and resources women used on the ground did not rely directly on the texts of international human rights law or on UN declarations. They did not seek to use human rights law through direct appeals to international bodies, nor did they refer to particular articles or sections of conventions. Indeed, we heard very little discussion of CEDAW. The work of these organizations suggests that they use women's human rights largely as discursive and aspirational resources without the authority provided by formal law.

The case studies for this project provide examples of each of these forms of vernacularization. The first, which focuses on the symbolic and aspirational dimension of human rights, appeals to a diffuse universalism of women's equality. It makes vague references to international standards, to the idea that women should stand up for themselves, that they should not be beaten. Yet, there are few if any explicit references to human rights in the day to day practices of the organization. Instead, much of the discourse is based on the national or local women's movement. For example, one organization in Baroda, India, that presents itself as working to promote women's human rights sometimes presents its messages through street plays using familiar folk characters and narrative forms. These plays rewrite traditional folk tales to expose social problems such as domestic violence or wife burning. For example, a street play called *Bandar Khel* (Monkey Show) uses conventional characters, songs, and performance to address dowry violence and murder. It features a snake charmer (Kallu Madari), a male monkey (Ballu Bandar), and a female monkey (Banno Bandariya). Our research team translated the play, of which we provide a segment.

Snake charmer: See brother, they both fall in love with each other. Now if they are in love, then we will have to get them married. But marriage is not a play like among children! In that, we need our elders! So brother you become a father of this heroine and you her mother and decide their marriage. (The theater is so arranged that Sahiyar members sitting amidst—and thus part of—the audience will become father and mother).

Father: We like the boy, but which religion does he belong to?

Mother: We like the girl, but what is her caste?

Snake Charmer: Oh! religion and caste prevail among human beings. These are petty animals. How would they know all these mental issues? At last, if groom and bride are ready, then what will the father do!

So Ballu (male) and Banno (female) get married. Let us see what happens in their house.

Banno cooks the food, Ballu eats the food.

Banno washes the clothes, Ballu wears the clothes.

Banno remains at home, Ballu goes to work and earns.

Oh! Today why is Ballu so upset? What happened? (Ballu says something in the ears of snake charmer and he conveys it to audience.) Listen, he says that he suffered from a loss in his business. He is in need of money. You don't even know from where the money will come? (Snake charmer to audience) Tell me, will any one of you give him money? No one is ready. What is so big in that? At last, the only solution is that. . . . Go and tell your wife to go to her father's house and bring money from there.

(She refuses.)

Snake charmer: Is she denying? What kind of a "man" are you! Can't you convince your wife on such a small matter? Go and tell her again and if then she is still not ready, slap her two or four times. Then she will definitely be ready.

(Monkey beats she-monkey, but the she-monkey refuses to go and ask for the money.)

Snake charmer: Now what happened? What kind of a "hero" you are! This guy needs to be taught everything. Go and buy kerosene from the market and burn her. Then there will be second marriage and you will get enough dowry.

(Monkey is scared and refuses to consider the idea.)

Snake charmer: Oh! Why are you so scared? Nothing will happen to you. Don't you read newspapers every day? Burned; killed; but has anyone been punished?

(Monkey looks at audience and says something in sign language to snake charmer.)

Snake charmer: Are you afraid of society? People will forget in two or four days. Even her own sister will be ready to get married to you!

(Monkey goes back, says something to she-monkey, and comes back again and whispers something in the ears of snake charmer.)

Snake charmer (to audience): Do you know what this he-monkey and she-monkey told me? They told me that to burn and to kill your own wife is such a lowly and cowardly deed that we monkeys do not do that even in a "show" (theater). Only a man can do such a thing.

Another example of this form of vernacularization was the organization's campaign against sex selection and abortion of female fetuses. The program paid poor women to make kites for the city's kite flying festival festooned with an anti-female feticide advertisement. As the kites drifted up and then fell down in a variety of places, they carried the message with them.

In Beijing, one of the organizations adopted an innovative approach to complaint handling: it brought in social workers to handle cases that did not have a clear legal basis but nevertheless represented people who needed help. The social workers brought with them an ethic of care that was inspired by human rights. They sought to treat the whole person, not just the specific problem, and to give everyone the same level of attention and respect, regardless of what in China is referred to as "quality."

In these two programs, the leaders saw a link to human rights in the way they thought about women's problems, but in their day to day work with women clients human rights were not mentioned explicitly. Diffuse notions of human rights, such as gender equality or protection from violence, were important, but activism is primarily based on national and local women's movements and the specific issues it foregrounds, such as dowry murders and female infanticide in India.

A second way human rights are used is as an explicit symbolic framework that allows programs to expand the boundaries of issues considered by national and local women's movements and connect with international allies. Explicit references to human rights help build alliances across local and national lines and open new problems to scrutiny and change. This approach more directly evokes the transnational consensus of human rights than the former does. For example, one of the organizations in Baroda, used human rights in its campaign for acceptance of alternate sexuality. Because lesbian rights are a relatively new issue in the Indian women's movement, the organization turned to the international community and the global language of "women's rights are human rights," CEDAW, and the Declaration on the Elimination of Violence Against Women. Other women's groups collaborated with this organization on other issues, like housing rights for slum dwellers; but less on sexual rights. In 2006, they extended support to two lesbian young women from a small town near Baroda. After they ran away together, a parent of one of them and her brother were arrested by the police to force her and her partner to surrender. The leaders of Vikalp intervened to get the relatives released. After the women were found, the local court gave an order saying that they were free to go anywhere since they were adults.

Vikalp adopted novel modes of communication to present this issue to the public. At the Gujarat World Social Forum, Vikalp helped sponsor a presentation by a gay and lesbian group that featured dance and testimonials about the difficulty of living as 'queer' persons in this community. It has also promoted a new mode of intervention by establishing a drop-in center for lesbians. In 2006, one of the leaders appeared on a national TV channel in a discussion program about gays and lesbians. In the same year, she published a book about the lives of working-class lesbians in India that garnered national attention (Sharma 2006). The national and international sexual rights movement is an important source of inspiration for the work of this organization. A poster developed by the program exemplifies its use of national and international symbols for the lesbian rights movement (see Figure 1). In this poster, traditional Indian folk figures are reconfigured to represent equally sized males and females and adorned with the Indian flag and the pink triangle as the poster announces that lesbian rights are human rights. Situated on a representation of the flag of India, the poster proclaims in several Indian languages as well as English that "Lesbian Rights Are Human Rights." The leaders of this organization are connected with the national lesbian rights movement in India as well as the international movement and take inspiration from both (see Bachetta 2002; Kapur 2005).

Another example of an organization that explicitly invokes human rights is a legal aid center in Beijing that was established in 1995, after the Beijing

Figure 1. "Lesbian Rights Are Human Rights" poster. Reprinted with permission of Vikalp/Parma Vadodara Gujarat India.

World Conference on Women that year. Inspired by this international gathering, the center provides services to women, particularly those facing domestic violence. It has gradually assumed a strong focus on human rights and an emphasis on pursuing class-action cases that may potentially have a strong impact, challenge policy, or reform social structures. For example, in one case the agency challenged a policy prohibiting married women with children from attending university. Staff members help battered women pursue their cases, but they are primarily interested in changing laws and practices. Litigation, public education campaigns, and policy reform are their main strategies. This organization receives a good deal of international financial and political support. Pictures of Madeleine Albright and Hillary Clinton adorn the walls of the office. The organization is led not by a party member, but by a powerful board of directors that includes high-ranking officials who protect the organization from government critique. It works on high visibility, policy-changing legal cases to promote human rights and women's rights in Chinese terms, with the goal of improving Chinese society.

A third type of vernacularization translates the core concepts of women's human rights into locally appropriate ideas and adopts human rights practices in newly created institutional settings. For example, in New York City, an organization of survivors of domestic violence that does advocacy for battered women's issues in city agencies has used human rights documentation as an advocacy strategy. The Voices of Women Organizing Project (VOW) is the first and only initiative of the Battered Women's Resource Center, which began in 2000 with the mission to enable survivors of domestic violence to become advocates on policy issues that affect battered women (www .vowbwrc.org, October 28, 2008). Members represent the geographic and racial diversity of the city, and include immigrant, lesbian, formerly incarcerated, and disabled survivors. Interviews with members suggest that working with VOW involved a distinct process of politicization and transformation in consciousness.

Forms of discourse observed in VOW reflect the traditions of the battered women's movement and community organizing in which it is embedded. The "survivor" is a central concept for the organization: a shared, collective identity for VOW members that expresses what they refer to as an ongoing process of overcoming their experiences of abuse. The organization is committed to giving "voice" to survivors and pursuing advocacy strategies based on their perspectives. Survivors are positioned to speak from a position of authority.

As a domestic violence advocacy organization, VOW does not have an independent agenda dedicated to "human rights." VOW members do not talk about "how to use" human rights, or about specific international mechanisms such as treaty articles and institutions. The primacy of the domestic violence advocacy agenda is reflected in the associate director's comment about the various human rights forums she has attended: "but you have to go back to your everyday work." However, staff and members have attended human rights trainings and have used human rights technologies in their political activism. Beginning in 2005, the Battered Mothers' Justice Campaign collaborated with the Urban Justice Center Human Rights Project to provide human rights documentation of the experiences of battered women in New York family courts based on qualitative and quantitative data. This project represents an explicit use of human rights practices. VOW staff and the Human Rights Project trained fourteen VOW members to interview survivors. In 2006, they interviewed 75 domestic violence survivors about their experiences in family courts. Women talked about losing custody of children to their batterers despite histories of being the primary caretaker, about inadequate measures for safety in the court building, and about unprofessional conduct of judges and lawyers against women raising claims of domestic violence. The data provided the basis for a report, *Justice Denied: How Family Courts in New York City Endanger Battered Women and Children* (VOW 2008) that documented these problems and identified the specific articles of human rights conventions that the Family Courts violated. It offered recommendations for change. The report was presented to city and state government officials and made available to the public on the web. Thus, although the organization relies primarily on the discourses of the battered women's movement in the U.S., it has creatively adopted some of the core information gathering and exposure strategies of the human rights system.

None of the organizations we studied appealed directly to the human rights system, although that is also a possibility. Some human rights organs have complaint mechanisms where victims who have exhausted national remedies can file petitions for action. In the field of women's rights, the major organizations open are the treaty committee monitoring CEDAW and the Human Rights Council. There are also regional human rights organizations. NGOs help victims take cases there, but the number of complaints is small. Such appeals represent a direct use of human rights law rather than a form of vernacularization.

One of the best-known examples is an appeal of a U.S. Supreme Court decision to the Inter-American Commission on Human Rights on behalf of a Colorado woman. In March 2007, Jessica Lenahan (Gonzales) filed a suit in the Inter-American Commission, an entity of the Organization of American States, concerning the failure of a Colorado police department to enforce a restraining order (Gardella 2007). This is the first time U.S. attorneys have used international human rights law to protect domestic violence victims and their children. In 1999, Jessica Lenahan, then Gonzales, had a restraining order against her husband in the town of Castle Rock, Colorado, although it allowed him some visitation. When Lenahan discovered that her daughters, aged ten, eight, and seven, were missing, she called the police for help. She continued to call the police from 6 p.m. until 3:20 a.m., when her husband drove to the local police department, opened fire on the building, and was killed by the police. The daughters were found dead in the truck, killed hours earlier. In 2000, she filed a $30 million lawsuit against the police department and three of its members, alleging that they violated her right to due process by failing to enforce the restraining order. The district court dismissed the case. On appeal, the Tenth Circuit gave her a property right to police enforcement of the order. The police department appealed this decision to the U.S. Supreme Court. In 2005, the Supreme Court found that she had no constitutional right to police enforcement of the restraining order (Bettinger-Lopez 2008: 183–93).

In 2007, Bettinger-Lopez and other lawyers from Columbia Law School's Human Rights Institute and Human Rights Clinic and the American Civil Liberties Union took the case to the Inter-American Commission of Human Rights, a body of eight human rights experts, claiming a violation of rights under the American Declaration of the Rights and Duties of Man. Even though the U.S. has not signed the American Convention on Human Rights and the Commission's decisions cannot be judicially enforced in the U.S., the Commission decided it had competence to examine this case. The U.S. State Department countered that the American Convention does not create positive governmental obligations. Nevertheless, it filed a comprehensive response to the petition (Bettinger-Lopez 2008: 183–93). The case had two hearings, one in October 2008. As of October 2009, the decision was still pending (Bettinger-Lopez, personal communication). Although the Commission has no enforcement authority over the U.S., its decisions have moral and political influence and contribute to setting international standards (2008: 185). This landmark case demonstrates the possibility of turning to international law when individuals feel that domestic law fails to protect their rights. The attorneys and Lenahan see this as a way to build consensus on domestic violence as a human rights issue and submit this case to the "court of public opinion."

Both rights and culture are changing all the time and are not oppositional. Rights are a dimension of transnational as well as national and local culture that is appropriated and redefined for local political struggles, reconstituted within the cultural understandings and practices of the place where they are adopted. Culture is clearly open to new repertoires for political action and mobilization. In other words, in practice human rights ideas provide political and moral resources to social movements, create allies, and establish an aura of universalism at the same time as they are tailored to fit into existing political and moral worlds.

The process of vernacularization, in all its forms, shows that the spread of human rights ideas is a process of appropriation and customization of both its discourses and practices. Rather than seeing human rights ideas and practices as opposed to "culture," it is clear that they are themselves cultural repertoires that are open to adaptation and use by people with a wide variety of cultural backgrounds. These are all examples in which local organizations creatively took those parts of the human rights system that seemed useful and symbolically valuable and used bits and pieces that seemed to fit and would be helpful. This is not a process of imposition or clash, but one of adaptation and agency. Vernacularization is a process in which there is an active creation of human rights by civil society groups. They appropriate and adopt the transnational meanings and practices of human rights, then use this collaboratively produced ideology to make alliances, to frame issues in ways that will travel, to expand issues, and to adopt new advocacy strategies. Thus, human rights gain strength and flexibility from the way they are vernacularized, even as their appeal rests on the magic of their claims to universality.

The woman oppressed by traditional culture who needs to be rescued by human rights activism occupies a critical rhetorical space that legitimates interventions and tells a narrative that ignores the more complex causes of poverty and disempowerment. The prevalence of the cultural explanation for their suffering displaces those that are systemic, related to economic processes that tie together the worlds of those who are injured and those who injure them. Rights arguments move the analysis in a different direction, pointing to state failure and lack of accountability, but often also move away from such economic analyses. Vernacularization returns the aura of the international and the universal to the terms of everyday activism within local communities.

Chapter 5

The Active Social Life of
"Muslim Women's Rights"

Lila Abu-Lughod

"Muslim women's rights"—something to fight for, debate, consider historically, see cross-culturally, make happen, organize around, fund, and examine
in action (as expressed or as violated)—have an extraordinarily active social
life in our contemporary world. As the concept circulates across continents,
traveling in and out of classrooms and government policy offices; UN forums
in New York and Geneva and local women's organizations in Egypt, Malay-
sia, and Palestine; television soap operas and mosque study groups; model
marriage contracts developed in North Africa and popular memoirs sold in
airport bookstores and instantly recognizable by the veiled women stamped
on their covers, we are confronted with the question of how to make sense of
its travels and translations across forms and forums, from websites to shelters
for battered women to inheritance disputes in rural villages.[1]

What would happen if we reframed the usual questions and instead
tracked "Muslim women's rights" into the multiple social worlds in which
they operate, paying particular attention to their mediations and transformations? What if we did not assume the ontological status of women's rights or
ask referential questions such as whether Muslim women do or do not have
(enough) rights, do or do not want rights, gain or lose rights through Islamic
or secular law, or need feminists or others to deliver them their rights? As
an anthropologist, I suggest that we might learn a great deal if we stepped
back from the usual terms of debate and instead followed "Muslim women's
rights" as they travel through various worlds and projects, circulate through

debates and documents, organize women's activism, and mediate women's lives in various places. The questions then become: In what debates and institutions do "Muslim women's rights" partake? What work do the practices organized in its terms do in various places, for various women? How, in fact, do "Muslim women's rights" produce our contemporary world?

I use the term "social life" here to suggest that Muslim women's rights are to be found only in their socially located places. By this, however, I mean not just the social circulation of the concept, as Appadurai (1986) might have taught us, or the social contexts of its reproduction, transplantation, or vernacularization, as Merry (2006) has usefully shown us for women's human rights more generally, but its differential mediation through various social networks and technical instruments, as Latour (1999) and the ethnographers of science might recommend.[2] To make my argument, I will take you to a few of the many sites where Muslim women's rights operate, to look at the social forms through which, in these sites, the term moves. Geographically, I will go to Egypt and Palestine.[3]

Egypt: In Shifting Fields

Egypt is a good place to examine the social life of "women's rights." It is well studied by feminist scholars, has a rich history of women's activism, and is the country in which I have done ethnographic research for years. "Women's rights" (not framed, for the most part, as "Muslim" women's rights—for good political reasons, given the history of nationalism and the mixed Coptic and Muslim population) have had a long and busy social life there, explicitly advocated for with the formation of the Egyptian Feminist Union in the 1920s but having been the subject of concern earlier in the mode of colonial feminism (Ahmed 1992) and turn-of-the-century nationalist-modernism, such as that of Qasim Amin, who wrote *The Liberation of Women*, a book read well beyond Egypt (as discussed by Badran 1995; Abu-Lughod 1998; Najmabadi 1998; Booth 2001; Elsadda 2001; Baron 2005).

After the critical period of state feminism under Gamal Abdel Nasser in the 1950s and 1960s, when independent women's organizations were shut down but sweeping legislation was put in place guaranteeing education, jobs, labor rights, maternity leaves, and various forms of state welfare, a new phase began under President Sadat (Hatem 1992, 2006; Nelson 1996; Elsadda 2001). Neoliberal economic reform and the opening to the U.S. starting in the 1970s led to the rollback of important protective legislation and paved the way for various civil society organizations from Islamists to women activists, many working through the paradigm and projects of "development," to play a more active part in society, not to mention picking up some of the pieces of social welfare now abandoned by the privatizing state under structural adjustment (Abdelrahman 2004: 51, 2007). A wave of new women's NGOs were formed in the 1980s and 1990s, enhanced by the full reentry of international NGOs such as the Ford Foundation, the Population Council, and UNICEF, and massive aid from European governments and the U.S. as part of the "peace" dividend. The traffic in women's rights was intensified with Egypt's participation in international conferences in the mid-1990s, most notably hosting the International Conference on Population and Development and sending delegates to the Fourth World Conference on Women in Beijing (Al-Ali 2000; 'Abd al-Salam 2005).

Significant international funds have ensured that women's rights and service NGOs have become a growth industry. There are currently tens of thousands of NGOs operating in Egypt, despite dire restrictions on civil society organizations and periodic government crackdowns (Abdelrahman 2004). When I turned my attention to women's NGOs in 2007–8, I found some important developments that reflect the transformation of the political and economic terrain in Egypt and confirm how critical the dynamics of transnational political organizing and economic exchange, local class relations, and national historical shifts are for the social life of "women's rights." Al-Ali's study of women activists in the 1990s noted the link between women's organizations and the wider context, suggesting that their debates and conflicts were "a mirror of Egyptian political culture" (Al-Ali 2000: 201). Debates about foreign funding were fierce, linked to "the struggles for political independence and especially the rejection of increasing American influence" (201), even though, as Abdelrahman (2004: 182–83) shows in her later study based on a survey of 60 Egyptian NGOs, foreign funding is highly sought after even while complaints abound about the way this funding constrains the choice of projects and forces local organizations "to tailor their objectives to suit the priorities of these agencies."

Yet I would argue that the larger political-economic contexts have affected "women's rights" most forcefully by determining the channels through which they operate and the technologies that mediate them. Arguably, the three most significant shifts in the social life of rights in Egypt since the 1990s have been (1) their governmentalization, (2) their imbrication with Islamic

institutions and religious discourse, and (3) their commercialization or association with the corporate world. Since Al-Ali did her research in Cairo in
the 1990s, not only have government organizations like the National Council
for Women or capitalist-style international NGOs come to mediate "women's
rights" differently, but the politics, projects, and self-presentations of groups
working for women's rights have shifted both to reflect the transnational appeal of human rights and to respond to the local situation in which religiosity
has gained tremendous legitimacy. This is all independent of whether Egyptian women have gained or lost rights, which I am insisting is the wrong kind
of question to ask.

The Governmentalization of Rights

The governmentalization of "women's rights" can best be seen in the establishment in 2000 of the National Council for Women (NCW) by presidential decree. Sakr notes, "under the auspices of Suzanne Mubarak, wife of the
Egyptian president, the Council was set up to advise the presidency and the
government on the effect of public policies on women" (2004: 166). Some of
the NCW leaders, like the leaders of its predecessor, the National Council
for Childhood and Motherhood (set up by Mubarak in 1988), are respected
individuals, even though they work with governmental organs. Yet Sakr, who
studied the situation just a few years after the NCW's formation, reports the
initial suspicions of many in the NGO world.

Rather than judging the NCW, I am interested in examining the role it
has been playing in "women's rights" in Egypt. According to my interviews
in 2008, NCW has tried to be inclusive, inviting the participation of many
women previously active in women's issues in Egypt, though not as representatives of their organizations but as individuals (thus weakening the NGOs).
The NCW has also been the recipient of significant funding from the Egyptian government, the UN Development Programme, and foreign sources including USAID that many of the smaller, more radical feminist NGOs will
not accept. The significant number of projects conducted under its auspices
suggests that the NCW is now an institution through which "women's rights"
get both visibility and practical existence.

NCW is a channel for funds that are then distributed along particular
social and political lines.[4] For example, the report on the United Nations Development Assistance Framework for Egypt 2007–2011 (UN/E 2006) (which

closely follows the outlines of the earlier Arab Human Development Reports, e.g., Jad/UNDP 2006)[5] specifies the partnerships that are to be established between the UN and various ministries and governmental and civil society bodies to implement development goals. The National Council for Women and the National Council for Childhood and Motherhood are prominent among those named as partners for improving women's status and rights. The funds for "women's rights" that the NCW can make use of are thus not negligible: the estimated cost to the UN system for the whole project is $340 million over the five years, which does not include the amount to be contributed by the World Bank (UN/E 2006: 22).[6] In taking a lion's share of development assistance, the NCW can determine many of the projects and people active in "women's rights."[7]

State organizations' involvement in defining and producing women's rights is not the only change we can observe in the social field of "Muslim women's rights" in Egypt. There has been a decided shift in the kinds of projects and languages that define work on behalf of women in Egypt due to the strong internationalization of "women's rights" in the NGO world. In a sense, the NGOs themselves are also part of what Halley et al. (2006) call "governance feminism," in which elites speak for women and use their gender expertise. One sign of the enmeshment in transnational feminist governance is the emerging hegemony of human rights language in women's rights advocacy.

International support for women's rights organizations has also merged the interests of educated professional women in Egypt with an international (hyper)concern about Middle Eastern and Muslim women's rights, leading to the proliferation of organizations and projects and the sort of transnational governance structures found in many countries of the global south. This is well illustrated by the Association for the Development and Enhancement of Women (ADEW), the organization founded in 1987 to provide micro-credit to women heads of household. On its website, ADEW claims now to have "emerged as both an influential grassroots organization and a leading advocate for women's rights."[8] ADEW boasts literacy programs, health services, and legal awareness seminars, operating from fifteen offices in five different areas with a staff of 200. In 2008–9 ADEW expanded its activities to women and domestic violence (in line with a worldwide trend, and one focus of the UN Development Assistance Framework cited above), opening a shelter and beginning an awareness campaign. Surprisingly keyed into the international community, ADEW's networks even extended to partners at Columbia University's School of International and Public Affairs in 2008–9.[9] ADEW's list of donors is impressive.[10]

Imbrication with Islamic Institutions and Religious Discourse

A new accommodation with religious institutions and ideology is the second characteristic of the social life of women's rights in Egypt. Although most of those involved in the official world of women's rights work think women's rights are under threat by rising conservative Islamist elements, there are various ways to respond, especially in a world of close social ties. The more explicit engagement with Islam can be seen clearly in the NGO world as well as in governmental organizations.

In March 2008, I went to the headquarters of a highly respected NGO that supports women's rights. Called the Center for Egyptian Women's Legal Assistance (CEWLA), it was founded in 1995 and is located in a poor and crowded informal neighborhood in Cairo. It had been set up there to help just this sort of population; now that it has so much more funding, it still refuses to leave the area because of its commitment to serving the community. This is an organization that started small, with just a couple of rooms and file boxes for furniture.[11] It is headed by a lawyer, Azza Sleiman. Many of the staff are women lawyers, graduates of the Egyptian universities where women, as in most institutions of higher education in the Arab world, constitute more than half of the students. Given financial support almost immediately by such organizations as the Canadian International Development Agency and Dutch Oxfam, and later by many others including the Now or Never Fund of the Global Fund for Women, the Ford Foundation, the Sawiris Foundation, and so forth,[12] CEWLA has expanded its mission: from giving legal aid to women the organization has moved to raising awareness about violence and children's rights, lobbying at the national level, conducting studies and publishing research, and providing direct services including adult literacy education, democracy training for children, and sexual and reproductive health education for teenagers. In CEWLA publicity material, the organization describes itself as dealing with topics from "a rights-based perspective," although in some of its other literature it claims to combine development and human rights perspectives.

CEWLA's latest initiative is taking the organization in a relatively new direction and represents a historically significant shift in the social lives and institutional mediations of "Muslim women's rights." The particular dynamics are Egyptian but, as I argue elsewhere, what CEWLA has been funded to do reflects a global trend that is taking a particularly novel form in the transnational social networking of cosmopolitan Muslim women (Abu-Lughod 2009a). The trend is toward highlighting the identities of women as Muslim, even though the NGOs are not faith-based or linked to any religious organizations. As Bibars (2001) and Abdelrahman (2004) have noted, there are Coptic and Muslim NGOs that have long provided services to women in Egypt; Bibars (116) is critical of them for their rigid expectations about gender roles and, in the case of Muslim welfare groups, their bias toward women who are heavily veiled and present themselves as "lonely, sick and poor."

The project that CEWLA was about to launch in 2008 was different: dedicated to demonstrating the compatibility of CEDAW and Shari'a, usually glossed as Islamic law. That this project is being taken up is an index of CEWLA's responsiveness both to the larger cultural-political context and the problems and concerns brought to them by the ordinary poor women, men, and youths they serve and in whose midst they have located their organization. Seham Ali, the lawyer who spoke to me about CEWLA, explained that people in Egypt are suspicious of anything that comes from the West. Some have accused CEDAW of seeking to destroy the family and undermine religion. This new project is intended to counter that ignorance. CEWLA had now routed itself through new institutional networks, enlisting experts in Islamic law, and particularly a respected and "noncontroversial" professor of Islamic philosophy at Al-Azhar University who had shown that 95 percent of CEDAW fits with Shari'a. Where there are points of difference, Ali added, there are often equivalents. She gave the example of adoption (which is not permitted in Islam). "We have something in Islam that resembles it called the duty to protect orphans (*kafala al-yatim*). We shouldn't accept anything that goes against Shari'a but. . . . " CEWLA's approach, she insisted, was simply to open up the subject for discussion: "Let's see if CEDAW is contrary to Islam." They would be running seminars and conferences, talking with media, judges, lawyers, and religious authorities (Ali 2008).[13]

That the concern with religion also comes from their "grassroots" base was clear from a point Ali made later in our conversation. Talking about the literacy classes CEWLA offers, she noted that they want to teach those who attend more than just reading and writing—legal literacy and knowledge about health were also important. She then mentioned that they also teach about religion. Flustered when I stopped her to ask why, she said, "No, not to teach them how to pray or do ablutions or anything like that. But sometimes they ask about whether something is religiously right or wrong (*halal* or *haram*). From the legal point of view and from Shari'a." She said she had studied a little Shari'a in law school; if she knew the answer she would respond. If not, she would tell them, "I'll try to get someone to talk to you about this."

CEWLA is not the only NGO to deal with Al-Azhar these days. In the UN Development Assistance Framework discussed above, Al-Azhar is mentioned as a partner of the National Council for Women and several ministries (including that of Religious Endowments) in the pursuit of two goals: changing perceptions of women's rights and combating gender violence (UN/E 2006: 30).[14] Twenty-five years ago, no one would have predicted that Muslim women's rights would be traveling so regularly in and out of Islamic law, Islamist parties, and the discourses and practices of moderation and reform within religious bounds (Abu-Lughod 2009a; Mahmood 2006).

The Commercialization of Rights

In one of the most dramatic shifts of the recent decade, and symptomatic of a global shift toward a neoliberal model for civil society, Iman Bibars, the feminist co-founder of ADEW who ran for Parliament in 2007 and holds a Ph.D. in development studies from the UK, in 2008 became coordinator of the Middle East North Africa fellows program of Ashoka, which describes itself as the global association of the world's leading social entrepreneurs. In a television interview, Bibars explained Ashoka's mission as looking for individuals who are "innovators" and who "think outside the box." "We are the venture capitalists of the social sector," she explained, in part because Ashoka accepts no government funding, looking for partnerships between corporations and foundations.[15]

The way women's rights talk in Egypt is thus also beginning to operate in a global commercial world—this third path in the evolving social life of "Muslim women's rights"—can be seen most clearly in a project of another NGO called the Egyptian Center for Women's Rights (ECWR), founded in 1996, only a year after CEWLA. This organization has been extremely successful in taking on a range of projects and issues beyond its initial concerns with legal aid. Its mission is described in the very contemporary language of liberalism: "CWR's work is based on the belief that women's rights are an integral part of human rights and are key to any substantive progress towards building a democratic culture and development in Egypt and the Middle East region."[16]

ECWR makes the novel appeal to socially responsible corporate sponsorship. This is, perhaps, the homegrown equivalent to the transnational NGO Ashoka. One of ECWR's latest campaigns is against sexual harassment on the streets. ECWR appropriated the slogan, "The Street is Ours," from a more radical coalition formed in summer 2005 after the scandalous attack by thugs with police approval/instigation on women protesters at a peaceful pro-democracy demonstration by the political movement Kefaya (Enough) (Al-Mahdi n.d.). Delinked from the ugly politics of government repression and violence by the security forces of which the incident of sexual harassment had actually been a part, ECWR's campaign focuses on anonymous harassment of women on the streets, which their survey alleged to be widespread.

Most intriguing are the innovative technologies ECWR mobilized for this campaign: one attempt to raise money was a proposal to develop a system for mapping harassment through SMS (text) messages. The proposal was submitted for the 2008 USAID Development 2.0 Challenge through NetSquared; the winner was to be determined by a jury after a popular vote narrowed the contestants down to fifteen finalists, à la *Star Academy* and *American Idol*.[17] On the ECWR website, besides noting the enthusiasm of young women volunteers for the project, they thank their "corporate volunteers"—Nile and Nugoom FM, Masrawy.com, Filbalad.com, Egyptsoft.org, Goethe Institute, and Netsmart Egypt—for having "given a life and professionalism to the campaign that was unmatched in NGO work in Egypt." The bid for mobile phone technology development, corporate cooperation, and popular voting fits perfectly in today's Cairo, where shopping malls, satellite television, ads for vying cell phone companies, and consumerism dominate the landscape (Abaza 2006).

This campaign marks another implantation in Egypt of the transnational trend to focus on violence against women, supported through various UN organizations, particularly UNIFEM and the CEDAW Commission. In Egypt, ADEW's new women's shelter is another node in the production of women's rights through this medium. Sally Engle Merry has shown that the campaign against gender violence has been, since the 1990s, perhaps the main issue on the agenda of the transnational feminist community (Merry 2006). There are those who have criticized this focus, noting how it universalizes and thus hides the divisions between feminists of the North and South. But the most interesting phenomenon is how many are building careers and profits on this issue that circulates beyond the halls of the UN and CEDAW hearings. To take just a few examples, Eve Ensler's *Vagina Monologues* is performed in Cairo as well as the U.S. and Beijing; the One in Three Women Global Campaign to raise awareness about violence against women encourages you to buy its cards, charms, and dog tags;[18] and Peacekeeper Cause-metics asks you to support women's causes by purchasing its lipstick and nail polish.[19] Although its focus has always been women's health, only a few years ago Peacekeeper Cause-metics also gave a fraction of its proceeds to fight "honor crimes" and other forms of cultural violence against women associated with the Muslim world.

Palestine: Other Violences and Inescapable Politics

The reference to honor crimes takes us to the next case and space of rights work: Palestine. One of the most recent "global" projects orchestrated in the name of "Muslim women's rights" is the Global Campaign to Stop Stoning and Killing Women! Launched in 2007, it quickly changed its name to the Global Campaign to Stop Killing and Stoning Women! (note the shift in emphasis).[20] It is coordinated by the network Women Living Under Muslim Law (WLUML), founded on a shoestring in 1984 by a small group led by anti-fundamentalist Algerian feminist Marieme Hélie-Lucas, which has grown to be a major international player in defending Muslim women's rights.[21] WLUML produces alerts, research, conferences, and publications, all of which are cast in terms of endangered or abused Muslim women. In its press announcement, the new campaign justifies itself by the alleged need "to address the intensifying trend of cultural and religious legitimisation of lethal violence against women" (WLUML 2007: 2). The campaign isolates, targets, and publicizes culturally specific forms of violence against women: violations of Muslim women's rights by Muslim regimes, Muslim fundamentalists, and local (Muslim) families. Individual cases of stoning or threatened stoning, whipping, and "honor crimes" merge on the campaign website as if they were instances of the same phenomenon, despite the differences among individual cases, countries of origin, reliability of information, and the legitimacy of the practices for Muslim thinkers, state legal systems, and ordinary people.

Violence against women is a serious problem worldwide. But to begin to see what is specific and perhaps peculiar about its deployment as an instance of the violation of "Muslim women's rights," we need to consider the context in which the campaign is being mounted. Two aspects of the context are critical. First is the dense terrain of similar sensationalizing projects to save Muslim women from their cultures, whether imagined as backward rural communities by educated youths or as governed by oppressive Islamic law by right-wing Americans (e.g., Spencer and Chesler 2007).

The second context, much in the news as I was working on this chapter in 2009, is that of violence against (Muslim) women inflicted in war and by militaries, not just in Afghanistan and Iraq, but in Palestine, as in the Israeli attack on Gaza that was launched in December 2008. In 23 days, more than 1,300 Palestinians were killed: buried alive in houses bombed by F16s, shot at close range in their beds, machine gunned from the sea, shelled by tanks using flechettes, and burned by white phosphorus, which acts like napalm (AI 2009; Hider 2009). One could ask where is the "global feminist campaign" against killing such significant numbers of (mostly Muslim) women? Women in conflict zones suffer and are killed in great numbers when armies, such as the Israeli army in this case, are not concerned about avoiding civilian casualties.[22]

Palestinian feminists have had to negotiate this situation for years, balancing their commitment to women's rights, as well as contact with feminists from other countries and regions as necessary for political and funding purposes, with an awareness of the larger political context in which they and the women for whom they advocate live and work. Despite widespread self-criticism about the depoliticizing effects of the NGOization of the Palestinian women's movement, which has brought on professionalization, hierarchization of expertise, diversion of energies to funders' desires for gender training and research reports, and deflection of women from political mobilization to grant-writing, the national commitments and constant attention to the larger political situation remain apparent in everything these women's rights advocates do (Carapico 2000; Hanafi and Tabar 2005; Jad 2005, 2008; Johnson 2008). Palestinian NGOs and projects, whether in the Occupied Territories or within the 1948 borders, may be funded by the Scandinavians, the Germans, the Ford Foundation, Open Society, WHO, and UNIFEM, just like so many of the Egyptian NGOs, but at the core of their efforts are the inescapable realities of occupation and militarization, and in the case of the Palestinian citizens of Israel, marginalization and discrimination.

One of the most moving studies I have encountered from this region is the report on some "action-research" on women and loss conducted during the second intifada. This report illustrates several features of women's rights work in Palestine that make it different, perhaps, from Egypt. The study was

designed to help produce effective psychological and social therapies for
women while at the same time giving voice to women's experiences of political conflict. As Shalhoub-Kevorkian (2004a: 5) argues in her chapter of
*Women, Armed Conflict and Loss: The Mental Health of Palestinian Women in
the Occupied Territories*, the project was to stand "at the crossroads between
human rights violations, mental health and research."[23] The long quotations
from individual women in the focus and support groups unfold wrenching
stories of trauma and coping in response to political violence (like watching your son's brain spill on the ground as Israeli soldiers trample his body),
house raids and demolition (watching your house blown up when you've
hidden your sons in the well at the center of the house), terror and sexual
harassment (soldiers molesting young women), gender-related violence (surveillance of martyrs' wives, births at checkpoints, unemployed and frustrated
husbands at home), and continuous fear and insecurity (17–31). The researchers from the Women's Studies Centre identify strongly with the women
whose rights concern them. Despite the differences in educational levels between the NGO feminists in general and the "grassroots," they are bound by a
national sensibility and solidarity.

Many committed feminists in Palestine cooperate with international and
governmental organizations to work for women's rights or empowerment.
Human rights claims, in particular, are recognized as a powerful tool for Pal-
estinians, claims they cannot forfeit even though they know the academic
critiques of human rights.[24] Jad chose to co-author the UNDP *Arab Human
Development Report 2005: Towards the Rise of Women in the Arab World*.[25]
Scholar-activists such as Nadera Shalhoub-Kevorkian assisted Human Rights
Watch in preparing *A Question of Security*, its 2006 report on violence against
Palestinian women and girls. In all this work, they never sidelined the subject of Israeli occupation or violence. Palestinian women's NGOs point to the
larger structural features that affect Palestinian women's lives even as they
participate in transnational women's rights institutions and networks that are
silent on such political features of everyday life. According to Johnson (2008:
125), scholar-activists like Shalhoub-Kevorkian who assist international organizations such as Human Rights Watch are sometimes dismayed to find
"that none of their analysis of violence of the occupation and siege and its
effects on women and families" gets included in the final reports. Johnson
charges that *A Question of Security* "isolates domestic violence and implicitly
gender relations and Palestinian families from all the contexts in which they
function." She charges that HRW 2006 fails to hold Israel accountable in ways

that are crucial; for example, it ignores the effects of occupation and siege on the Palestinian Authority's ability to enforce law and it does not take into consideration the effects of pervasive violence and economic strangulation on Palestinian family relations (125).

If governance feminism best characterizes Egyptian women's rights work of the last decade, Jad (2008) has similarly suggested that the establishment of the Palestine National Authority in the West Bank and Gaza, particularly its patronage of "femocrats" alongside the proliferation since the 1990s of foreign-funded NGOs, has led to the "demobilization of the Palestinian women's movement." Paying careful attention to the types of work, forms of organization, hierarchies, and social networks the new means of pursuing women's rights have entailed, Jad concludes that there has been a gradual disempowerment of women activists. She is most concerned about how this has left the field of "grassroots" women wide open for Islamist mobilization, but I think she underestimates the distinctive way the "depoliticized" NGO technologies of gender training courses could still, in the Palestinian national context, intersect with and enhance other sorts of women's rights work carried out in more activist veins.

A hint of this can be gleaned from the story Aweidah (2004: 102) tells about her first encounter on a trip to the Jenin refugee camp that formed the subject of the study of women's loss described above. The multinational delegation, organized by the Union of Palestinian Medical Relief Committees, was greeted by some young men doing medical relief. When these young men found out there were two "Arabs" accompanying the international delegation, they were excited to hear that they came from women's centers because they had previously had some gender training by the Jerusalem Women's Studies Centre. They even recognized Aweidah's name from their training course materials. Such crossovers from gender training to therapeutic and political work characterize the field of women's rights work in Palestine because of the particular national context. It is precisely such particulars that must be tracked if we want to understand the social life of "Muslim women's rights" as they operate in a larger international context that silences the particular political claims of Palestinians and deals in generalizations about patriarchal culture, especially Islamic.

Hybrid Circuits in Everyday Life

If the previous two sections analyzed the shifting fields of women's rights in Egypt and the tight nexus of women's rights and national politics in Palestine, this final section explores how we might begin to account for the mediations of women's rights outside the direct reach of advocates and defenders of women's rights. For all these professionals, there are women (not themselves) who are imagined as the targets of their efforts. How do Muslim women's rights circulate in the lives of those often characterized as the "grassroots" beneficiaries?

I will take you to one village in Upper Egypt to look at the mediation of women's lives through the social instruments of "rights." I invoke some village women's stories to explore the way the circuits of "rights" in such villages intersect with—and diverge from—those we have been following in elite urban and international sites. For the past eighteen years I have been going back and forth to a village in Upper Egypt that relies on a mixed economy of agriculture, tourism, and migration. I used the village as a base to do research on Egyptian television soap operas and the role they play in shaping a sense of national community and a way of thinking about politics, religion, womanhood, and citizenship (Abu-Lughod 2005). In March 2008, when I was doing some new research on women's rights organizations and people's everyday thinking about "Muslim women's rights," I went back to some of my women friends to talk about this new project. All had immediate responses to the concept of "women's rights" (*huquq al-mar'a*).

For example, a couple of sisters I'd known since they were young girls (they were now fifteen and twenty-two) immediately launched into an animated discussion of a popular television serial that they, along with the rest of the country, had just finished watching during Ramadan. It featured Egypt's biggest star, Yusra. They told me the plot: a few young guys kidnap a female doctor and some nurses on their way home late at night and rape one of them. The show was about bringing these rapists to justice. They wanted me to know that rape is punishable by death.

That they had paid attention to the message of the television serial and were part of a national conversation is significant, but nothing new. Egyptian TV serials often take up important social issues. This serial, *A Matter of Public Opinion*, had launched public debates on violence against women. After it was broadcast, the television serial became the focus of an event in Amman, Jordan, that was part of the UNIFEM celebration of the global campaign, Sixteen Days of Activism to End Violence Against Women.

That national television had mediated women's understandings of "women's rights" in the village was apparent in the response of another young woman. In answer to my question about what she knew about "women's rights," she just said, "It's something Suzanne Mubarak is working on. It's about female circumcision." Indeed, one of the key projects of the National Center for Childhood and Motherhood, which addresses violence against girl children is the push for circumcision-free model villages. This young woman knew nothing about such villages.

However, other discussions revealed the multiple mediations and registers of "women's rights" in this village. 'Aysha, a woman in her forties from a poor and troubled family whom I had met in a literacy class in the mid-1990s, gave me the best evidence of the hybridity of the concept of "Muslim women's rights" in this rural village and the multiple institutional circuits through which "rights" are produced and pursued. The literacy classes where I met her were themselves part of the national machinery of women's rights: sponsored by the government for a couple of years, with local women graduates hired to teach, then for no reason, discontinued.

When I told 'Aysha that my new project was on women's rights in Egypt, she exclaimed,

> Let me tell you, the woman in Egypt enjoys the highest level of rights. Truly. . . . Do you know, Lila, that we have women ministers in the cabinet? Ministers! The Minister of Social Affairs. The head of the Finance Ministry. All of them are women. Here in Egypt the government has given women their rights, one hundred per cent.

But then she went on to qualify this:

> But people, a woman's family, they are the ones who undermine her rights. Say it happens that my father leaves me three acres of land. Her brother comes along and says, "No, she shouldn't take it. The girl shouldn't take the land." Here, the government gives her her rights.

Picking up on the shifting pronouns—my father, her brother—I asked if this happened to her. She laughed. "This is just a for instance. Praise be to God [so as not to complain about her fate], my family doesn't have any land!" Then she continued, "So the brother takes his sister's land. It happens. In some families. Not all because some families give to the daughters. . . . He says, 'I want the land. I'm a man, I should take the land.'"

Her response to this imagined brother was, "But God, Glory be to Him, gives women an inheritance." She then quoted the Qur'anic passage that mandates that women inherit.[26] She concluded, "So if God sent down in the Qur'an word that a woman is entitled, that the woman should get her inheritance, how dare you fight this?"

When I asked what a woman would do in these circumstances, she responded, "She goes to the government." Only a few seconds later, she modified this: "Well, first she goes to complain to the family. To the elders." Immediately after that, however, she gave a different example that related to her own village. She reminded me that they had an important religious figure in the next village, a respected man whose father and grandfather had also been religious figures. She said, "We go to him with any problem like this. Women do." Just then, her older brother walked into the room and she confirmed with him, "Isn't it true that a girl goes to the Shaykh if she has a problem with her uncle or her brother? Yes, she complains to him. It's normal. And he listens to her." Her brother nodded and then went on to tell a story of a major problem that the Shaykh had resolved, interestingly, not between a girl and her family, but between a Christian and some Muslim families in a dispute over land. This showed the Shaykh's enormous grace, generosity, and wisdom and suggested why he had the respect of all in mediating arguments.[27]

In this one conversation, 'Aysha talked about rights in multiple registers: she invoked national legal rights for women; she assessed women's rights in terms of political representation; and she talked about local conflicts within and among families; and then, finally, she talked about the God-given rights granted to women in the Qur'an, or what we call Shari'a. In another conversation a year later, she defended "Islam" in general. She insisted that Islam says that women are free to work and free to go to school. She then gave examples of important women in the Prophet Muhammad's time: Nafisa, who was a teacher, and 'A'isha, who transmitted *hadith*s, the sayings of the Prophet. But, she added, some women had decided that freedom meant wearing short dresses with short sleeves and walking around the streets naked. There is too much freedom now, she concluded. Mixing yet again several registers of rights, she explained that this kind of "freedom" was not what Qasim Amin had meant. Here she invoked the classic turn-of-the-century Egyptian modernist reformer who wrote *The Liberation of Women* supporting women's limited education and unveiling. She also referenced in her discussion the multiple institutions that mediate "rights" in Egypt. These are the forums through which individual women might seek justice: the courts with their lawyers, legalities, and papers; local family arbitration with its pull of emotions, hierarchies, and cross-cutting ties; and the institution of the local religious figure who would intervene in the name of Islamic rights and morality if a woman was wronged by her family. She did not mention NGOs. Like the other women and girls whose conversations about women's rights I have quoted, 'Aysha has learned these multiple ways of framing lives and asserting rights from television, from school, from religious study, and from the everyday lives of people in her community, about which community members tend to have intimate knowledge.

In a study of the interaction between a Scandinavian feminist NGO and the village women's organization it supported on a tiny island off the coast of Tanzania, Christine Walley (n.d.) has argued that a universalizing term like "rights" actually accumulates meanings from multiple sources. She shows that for the Muslim women in the community in which she worked, the KiSwahili term translated as rights (*haki*) could refer to prerogatives and obligations found in Islamic law as well as suggesting what was just in a customary sense. But she also found that *haki* had accumulated other meanings in the independence and socialist periods, meanings tied to citizenship. Most recently, the term was also coming to reference international human and women's rights frameworks encountered through their leaders who were sent to conferences by funders. When a village woman asserted or claimed her "rights," therefore, one simply could not know what register she was using, or which meaning(s) of rights she was referencing, or whether in fact these all inflected each other, producing a dense sense of rights.

Walley's challenging presentation of the way conceptions of rights are layered in one concrete "grassroots" situation is intriguing, and seems to describe well women's mobilizations of "rights" in Egyptian villages too. What Walley did not pursue is what I have been trying to showcase: the need to do more sociological tracking of the networks, institutions, and technologies that mediate "Muslim women's rights." In the Egyptian village from which I have been drawing my examples, it is clear that even though there are no women's rights organizations, comments like 'Aysha's suggest that the larger national and international enterprise of "women's rights" has shaped local conceptualizations of rights and made certain institutions, such as schools and governmental organs and legal sites, central to their communication and pursuit. However, her comments also reveal how many social institutions and imaginative frameworks outside of the dominant work of NGOs and government are in addition part of local women's active pursuit of justice and rights. The religious idiom of Islamic law (only now becoming in the capital a track for rights, as we saw in the case of CEWLA) and the local moral force of popular religious authorities, alongside the extended family that remains the most significant social form, exceed the frames and social institutions of more official women's rights work in Egypt.

I have been trying to argue that we need to find new ways of analyzing "Muslim women's rights," surely one of the most sensationalized issues on the current global stage, entangled variously with military intervention and transnational feminism, progressive foundations and right-wing think tanks, elite careers and welfare administration, literary commerce and marginal lives. An ethnographic approach that tracks the many social lives that the concept partakes in may be more useful for understanding this subject and the historical moment we are living than moral posturing that traffics in judgments of the work of women's rights as either a form of collusion with imperialism (to be denounced) or a hopeful sign of universal emancipation and progress (to be celebrated). I argued in the introduction that it might be fruitful to examine how "Muslim women's rights" makes and remakes the world. How, when, and where is the concept deployed? What transformations of social life and individual lives are produced in its name? Who enables that work and is in turn enabled by it? What new paths of power and channels of capital, financial and cultural, does it open up?

Anthropologists who study rights have urged us to take the "social practice of rights as an object of ethnographic inquiry" (Goodale 2006: 3) and to produce "closely observed studies of rights talk and implementation" (Wilson 2006: 81). I have argued here for something more: that we track carefully, across multiple terrains, the way both practices and talk of rights organize social and political fields, producing organizations, projects, and forms of governing as much as being produced by them.

If we take this approach, there is no alternative but to go into the details of "Muslim women's rights" as they move in and out of particular locations and communities. In Cairo, as I showed in the first section, the women's rights industry creates careers, channels funds, inspires commitments, gives credibility to new actors, creates and disrupts social networks, and legitimizes intellectual and political frameworks and ideals. Women's rights provide a conduit for foreign intervention and government involvement in ordering the daily lives of both the middle classes and those at the margins. The object of struggle among religious institutions and organizations, women's rights are also the subjects of corporate sponsorship and adopted as a symbol of modernity.

Juxtaposing the Egyptian to the Palestinian case reveals how dependent the operation of "Muslim women's rights" is on the larger political situation, the organization and resources of the local states, and the configuration of international interest. Palestine may have just as well-funded women's NGOs as Egypt, again as part of the "peace dividend," but the nature of the work they do, the social networks they forge or on which they are built, their relationship to international and national institutions and projects, and even the class relations and solidarities—many political—among the women and their beneficiaries, differ dramatically from the Egyptian case.

Finally, in a somewhat unusual move, this chapter tracked "Muslim women's rights" out of the arenas where it is mobilized explicitly and in turn configures the social field, into one village. This is a village that houses the kinds of socially marginal women often imagined to be the "grassroots" beneficiaries of rights work: the "traditional" or "oppressed" women in need of rights and empowerment. The women in this village that I have come to know over the past eighteen years are not members of any women's rights organizations or recipients of their funds; they have not been the objects of "rights" interventions in the current era except through a short-lived government literacy program for women in the 1990s and equally short-lived initiatives for handicraft production by individual Europeans. What the fragments of conversation I had with them on the subject of "rights" demonstrate, however, is that no one is unaffected by the circulation of discourses of "Muslim women's rights" and the practical ways their pursuit is being negotiated. At the same time, these fragments indicate that the framework and projects of "Muslim women's rights" do not begin to exhaust these women's conceptions of rights and their experiences of trying to assert them in everyday life. Only ethnography can reveal the different place of "rights" in these lives, and the multiple registers and tracks they follow in specific locations.

Chapter 6

How Not to be a *Machu Qari* (Old Man): Human Rights, Machismo, and Military Nostalgia in Peru's Andes

Caroline Yezer

> When I was younger, the old folks were so organized. The
> whole village would show up for a work project and sweat
> together. And, when there was adultery, there would be
> a village assembly . . . [they would] make the adulterers
> strip, put bullhorns on them and make them run around
> the plaza. . . . But now, we are more knowledgeable. We
> know the laws. And that is why there is no obedience.
> Tell me, how can a *pueblo* advance when it is like that?
> —Don Pedro, fifty-year-old villager and
> ex-civil defense patrol member

Over the ten years of relative peace following the end of Peru's dirty war, fought between the state and the Maoist rebels known as Shining Path (1980–2000), indigenous peasant communities of the Ayacucho highlands have undergone fundamental changes in the ways rights are understood and claimed. Far-flung villages that had been under martial law since the early 1980s became the focus of aid organizations, human rights groups, and other post-conflict projects funded by or coming from abroad. Following these changes, military reform, disarmament, and the retreat of state troops and army bases from much of Ayacucho marked a sharp reduction in state presence in the highlands.

One might think that these poor farmers, for many years the targets of state violence, would view association with the military dimly, and welcome the demilitarization of their villages and an international discourse of human rights. Negative memories of the state have by no means vanished in an area where many peasants had at least one relative killed by the military or by rebel guerrillas. Yet some villagers, such as Don Pedro (quoted above) experienced the recent interventions of human rights law as a destabilizing force, and even showed nostalgia for the macho military discipline of the recent past. During my fieldwork in Wiracocha, a small peasant community located in what was once the heart of Peru's war zone, other men and women mourned the social solidarity they perceived had been lost since the war.[1] They expressed these insecurities through an idiom of gender and authority, one that equated male virility with social strength and communal autonomy. If Wiracocha's past village leaders ruled effectively because they were masculine and strong in the midst of war, today's villagers claimed they were "all just *machu qari*" (Quechua for "old man/men")—too weak and ineffectual to ensure the continued survival of their community.[2]

This chapter explores how people in Wiracocha experienced shifts from militarization to human rights reform, in ways that are crosscut by changes in gender roles and indigenous peasant citizenship in post-conflict Peru. During the war, villagers in Wiracocha were able to find some measure of security and even pride in their cooperation with the military, especially when confronted with the authoritarianism of Shining Path rebels (Starn 1998). At that time peasant men began to, as one patroller put it, *ponerse macho* ("make themselves macho"), by forming their own counterinsurgency patrols that were later subsumed by state forces (Del Pino 1991).[3] Militarization of villages went so far as to replace certain customary forms of leadership and justice that had diminished during the war.

The combination of soldiering with local traditions allows for an unusual vantage point to observe the cultural links between militarization, citizenship, and masculinity today. In Peru, as in other Andean contexts where indigenous highlanders are denied basic rights, joining the military has been a limited, yet significant way indigenous men can claim rights as citizens, for themselves and their families (Gill 2000: 105–8).[4] This militarized culture of rights has clashed, however, with the turn to peace-building and international human rights laws. In Peru, the deployment of human rights has brought with it an ideological shift in the ways rights are understood and regulated, from a nation-state soldier-citizen model to a transnational one based on the universal human rights of the international citizen. Villagers express and experience this change through cultural understandings of gender. As well, they experience this shift differently across the gender divide. Men who had served in Wiracocha's counterinsurgency and sided with the state against Maoist rebels experienced the shift from military justice to international human rights as disorienting and potentially dangerous. Their service in the military or *rondas* had guaranteed (theoretically) their rights as Peruvians; now rights were to be managed through deterritorialized parastate organizations (NGOs and international bodies like the United Nations) mysteriously beyond the sovereignty of Peru. At the same time, human rights discourse resonated with women's growing economic and social independence after the war. Within their homes, women were able to use the human rights interventions to create a space from which they could make political demands for decision-making, especially to control their reproductive rights.

Peru's uneven and sometimes contradictory transition from one culture of rights to another also speaks to broader patterns of governance, in which states transition from Keynesian welfare programs to what some have called "neoliberal governmentality" (Gupta and Ferguson 2002). This term describes the recent trend of states to privatize and outsource the regulation and management of their populations far beyond the space and authority of the nation. The consequences of neoliberal reforms are especially dramatic and difficult to evaluate in Latin America. On the one hand, transnational networks of human rights organizations and international NGOs are an important source of solidarity and external intervention for local activists (Escobar and Alvarez 1992). The new forms of governance that come from privatized NGOs have played a progressive role in revealing hidden state violence such as death squads, torture, and "disappearances" in order to hold oppressors accountable for these deniable crimes (Shaw 2005; Yezer 2008). International networks are also a source of aid and solidarity in countries with large indigenous populations like Peru, where watch-dog groups may be all that stands between state or private interests and the territories, rights, and lives of indigenous citizens (Stavenhagen 1995; Youngers 2003).

But while transnational alliances have helped combat state atrocities, anthropologists caution that they can also fit well in neoliberal reforms that may take away access to indigenous resources formerly protected by the state. Research on indigenous social movements, for example, cautions that at times multiculturalism and human rights law may, paradoxically, rein in indigenous autonomy (Gill 2000: 137; Hale 2006; Postero 2006; Speed 2005; Speed and Collier 2000). For example, anthropologist Charles Hale writes that in Mexico "neoliberal multiculturalism" may co-opt more radical activist projects among indigenous peoples, ironically giving states more paternalistic control over indigenous lands and resources than in the past (Hale 2006).

By the same token, the case of Wiracocha shows us that the dominance of human rights in struggles for social justice must also take place, as Hannah Arendt once argued, at the level of belonging to a nation. In this analysis I use feminist critiques of militarization to understand how indigenous peasants struggle to do this by maintaining some ties to their war past. These scholars have argued that an analysis of the relationship between marginalized people and state forces as solely oppressive does not capture the complexity of war or the options for citizenship offered by conscription. Equally important are the ways desire, power, and cultural capital are bound up in military service (Enloe 1983; Gill 2000, 2004; Lutz 2001; Nelson 2009). Lesley Gill has explored the ways that indigenous men in Bolivia view military service as a way to improve their status within a society that excludes them (Gill 2000: 107).[5] Even though they face racism of the whiter, mestizo officers and are forced to occupy the lowest rungs of military service, subaltern men become soldiers, she argues, because, among other things military service is one of the few ways to gain official citizenship (Gill 2000: 117). In Wiracocha male villagers use their strongest claim to the nation—their military service, to ensure that they keep this fundamental connection to this essential "right to have rights" (Arendt 1968).

Shining Path and the Peasant Counterinsurgency

Peru's internal war hit villages like Wiracocha especially hard. In the 1980s almost all Wiracocha's residents fled their homes several times, escaping the assassinations and massacres that plagued the countryside. The military was brutal in Wiracocha because the region had been stigmatized as an area of rebel sympathies.[6] This reputation was due to the early presence of Shining Path rebels, who recruited some younger villagers. But when rebels became more authoritarian in their methods, villagers learned Shining Path's violent and top-down brand of Marxism, which demanded a blood quota from its members and dismissed all other movements as enemies (Degregori 1990; Gorriti 1999; Poole and Rénique 1992; Starn 1995). In Wiracocha the situation reached a breaking point when rebels began to assassinate anyone not in complete agreement with their cause. At the same time, state forces viewed villagers as subversives, and disappeared them indiscriminately.

Wiracocha was finally repopulated when villagers decided to form a *ronda* (defense patrol), as some of their neighbors had already done. These patrols were based on rondas created before the war, by peasants in Peru's northern provinces. The original purpose of the rondas was to control crime and dispense justice in areas abandoned by the state, but in Ayacucho rondas patrolled the village or went on longer offensive expeditions to confront rebel columns.[7] Wiracocha's patrols consisted of men between ages sixteen and sixty and were ill equipped, with only two Mauser rifles, knives, a few slingshots, and homemade guns made of wood and metal pipe.

When news of these patrols reached the cities, many on the left were wary that the rondas could degenerate into death squads or vigilante groups, as they had in Guatemala (Nelson 2009). These fears grew as Peru's armed forces took over the peasant patrols and militarized them as part of a new strategy to win the support of the peasantry. While many indigenous men volunteer for the armed forces, the state's new strategy also seemed suspicious in light of Peru's "*levas*," the seasonal military ambushes in which young men from the rural Andes and urban shantytowns were rounded up, kidnapped, and forcibly drafted (González-Cueva 2000). By the mid-1990s, however, analysts argued that many Ayacucho rondas were grassroots or at least semi-autonomous actors, motivated to join the counterinsurgency as much by their own frustration with Shining Path attacks as by pressure from the state (Degregori et al. 1996; Starn 1998; Del Pino 1991).

The state's strategy of including villagers in the counterinsurgency rather than targeting them as enemies finally paid off as the rondas became essential to rebel defeat. Villagers knew the craggy terrain and its hiding places more intimately than the soldiers did. This superior knowledge provided an advantage, allowing them finally to drive rebels back into the jungle where the army had failed. For a time patrollers even reached the status of national heroes due to their important role in the state's victory over the rebellion (Degregori et al. 1996). This representation as patriots was especially important in Wiracocha, where it counteracted the community's earlier stigmatization as a treasonous place of rebel support. Even after the war, the narrative of patrol service has remained an important way that villagers stake a claim in debates about reparations and political representation (Yezer 2005).

The counterinsurgency began to win the war with the capture of Shining Path's leader in 1992. Five years later the rondas managed to push rebels back to the remote jungles, making the war an official victory for the state.[8] By 1999 President Fujimori, eager to show the war had been won on his watch, as well as to combat his government's reputation as a human rights violator, began to demilitarize the countryside. He cut back on patrols in the former emergency zone, closed down army bases in much of Ayacucho, and planned to make military service voluntary and redirect military aid to other sectors. These changes, at times superficial, were meant to mark a clear transition from war to peace in the countryside, and a return to the ideals of modernization and economic development, as it legitimated the state.

By 1999 Wiracocha's rondas had ceased almost all their patrolling activities and were under orders to turn their arms over to state forces, including arms purchased by villagers themselves. The state also declared that the patrols, known officially by the military as Civil Defense Committees (Comites de Auto Defensa) would be renamed and reorganized as Civil Development Committees (Comites de Auto Desarrollo); their main jobs would be to help their village advance economically. Many of the villagers still in exile returned to claim their lands and begin rebuilding their lives as a peasant community.

From Customary Justice to Ronda Justice

When they returned to Wiracocha, villagers faced the challenge of rebuilding their fields, homes, and system of government, but fifteen years of violence had destroyed systems of communal authority. These included officers called *varayoq* (Quechua for "staff-bearers," for the staffs they carried to signify their authority) who administered justice, serving as informal internal police.[9] The office of the *varayoq* was originally part of an indigenous political order, cultivated by the Spanish to be a dual system of governance that would better control the conquered population. Scholars differ as to what extent indigenous villagers embraced or avoided the office, but some historians as well as the villagers I interviewed in Wiracocha see the survival of the *varayoq* into the 1980s and later as a symbol of Andean cultural continuity and resistance (Heilman 2010, 104; Thurner 1997). However, in Wiracocha, as well as in other villages in the warzone, the *varayoq* diminished or disappeared as a result of selective targeting of village administrators and leaders for assassination (Mitchell 1991).

During the war and afterward, the role of the *varayoq* were partly filled by the rondas. The Peruvian constitution allows some autonomy in prosecuting minor offenses in official peasant communities, as long as they come from traditional *usos y costumbres* (uses and customs) and do not violate international human rights law. However, the law is notoriously vague about exactly what kinds of customary punishments are acceptable, and the state has had to create a special law for those who implement corporal punishments that violate human rights unintentionally. In the past the state looked away from the forms of punishment used by peasant communities to deal with misdemeanors and other infractions, even if they involved corporal punishment. Similarly, under the state of emergency, the Ayacucho rondas were given tacit encouragement to use violence to maintain order. As the rondas slipped into the role of the "traditional" *varayoq*, the physical punishments meted out by ronderos in the village merged with physical punishments prescribed by customary justice. Eduardo, a thirty-year-old who lived part time in the *ceja de selva*—the high jungle where coca is grown and crime is high—explained: "We need the rondas, just to maintain the peace, even if it is only among ourselves."

After the war ended, the Wiracocha rondas ceased almost all their activities and the patrol leaders lost their authority. In 2003 the nostalgia for previous village order was so strong that Don Eugenio, the village president, presented a proposal to bring back the office of the *varayoq* at a community meeting. Villagers overwhelmingly voted to reinstate these traditional leaders, and Don Eugenio concluded: "All the old rules and customs of the village, they have all been burned, lost, who knows, during the violence. We used to have rules, but now we don't any more and that is why we have to re-do them. . . . The *varayoq* used to take care of the fields like foxes. They would lie in wait 'til your animal would graze in someone else's field, and then—*bam*! The whip. *That* was respect, in those times."

For many villagers, the militarization of the war years had stood in for this swift "traditional" justice of the *varayoq*'s whip that Eduardo described. The corporal punishment administered by the rondas was in fact resonant with villagers' customary justice, which emphasized reconciliation and restoration of erring village members back into the community, rather than expelling them from the community or turning them over to the state.

Village Solidarity, Discipline and Military Nostalgia

By the time I began my fieldwork in 1999, the rondas had been almost completely disbanded and the last military base removed from the district capital closest to Wiracocha. Nevertheless, men I interviewed (especially those who had served in the patrols) expressed nostalgia for the way the village operated during the war. Many felt that their militarization had disciplined and organized village life and now served as a crucial ingredient in communal solidarity.

Nostalgia for militarization was partly shaped by what all villagers perceived as an increase in crime in rural Ayacucho. Both men and women believed that this rise was due to a lack of the rural governance and discipline that were in abundance during the years of militarization and ronda activity.[10] Because rural misdemeanors were often handled informally, reported in the "yellow" press but not studied and counted, I could not verify this crime increase. Yet everyone in Wiracocha complained and worried about it. In my interviews, villagers marked this increase in the rise of new crimes, including livestock thefts and wars among the cocaine traffickers who traveled the paths of the altiplano above the village.

Villagers also perceived a rise in crime among neighbors, including an increase in the frequency of adultery. The state did not intervene in these problems, as the remoteness of Wiracocha made such crime invisible, or ignorable. For most misdemeanors, the village was in charge of governing itself. Both men and women despaired that crime and corruption in the village was getting out of hand. "We are morally degenerating," Don Julio, the village justice and head of the Pentecostal village church, complained to me. "We have more and more *maldad* ("immorality, evil") here—every day, it continues."

Against this moral decay, most men saw the discipline of even a warridden past in a rosy light. Daniel, a former rondero commander, recalled with some pride, "Before it was—you didn't show up to your patrols? Well, *straight* to the village jail." Prudencio, another former rondero, exasperated at trying to get villagers to attend village *faenas* (obligatory communal work projects), explained that in wartime, when villagers did not perform their community obligations, they were whipped in the plaza. For greater offenses, they would be made to stay awake all night standing in a deep trench filled with freezing water. Now that these physical punishments were discouraged or outlawed by recently implemented human rights laws, leaders resorted to monetary fines to deter and punish crimes committed between neighbors. But Prudencio, plagued with his failed *faena*, said disgustedly "They just don't pay the fine. Why should they, when there is no whipping to enforce it?"

Moreover, military discipline was valued for the ways villagers appropriated it to serve local needs—a use that was not necessarily in accord with the state. A militarized defense was necessary now more than ever, Eduardo told me, because "without the rondas they [criminals] think they can come into the countryside to rob." The patrols were also seen as potential protection from the state. Julian, for example, explained that the rondas might have stopped recent cases of police brutality in the village. Due to a rise in Peru's coca production in 2000, traffickers increasingly used the mountain paths in the altiplano above the village to bring cocaine paste and illegal coca leaf to the coast.[11] As a result, police from the provincial capital made surprise visits to threaten and physically intimidate local leaders for "allowing," as they phrased it, the trafficking to take place. Anti-drug police approached Don Felix, a church elder, on a regular basis. Shoving him around one day to prove their point, the policemen yelled that if any drugs passed through town they would hold Felix responsible. Julian explained that, during the war, the rondas would never have allowed that to happen: "You know, the police are lucky because, in some places, when people come in—without authorization from the city? The rondas shoot people like that."

Of course no one missed the terror or violence of the war. But many men lamented a loss of village solidarity, consensus, and discipline that seemed to arise from wartime crisis, when neighbors banded together in the face of a common enemy. Eduardo explained to me that the rondas ensured intercommunal service, "if something happened in one part others would come to their aid. Even if there was someone who was a *desconocido* [stranger] then they would go to investigate." Prudencio, the frustrated director of the work project, explained, "those days [during the rondas] it was so much stronger, there were stronger leaders. People were afraid not to attend the assemblies and the patrols. Now with the pacification, no one does a thing; there is much less participation." Compared to the glory days of the rondas, men lamented that they were now *mana kallpayoqchu* (Quechua for "without force, weak") and *desorganizada* ("disorganized" and incapable of reaching any consensus).

Gender, Power, and Village Sovereignty

Because men tended to equate masculine strength and militarization as an inherently positive aspect in a good village society, I assumed village women would not agree. As anthropologist Kimberly Theidon has shown in other villages in Ayacucho, the macho narrative of ronda patriotism left little room for women's representation (Theidon 2003: 69). I was surprised when Dona Julia and her neighbors shared this critique of men's meekness. Much like the men, women were vocal in their complaints about a general lack of village order and discipline. But, whereas men blamed demilitarization for many of their woes, women blamed leaders directly for a loss of solidarity and an increase in crime. In fact, every woman I interviewed blamed male village leaders with gusto and in a colorful language that extended and exaggerated the metaphors of virility and meekness. According to women, the loss of village order was due to men's weakening since the war; men's laziness as authorities was not only dramatic in comparison to the courage and activism of previous leaders, but symptomatic of the general village decline.[12]

Some of the more outspoken women took pleasure in insulting the masculinity of post-war leaders in some of the harshest Quechua: for being *quella* ("lazy") or having *loqlo runtu* ("putrid balls"), lacking the masculine qualities they defined as courage or virility. Mostly I heard these comments when men were not around, but some women would utter them under their breath in village meetings, when they thought male leaders were not being sensitive to women's concerns. These insults were leveled at leaders who did not want to hear from elderly women who presented a complaint during a communal assembly, or did not follow up on women's complaints about the budget for the communal kitchen they were running, or about neighbors who stole their crops, for example. Such male leaders were too *quella* to trudge up the mountain fields to investigate, Mari, a sixty-year-old widow, told me, to determine which burro was eating the crops. Or they were just too permissive to villagers who were accused of misdemeanors because they allowed a physically abusive husband off with merely a warning instead of a physical lashing.

While women blamed men for being meek instead of manly, some of the more self-critical men agreed with them, saying that they would *like* to be stronger, to do better now. As counterinsurgents, village men found a coincidence between their roles as authorities and protectors of the nation. If during the war they were powerful patriots fighting treasonous terrorists, now men complained they were simply *machu qari*, incapable of instilling fear or meting out punishment. Almost every man explained that he could not do better because leaders were fettered by new limits placed on their authority, due to demilitarization (the loss of military outposts, the order to turn in patrollers' rifles) and, even more fundamentally, human rights. In the village, men understood human rights to be a foreign legal system imported through international NGOs that constrained male authority and even endangered village sovereignty.

NGOs in Ayacucho

Throughout the 1980s and the Alberto Fujimori presidency in the early 1990s, Peru's state and military officials, along with the conservative sectors of the Catholic Church, opposed aid and human rights groups, which they categorized as shelters for terrorists.[13] Human rights talk was suspect, especially in Ayacucho, where the state of emergency allowed state forces to disappear rights advocates (Smith 1992; Burt 2006).[14] For its part, the Shining Path also targeted human rights activists (along with union leaders and other leftist organizers that rebels categorized as revisionists). Nevertheless, by the mid-1990s, Peruvian NGOs, Protestant church groups, and progressive Catholics in Lima had formed a formidable national coalition for human rights (Youngers 2003). International and domestic private NGO aid projects proliferated in Ayacucho's urban centers at this time. These changes quickened in 2000 when, amid corruption charges and shady arms deals made by his chief intelligence officer, Fujimori left the country and faxed his resignation. In the interim a transitional government sympathetic to human rights reform took over and began to implement Peru's Truth and Reconciliation Commission, mandated to investigate and educate about the human rights violations of the dirty war. Without Fujimori's opposition, an influx of human rights *capacitaciones* (workshops) accompanied the proliferation of state aid and NGO programs into the Ayacucho countryside.

It would be hard to overestimate the novelty of these workshops to peasants in rural Ayacucho. Of course human rights discourse did not mark a rural awakening of feminist or indigenous consciousness where there had been none before. Irene Silverblatt has documented how Andean women have long exerted their power over highland politics, especially before the Inca empire (Silverblatt 1987). Nor do I mean that peasants were somehow so remote, or so unattached to the rest of the world that villagers had no conception of "rights" at all. *Derechos* ("rights") on the national level were not a new concept: villagers knew when they did and did not have the right to *quejar* ("place a complaint"); when they had the right to own land, or the right to sue; they had been making use of the court system and filing formal complaints to the endless bureaucracy of police and lawyers for decades. They also knew when those rights were taken away, as they were in the state of emergency during the dirty war. But *derechos humanos* ("human rights") were a new breed. Aid workers introduced human rights to villagers as a radically new system of justice. And, in theory, they were: unlike rights guaranteed by the state, human rights involved new kinds of sovereignty that could bypass a corrupt state, where state abuse could not take place because accountability would be assured by an unseen international community. For their part, villagers talked about human rights as a novel and abrupt change, an import whose sudden appearance in the countryside could almost be narrowed down to a precise moment.

A Woman-Focused Humanitarianism

The institutions that introduced this new system of justice and accountability targeted women's groups for consciousness-raising workshops about their rights within the home and village.[15] Probably this feminine focus was not meant to exclude men, but was tailored to practical concerns in the field as well as larger demands in the international economy of humanitarian aid. In the field women were more available for interviews or workshops than men, especially during the day. Women's activities were more likely to take place at a time and location near the village center, making them easier to convene when NGOs visited, while men were often far off in the fields, or on seasonal labor migrations in the cities or jungle.[16] Transformations in international aid also made women's organizations better options for local aid agencies and rights groups. The increased interest in gender-based projects among international funders and local investigators in the late 1990s, after the 1995 Beijing Conference on Women's Rights, was one such change. During my fieldwork in 1998, many city-based NGO fieldworkers had been inspired by the Beijing Conference and what they saw as the need to account for women's situation in the wake of Peru's conflict. External demand for projects on gender created a supply of local projects that focused on women's issues, as such projects were more likely to appeal to powerful international funders like USAID. But demands for women or gender-based aid projects could also be confining for fieldworkers. In 1998 when I traveled with aid agencies to various returning refugee villages throughout Ayacucho, local NGOs were implementing women's projects not because that was the sector they determined needed the most aid, but because, as one Spanish aid worker told me, "that is what *your people* [USAID] want."

In Wiracocha, human rights workshops focused on the Clubes de Madres ("Mothers' Clubs"). Begun by women in the 1970s, the clubs multiplied to share resources made scarce by the war, as well as by Peru's excessive inflation in the 1980s and soaring utilities during structural adjustment programs of the 1990s. In Ayacucho and Lima, women also took the lead in organizations of the relatives of the disappeared, communal soup kitchens, and the Vaso de Leche ("Glass of Milk") program—in response to wartime violence and the needs of woman-headed families. These and other women's groups were sped up by the war, as widows and single mothers—often refugees from the countryside—coordinated solutions to their economic desperation (Blondet 1991, 1995; Coral Cordero 1998).

Changes in Women's Rights in the Home

Unlike the men I spoke with, most women in Wiracocha looked on the interventions of human rights workshops favorably, explaining to me that "human rights" gave them someplace to voice their complaints and helped restructure their power in the home. "Before we were ignorant here," Cecelia, president of Wiracocha's Mother's Club, told me, "but now we know we have rights, and we can complain." Other women explained that they were less afraid to make complaints about rape or spousal abuse because of the availability of human rights organizations that had opened up offices in the provincial capital. Such organizations would put pressure on the mostly male authorities to investigate and back women's claims if the local *juez de paz* did not follow through in prosecuting offenders.[17] Women also valued the new discourse of rights when it intervened in family planning, a topic that has been a source of conflict between domestic partners for as long as anyone could remember. At a Mother's Club meeting Cecelia explained to the assembled women, "Ever since we have human rights. . . we can have the number of children we want; now it has to be decided by *both* spouses, the man and the woman." The women around her nodded, saying, "That's right!" "That's very good."

That women leaders might be more enthusiastic about these human rights reforms than men were was foreseeable. After all, men's frustration with human rights could be at least partly attributed to their own loss of power over family planning and other domestic concerns as women's power increased. Before the war, for example, it was not unusual for husbands to have the final say in how many children they would have. In the highlands, husbands are still considered to be, at least in theory, the de facto head of the household, and therefore the ultimate authority in decisions that concern the family. Women I interviewed credited the consciousness-raising human rights workshops they had attended for what they perceived as increased control for women in reproductive decisions.

Rights workshops also gave village women the legitimacy they needed to fight domestic violence. To be sure, no men in Wiracocha defended wife beating, and leaders were even strongly vocal against it. Yet, as in much of the country, violence between spouses or between parents and children is nevertheless one of the most frequent and widespread forms of community conflict. This trend is not confined to the countryside; according to one study, over half of all Peruvian women will have been beaten by a male partner at least once in their lives.[18] However, domestic violence did surge in villages like Wiracocha that were in the heart of Ayacucho's war zone (Reynaga 1996), as did alcoholism among male abusers (Theidon 1999). In response, the state passed a law in 1993 that outlawed domestic violence and punished perpetrators. But the law did little to stop familial violence in the cities and even less in the countryside (Boesten 2006). As in many highland communities, in Wiracocha there is no incarceration for wife beating; the customary procedure is to resolve domestic violence by keeping the family together and reintegrating the erring member into the village at all costs. In the city the 1993 law is undermined even among higher-court judges, privileging conservation of the family unit above the protection of an abused partner.[19] Given these conservative trends, it was not surprising that village women expressed appreciation for the ways the discourse of human rights helped them criticize the presence of domestic abuse, even if most women told me that the effect of these policies had yet to be seen on a practical level.[20]

The Paradox of Human Rights and Customary Justice

While woman praised the new regime of human rights for its potential to intervene on their behalf in the home, they took an unexpected stance on the intervention of human rights law into village sovereignty outside the family. This was especially evident when villagers who were charged with infractions sought the intervention of human rights agencies to oppose the decisions of village authorities.

According to one survey, 80 percent of conflicts in the rural highlands are resolved through local custom.[21] Yet, as anthropologists Shannon Speed and Jane Collier have shown in the case of Mexico, many local customs rely on physical punishments that would be considered illegal by international human rights standards (Speed and Collier 2000). In Peru customary punishments ranging from public shaming to whippings have blurred the boundaries between legal and illegal for hundreds of years. The modern state has continued this implicit policy by turning a blind eye to village corporal punishment, even if these punishments are theoretically illegal. From the perspective of international human rights law, the partial autonomy given to village leaders can be cause for alarm. Without a higher system of checks and balances, autonomous village justice may be exploited by abusive or corrupt leaders who are accountable to no one, especially in the socially and spatially marginal places like Wiracocha.

But for many of those living in what some have called the "margins of the state," village customary justice may offer a kinder, gentler resolution to local conflict when state presence is minimal, or where judicial systems have been corrupted by too many years of "dirty war" violence to have any objectivity (Poole 2004). In this case, human rights agencies offered villagers an alternative to submitting themselves to customary justice. Villagers who were given a typical local punishment—for example, a public whipping for several counts of adultery—could now go to the Defensoria del Pueblo (Public Defender's or ombudsman's office) to help initiate legal proceedings against the local village judge or president who had prosecuted the villager. The Public Defender could not initiate a complaint against the village, but it could counsel villagers on the legal interpretation of human rights, and the proper way to challenge local authorities.

Given the difference between men's and women's perceptions of human rights reforms on the whole, I imagined that women, who were sympathetic to interventions in the home, would also support them in other contexts. Instead, with the exception of the defendant who sought external support, everyone in the village condemned this action. On two occasions when state representatives were forced to take action against punishments that went against the letter of international human rights law, women as well as men expressed outrage at the defendants, and even spoke of having them thrown out of the village.[22]

Losing one's membership in the community was the worst punishment that could be imposed in peasant villages like Wiracocha, and testified to the seriousness with which villagers treated attempts to bypass local leadership. Unlike a whipping, which, while horribly painful, at least reintegrated villagers back into their community with the assurance that all debts to society had been paid, banishment was the one form of punishment that was not based on reintegration and restorative justice. Banishment entailed the divestment of the defendant's lands and possessions, leaving the guilty party cut off, without economic or social resources. Ultimately, however, both punishments were successfully sidestepped by the guilty parties, who got enough support from the Public Defender to draw up papers informing local leaders that they were in violation of international human rights laws. Although the majority of villagers supported banishment, the village president decided to drop charges rather than face the embarrassment and red tape of the state court system.

These interventions might work on the part of villagers who were unduly judged by corrupt leaders. But literal interpretation of human rights law could also backfire for abuse victims. For example, the same literal interpretations of human rights law that requires local authorities to intercede in domestic violence might serve to limit village leaders' ability to impose strict physical punishments on those men that were wife beaters. Without immediate access to state police, military, or even a jail, even the confinement of criminals is a difficult process. Simply detaining a cattle thief in a classroom, for example, could violate human rights law if there were not access to a mattress and a toilet or latrine—both uncommon luxuries in the Ayacucho countryside.

Villagers referenced these cases when they explained why "human rights" turned some villagers into *machu qari*. The rights protocol interfered with their ability to make judicial decisions and enforce punishment at the village level. Without some form of customary punishment, many felt that the village could not recreate the sense of communal cohesion and rule of law that had been destroyed in the years of the dirty war. Rather than a failure of rights, for many men militarization actually enforced rights, order, and security by taking over the physical punishments of customary justice. In turn, the state tacitly approved leaders' sovereign right to punish, defining punishment first as cultural tradition and later as martial law.

When the votes were counted in Peru's 2006 presidential run-off election, analysts were stunned that an Ayacucho ex-army officer, Ollanta Humala, had won a majority of votes in the region's former war zone. At the time, the candidate was under investigation for the torture, kidnapping, and killing of civilians during the dirty war, as were many of the officers in charge of areas where state brutality occurred. Although Humala eventually lost to former president Alan García, his lead was very strong precisely in the areas that had been hardest hit by state violence: in villages that had suffered some of the most infamous massacres by state forces. Most surprising was the news that Accomarca, a village in southern Ayacucho where, just twenty years before, state troops massacred more than 60 civilians, had voted 72 percent in favor of Humala in preliminary runoff (Páez 2006).

Humala's success is less surprising, however, when we consider the ways the armed forces have informed the culture of rights in rural Ayacucho. Unlike Peru's criollo or white upper classes, whose citizenship is less questioned, marginalized Peruvians in Ayacucho have had to earn these rights through participation in the rondas or army. For indigenous people, soldiering provided some a small foothold into the security of the rights of citizenship. In addition, the hybridization of cultural practices and village offices with military ones over the course of the war has guaranteed that the experience of hard-handed local justice is now tied to villagers' understandings of village autonomy, solidarity, and even their own cultural survival.

These overlaps between citizen rights, patriotic masculine pride, and local traditions and sovereignty are difficult to perceive at first glance. This is partly due to the tendency in the social and political sciences to understand rights and culture as spheres of social life that are mutually exclusive and inherently conflictive. These links between a culture of human rights and the rights of military culture are harder to accept as well, especially because they require an analysis of the gray zone between victims and perpetrators at a time when the transition to peace and a form of governance free of violence and arms is urgently needed to ensure that cycles of violence stop. After more than a decade of military rule, international aid and national human rights institutions have tried to shift the institutions responsible for governing and defending the rights of highland villages to civil society. They hope, at least in theory, to transfer the oversight of human rights to a broader, international community that may hold the Peruvian state as well as others accountable for rights violations. Yet the fact that so many rural highlanders depend on this military model has stymied some demilitarization efforts, which assume that the relationship between villagers and soldiering is only one of state oppression. As human rights reforms have been deployed in Ayacucho, they affect the ways village justice, gender roles, and solidarity are articulated. In some ways the conflicts between human rights and self-governance are a foreseeable result of the swift change in forms of regulation: one that almost overnight replaced ideals of masculine military patriotism with a cosmopolitan discourse of transparency, democracy, and human rights.

In his presidential campaign, Humala promoted the model of the armed services as a positive, anti-racist, socially equalizing force in the country. Promoting himself as a military leader fighting against foreign imperialist interests, he was able to claim an almost socialist alternative to the disappointingly superficial "democratic reform" that accompanied the free market, neoliberal adjustments demanded by foreign investors and multilateral lenders in post-conflict Peru. That the former military captain was capable of advancing these ideas in areas hard hit by state violence testifies to the fact that the culture of military justice and militarized citizenship is still perceived as the best insurance of rights for some of Peru's most marginalized citizens. While human rights consciousness-raising workshops in rural Ayacucho open some important spaces for women to use and legitimate their own demands for equal rights, my own research shows that interventions have yet to offer villagers a full substitute for state presence and citizenship rights that were at least somewhat guaranteed when villagers participated in rural militarization.

This is not to say that militarization is a better way of integrating the peasantry into the national imaginary, or more conducive to peasant life today than human rights reform. Rather this research shows that, even among marginalized populations that were targets of state violence, human rights reform may be experienced less as a guarantee of basic rights, and more as a contradictory process that increases feelings of insecurity even as it opens new empowering solidarity networks. Part of this insecurity comes from the nature of globalization and neoliberalism, in which governance is diffused among bilateral lending institutions like the World Bank on one hand, and NGOs and solidarity groups on the other. Compared to the concrete proximity of the military barracks, the office locations of neoliberal regulation seem deterritorialized, the staff and funding transitory, and the ability to implement law and dispense justice too theoretical still, to be predicted or trusted.

Chapter 7

"These Are Not Our Priorities":
Maasai Women, Human Rights,
and the Problem of Culture

Dorothy L. Hodgson

"MWEDO urged to step up fight against female genital mutilation," read the headline in the *Arusha Times*, a weekly newspaper in northern Tanzania (August 19–26, 2006). Since Tanzania made female genital modification (FGM)[1] illegal in 1998, there have been constant articles in the English and Swahili language press outlining the dangers of FGM, announcing yet another campaign to stop it, praising the successful eradication efforts of local, national and international women's organizations, and lamenting the stubborn persistence of the practice among certain ethnic groups, most notably Maasai.[2] So as one of the two main NGOs working with Maasai women, it seemed only natural (to the national press and most Tanzanians) that MWEDO (Maasai Women's Development Organization) would join the fight to eradicate FGM. But the fact that MWEDO was being "urged" suggests that the organization was somehow slow or reluctant to get involved in the FGM campaigns. And, indeed, it was. Most Maasai women leaders, including the leaders of MWEDO, have tried to resist demands to focus their efforts and resources on eradicating FGM, insisting instead on the need to address a different set of priorities and human rights—namely, economic and political empowerment.

The differences between the agendas of MWEDO and those of the dominant Tanzanian society (who Maasai call "Swahili"), including prominent national and transnational women's organizations, on the matter of FGM point to larger tensions over culture, power, and human rights. As international campaigns to end the practice of FGM have shifted from framing the practice as a health concern to a human rights violation in order to justify their interventions (Shell-Duncan 2008), they have broadened and intensified the pressure on "grassroots" organizations like MWEDO to join forces. Moreover, both the health and human rights frameworks have downplayed the history and complicated cultural and social meanings of the practice for societies like Maasai, condemning FGM outright as a "traditional oppressive practice," a "harmful cultural practice," and, now, a form of violence against women (cf. Hernlund and Shell-Duncan 2007). Simultaneously, cultural rights have become an increasing focus of the international indigenous rights movement, which Maasai, like several other pastoralist and hunter-gather societies in Africa, have joined. Thus, as Maasai women have formed their own NGOs over the past ten years, they have had to navigate an often contradictory path between the women's rights movement and the indigenous rights movement. Although both are derived from international human rights legislation, they assume, invoke, deploy, and advocate very different ideas of culture, gender, power, identity, social change, and citizenship. These tensions become starkly apparent in debates over FGM and development priorities, where ideas of "culture" and the proper roles, responsibilities, and rights of men and women often contrast sharply. Do indigenous women then invoke their rights as "women" or as "indigenous people"? What ideas of "progress" and visions of the future do they advocate? This chapter explores the history, objectives, agendas, and practices of MWEDO in order to probe how it has negotiated the differences, and often contradictions, in the assumptions, meanings, and practices of each social movement. My purpose is not to explore the practice and meaning of FGM for Maasai women and men, which I have done elsewhere (Hodgson 2001a, 2005), nor to trace the history of campaigns against FGM (Boyle 2002) or for "women's rights as human rights" (which Merry 2006, among others, does very well; see also Hodgson 2003). Rather, I seek to analyze the consequences, or "perils and pitfalls" (Shell-Duncan 2008), of the international anti-FGM campaign and the larger "problem of culture" for the agendas and struggles of Maasai women leaders, activists, and community members, especially now that FGM has been reframed as a human rights issue.

Exploring the consequences of the reframing of FGM as a human rights issue for the lives of African women is important for several reasons. The chapter contributes to a growing body of feminist scholarship that explores

the limits of a human rights approach to gender justice. Clearly the inclusion of women's rights as human rights has helped women throughout the
world challenge oppressions of various kinds (e.g., Hodgson 2003; Merry
2006; Agosín 2001; Hesford and Kozol 2005). But such rights-based approaches to justice, with their assumptions about privileging the individual
and the power of secular law, often make it difficult to recognize and address
the structural causes and context of gender injustice, such as the disman-
tling of health care, education, and other social services and deepening impoverishment produced by the adoption and implementation of neoliberal
policies and practices. Moreover, "culture" is often depicted as an obstacle to
"progress," thereby, at times, undermining women's power and autonomy by
ignoring cultural practices and beliefs that serve to empower women, while
stigmatizing others, like FGM, that are often central to rites of passage or
ritual transformations. But, as the chapter will show, the "problem of culture"
is really a problem of power—of the continued assumption by many Euro-
American donors and activists, and, increasingly, by African elites, that they
can speak for (rather than listen to) rural, poorly educated women or even
well-educated African women who are deemed culturally "other." Even if we
acknowledge the interconnection of all rights (including economic, political,
cultural), the question still remains as to who decides which rights to pursue
at any given time.

Becoming Indigenous Women

Since the late 1980s, growing numbers of historically marginalized minority
groups in Africa, such as Maasai in Kenya and Tanzania and !Kung San in
Namibia and South Africa, have come to identify with and join the transnational indigenous rights movement. These groups have become "indigenous"
to gain international support for their ongoing struggles for political, economic, and cultural self-determination within their respective nation-states
(Hodgson 2011, 2009, 2008, 2002b,c; Sylvain 2002; Saugestad 2001). They
have received tremendous financial and logistical support for their efforts
from transnational advocacy groups and donors. They have participated in
ongoing deliberations at the United Nations and in innumerable international conferences and workshops to draft, promote, and ratify international
legislation that specifies and supports the rights of indigenous peoples. But
most of these indigenous groups have been organized and led by elite, ed-

ucated men, who paid little attention to the concerns and demands of indigenous women. Moreover, their elite, male visions of "traditional" culture often reified, reproduced, and enforced a deeply patriarchal gendered order (Hodgson 1996, 1999, 2001a).

Simultaneously, increasing numbers of African women have been rethinking and rearticulating their political struggles in the new terms provided by the expanding international "women's rights as human rights" movement (Bunch 1990; Schuler 1995; Hodgson 2003). Key events in this transformation were the UN Decade Conferences for Women in Nairobi (1985) and Beijing (1995) and the support of transnational feminist organizations, international human rights organizations, and donors. Although not without limitations, the language and paradigms of women's human rights have enabled African women to develop new strategies to circumvent and reframe enduring debates about women's empowerment mired in the potent, contradictory terms of "culture," "tradition," and "modernity" (Hodgson 2003; cf. Merry 2006).[3] But this movement has also been organized and led by a specific social group, elite African women, who rarely encouraged the participation of indigenous women or attention to their rights and needs.

In Tanzania as in other parts of Africa, indigenous women have organized themselves at the nexus of these two movements into NGOs that work for economic security and improvement as well as the protection of certain cultural rights and customs. A transnational indigenous women's organization, the African Indigenous Women's Organization (AIWO), was instituted at the First African Indigenous Women's Conference held in 1998 in Morocco to link, strengthen and coordinate more localized efforts.[4] As the first continent-wide meeting of indigenous women from Africa, the timing of the meeting was remarkable for several reasons. First, numerous African women had been very active in the international women's rights movement for almost 15 years, since the 1985 UN Decade Conference for Women was held in Nairobi, Kenya and certain long-marginalized African peoples like Maasai had been participating in the indigenous rights movement for more than a decade. In fact, Moringe Parkipuny, an educated Maasai man from Tanzania, was the first African to formally address the UN Working Group on Indigenous Populations in Geneva in 1989 (Parkipuny 1989; see also Hodgson 2009). In addition, indigenous women from other parts of the world such as the Americas and Australia had been meeting in regional and international gatherings since the late 1980s and issued several declarations, including the well-known 1995 Beijing Declaration of Indigenous Women.[5] In other words, the fact that it took until 1998 for indigenous African women to meet marked their triple marginalization at the time: from the international women's rights movement, the indigenous rights movement, and even the indigenous women's movement.

Briefly, there were several reasons for their triple marginalization. First, most of the African women who participated in the NGO Forum that accompanied the 1985 UN Decade meeting in Nairobi and those who subsequently became active in the international women's rights movement were elite, educated urban women—often activists, lawyers, and academics from dominant ethnic groups. They tended to share the modernist perspectives of their Western feminist counterparts—that indigenous women like Maasai lived as victims in patriarchal worlds shaped forcefully by the drudgery of endless household labor, domestic violence, and primitive "cultural" practices like polygyny, arranged marriage, and female genital modification (e.g., Aina 1998). Indigenous women were associated with "culture" and "tradition," precisely the domains the international women's movement was trying to challenge with its liberal claims to universal human rights and values, premised on notions of individual agency and autonomy. Indigenous women could be spoken for and helped, but certainly had little to contribute to the struggle for women's advancement. Although similar to the recurring tensions between elite, urban women and uneducated, rural "grassroots" women described by many authors (e.g., Hodgson 2003) the marginalization of indigenous women like Maasai was heightened by their seeming "excess" of culture.

Second, the structural dismissal of Maasai and other indigenous women from the international women's movement was mirrored by the general exclusion of their ideas, concerns, and experiences from the indigenous movement in Africa during this period. In Tanzania, the indigenous movement quickly grew from just two NGOs formed in 1989 and 1991 to more than 100 by 2000. During the early period, these indigenous NGOs were formed and run almost exclusively by educated Maasai men considered "junior elders" in the Maasai age system. Maasai women, with few exceptions, were relegated to the sidelines in the name of "culture" and "tradition." A vivid example of such gender politics occurred at the First Maasai Conference on Culture and Development, which I attended in 1991 as an "invited observer." The organizer, an educated junior male Maasai elder, decided that while the conference debates were taking place among men in the large hotel meeting room, Maasai women would display their beaded jewelry and other crafts on the outside balcony as part of a Maasai Women's Cultural Exhibit. When I questioned him about this gender divide, he explained that it was part of "Maasai tradition," in which women did not participate in political gatherings and debates. "But when," I responded, "was a 'First Maasai Conference on Culture and Development,' held in a well-known tourist hotel, ever a 'traditional' event'?" During the actual meeting, a few younger, educated Maasai women participated. And on the last day, the older, mostly illiterate Maasai women who had been relegated to the balcony to display their crafts walked into the conference and demanded to know why they had not been included: "Are we not Maasai?" they asked.[6] Not surprisingly, similar dynamics were present at the global level, where few women participated in the African delegations attending meetings of indigenous peoples such as the annual UN Working Group on Indigenous Populations (IWGIA 1998: 319).[7]

The First African Indigenous Women's Conference was held, therefore, to counter this history of triple marginalization, "to [break] through the isolation of indigenous women in Africa" (IWGIA 1998: 320). And by all accounts, it was successful; "for most participants, it was the first occasion to meet and to share experiences as indigenous women with their sisters from other regions of Africa. The participants took this opportunity to learn from each other's experiences by exchanging stories, information and strategies" (IWGIA 1999: 347). After several days of discussions and workshops on the two framing subjects, "the role of African indigenous women as treasurers of the cultural and intellectual heritage of their people" and "violence against African indigenous women" (Van Achterberg 1998: 11), and several minor subjects (including legal situations, biodiversity, and traditional medicine), the participants decided to form an organization to follow-up on their discussions—AIWO—and listed seven objectives to serve as AIWO's initial mandate. These included "the defense and promotion of the rights and interests of African indigenous women," protection of indigenous languages and identities, preservation of indigenous knowledge and natural resources, prevention of genocide and ethnocide, guarantee of the property rights of indigenous women, monitoring of sustainable economic development initiatives, and organizing training sessions for African indigenous women (Van Achterberg 1998: 13–14).

With the formation of AIWO, African indigenous women did indeed come "out of the shadows," as the report from the First African Indigenous Women's Conference was titled (Van Achterberg 1998). Although AIWO itself soon confronted the logistical challenges shared by other transnational

networks—including bridging multiple languages,[8] an inadequate and expensive communications infrastructure, scarce resources, and an uncomfort-
able dependence on donor funds and susceptibility to donor agendas—the
formation of the organization brought attention to the energy and issues
of African indigenous women, helped several women achieve international
prominence in the global indigenous rights movement, and prompted other
donors and advocacy groups to demand that all African indigenous organizations and international indigenous women's organizations reform their
structures and agendas to include African indigenous women. As a result, in
part, of these changes, increasing numbers of indigenous women's organizations were formed at the local level, including MWEDO in Tanzania.

Toward Equal Rights for Women: MWEDO

MWEDO was registered as an NGO in 2000 "to work towards the empowerment of disadvantaged Maasai women economically, politically, culturally,
and socially through implementing activities in capacity building, advocacy,
and promotion of human rights within the Maasai community" (MWEDO
2005: 6). In 2006, it described its primary program areas as human rights and
advocacy, household economic empowerment, public services development,
and cultural citizenship. Work was conducted by a staff of five from a central
office in the regional headquarters of Arusha through more than 35 village-
based membership groups spread throughout four of the five so-called "pastoralist districts" (Monduli, Simanjiro, Kiteto, Ngorongoro, and Longido).

One of the founders and the first executive director, Ndinini Kimesera
Sikar, is an educated Maasai woman who was taken from her rural Maasai
homestead in Namolog (Kiteto District) as a small child to live with her uncle
in the large city of Dar es Salaam for health reasons. She was educated and
easily assimilated into the guiding norms of urban, elite, "Swahili" society, yet
maintained strong ties with her rural base. After secondary school, she studied finance and then worked as a banker for several years before marrying an
older Maasai man, moving to Arusha, and helping start MWEDO.

I first met Ndinini at the United Nations in New York in 2004, at the annual meeting of the UN Permanent Forum on Indigenous Issues. She was
browsing through a table of pamphlets and posters outside the main assembly
room, dressed in a stunning rendition of customary Maasai dress, with a long
beaded skirt and cloak, headdress, and jewelry. I approached her and greeted

her in Maa, which surprised and pleased her. We spoke for a while, then continued to meet and talk throughout the week-long session. We discussed many things, including news about mutual friends in Tanzania, her unusual life as one of the few well-educated Maasai women, MWEDO's work, and current policy debates in Tanzania. At the time, Ndinini felt very drawn to "indigenous rights" as a useful frame for pursuing Maasai political struggles; "it allows everyone to work together to pressure the Tanzanian state without making it an 'ethnic' or 'tribal' issue. But the problem is that everyone has to get along." She had only just learned about the UN Permanent Forum at a recent meeting for East African Pastoralists in Nairobi, and IWGIA, based in Copenhagen, had sponsored her trip to New York. But she was very disappointed that she was the only representative from Tanzania at the Permanent Forum that year, in contrast to the many Kenyan Maasai present.

Ndinini has continued to maintain contacts with IWGIA and occasional involvement in the international indigenous rights movement (including attendance at the 2007 UN Permanent Forum). As evidenced by MWEDO's program in "cultural citizenship"[9] and use of the Maa language in workshops and meetings (despite government injunctions that only Swahili be used in such venues), she seeks to promote and protect Maasai culture and language in the face of radical social and economic changes. But her primary concern is with the political and economic empowerment of women. According to MWEDO's 2005 five-year strategic plan:

> MWEDO was initiated in 1999 by three Maasai women inspired by the government efforts towards achievement of the goal of sustainable and equitable human development. But the patriarchal relations, attitudes and practices between men and women and between elders and young in Maasai land prevent these efforts. The women realized the need for doing something to support the government's efforts in transforming and operationalising a qualitative shift in Maasai land and national development so that gender equality is recognized in Maasai land. (MWEDO 2005: 4)

As the cover of MWEDO's brochure states, beneath a picture of a group of seated Maasai women, "women have equal rights within the society."

The creation of MWEDO and other local pastoralist women's NGOs is timely, given the increasingly dire situation of pastoralists in general and pastoralist women in particular. As a nation, Tanzania has not only embraced the Millennium Development Goals, but set out an even more ambitious set of goals in two key policy documents: Tanzania Vision 2025 (which outlines a "new economic and social vision for Tanzania," including good quality lives for all, good governance, and a competitive, neoliberal economy); and MKUKUTA (the 2005 Poverty Reduction Strategy Proposal). Although both discuss the need to direct resources and thought toward overcoming pervasive economic inequalities among Tanzanians, neither addresses the specific social, cultural, or economic needs of pastoralists, who currently number more than 1,000,000 of a population of over 34 million (including Maasai, Sukuma, and Barabaig). Moreover, the strong neoliberal assumptions and goals of both documents, and recent related sectoral policy initiatives, suggest a bleak outlook for pastoralists as their land, livestock and livelihoods come under increasing threat from national and international economic interests. Under pressure from the World Bank, IMF, and northern countries to meet global demands for increased competition, the Tanzanian government has privatized key industries, revised land regulations to encourage the sale and alienation of land, promoted large-scale commercial agriculture, expanded the highly profitable wildlife tourism and big-game hunting sectors, instituted service fees for health care (primary school fees were instituted then revoked), withdrawn support for education and other social services, and encouraged pastoralists to replace transhumant pastoralism with more "productive" and less "environmentally harmful" modes of livestock "farming" (as opposed to "herding"), such as ranches. As a result, there has been increased alienation of pastoralist lands (especially drought and dry season grazing land), competition for water sources and other livestock-related resources, decline in the use of health facilities, and increased impoverishment (Hodgson 2001a, 2008, 2011). As pastoralism becomes less economically viable, growing numbers of pastoralist men have left their homesteads to seek work as miners or guards and laborers in towns like Arusha and Dar es Salaam (May 2002; May and Ikayo 2007).

Pastoralist women are often now the de facto heads of household, although their increased workloads and responsibilities are rarely matched by increased rights and decision-making control. Historical evidence suggests that Maasai gender relations were complementary: each gender-age category had distinct roles, responsibilities, and rights, all of which had to be accomplished successfully for their households and homesteads to prosper (Hodgson 2001a). In addition to childcare, cooking, and other domestic duties, adult women shared use and access rights to family herds with their husbands, traveled widely to barter livestock products for food and other household goods, managed disputes among women and influenced the political decisions of male leaders, and were recognized as the moral authorities (Hodgson 2001a, 2005). Over the past hundred years or so, however, as resources like land and livestock have become commoditized, men have been targeted as political leaders, household "heads," and livestock "owners" by first colonial then postcolonial authorities; and women's moral authority and spiritual significance have been dismissed; pastoralist women have occupied increasingly vulnerable and dependent positions in their households and homesteads.[10] They now hold only limited rights to livestock, lack inheritance rights and significant decision-making power, and have few ways to earn cash. Yet they are increasingly responsible for feeding and caring for their children, including paying any school fees or health care costs. Very few are literate or speak Swahili, the national language.[11]

The precarious position of pastoralist families, especially pastoralist women and girls, has been exacerbated by the disproportionate impact of neoliberal economic policies on pastoralists' access to quality education and health services, among other sectors.[12] In 2000, for example, while 78 percent of children were enrolled in primary school nationally, only 8 percent of eligible children were enrolled in Monduli District, a large district comprised of mainly pastoralist Maasai. Moreover, the ratio of boys to girls in primary school in Monduli District in 2005 was 222 boys for every 100 girls, as compared to the national average of 98 boys to 100 girls (MWEDO 2006: 7; URT 2006). The discrepancy when attendance and completion data is considered is even more marked: in Simanjiro District in 2003, there were a total of 2,759 boys and 2,115 girls enrolled in Standard I, as compared to only 729 boys and 527 girls in Standard VII—a dramatic decline suggesting a completion rate of approximately 26 percent (Simanjiro District Report 2005: Table 38). In terms of secondary school, pass rates on the national exams are much lower in the pastoralist districts than the national average of 22 percent, and the stark lack of secondary schools in pastoralist districts (in 2005 there were two in Simanjiro, two in Kiteto, four in Monduli, and four in Ngorongoro, compared to 22 in neighboring Arumeru District, which is densely populated with settled farmers), means that the few pastoralist children who pass the exam and obtain secondary school placements must attend boarding schools far from home.

Health indicators in pastoralist districts are severely underreported, in part because they do not include deaths outside health facilities. Traditional birth attendants assist about 90 percent of deliveries, and few report maternal or infant deaths to health centers (Simanjiro District Report 2005). Moreover, Mother-Child Health (MCH) clinics are not offered at all health facilities, decreasing the likelihood of referrals and routine data collection. The recent introduction of fees for health services (except for MCH clinics, which are supposed to be free) and escalating costs of medicines have created further barriers to health care for poor pastoralist women and their children, who must often ask their husbands for money. Even those who try to use the health system face innumerable challenges and frustrations, including absent doctors, cancelled clinics, and lack of medicines. Many women must still travel long distances for more than rudimentary health care, such as in difficult pregnancies and deliveries, further contributing to maternal and infant mortality.

The top causes of morbidity and mortality in pastoralist districts are malaria, pneumonia, diarrhea, and tuberculosis. While the national average in 2004 for under five and maternal mortality was 126 children per 1,000 births and 1,500 per 100,000 respectively, research and experience suggests that these figures are substantially higher (and seriously underreported) in pastoralist districts.[13] Pastoralists are at a significant disadvantage because of their remote, dispersed locations. For example, in 2007 there was only one health facility per 780 square kilometers in Ngorongoro District, versus one per 31 square kilometers in Arumeru District (Arusha Regional Commissioners Office 2009). Even today, there is a notable lack of health centers and hospitals, with only three serving the five pastoralist districts. These difficulties are further magnified by the poor roads and lack of reliable transportation in these districts.

To date, MWEDO has pursued three primary strategies to promote women's empowerment and equality in the context of their increasingly difficult lives. First and foremost, MWEDO has worked to strengthen the economic capacity, income, and autonomy of women through providing small start-up grants for group income-generating projects and training on how to keep accounts, run small businesses, and market their products. Many MWEDO groups, like those in Longido and Kimokowa, have used the money to start projects that produce beaded jewelry, ornaments, and other items for the tourist market. Others have purchased goats and even cattle to raise and sell for a profit. These projects are not without their problems (especially how to market beaded crafts to transient tourists in a flooded domestic and international market), but Maasai women, as discussed below, have clamored to get involved.[14]

Secondly, MWEDO has supported the education of pastoralist girls in secondary school and beyond through provision of full financial support for tuition, room, board, and other needs, including a year of "pre-form I" training[15] where necessary. In 2005 45 girls were supported, selected by committees from all the "pastoralist" districts based on school performance, exam scores, teachers' recommendations, and financial need. Funds have come from donors but also Maasai community members; MWEDO has met with community members and leaders, both men and women, to convince them of the need to educate Maasai girls and encourage them to contribute to the Pastoralist Girls Education Fund. In 2005, they organized a huge community-based fund-raising campaign for the Education Fund involving *ilaigwenak* (leaders of male age-sets), women leaders, politicians, and others. By August 2006, they had received over 6 million shillings (approximately $5,000) in contributions and pledges.

Finally, MWEDO has conducted workshops and awareness raising sessions on aspects of women's rights. In 2005, these included a large, USAID-sponsored workshop on human rights and democracy designed to educate women about their legal and political rights, including their right to vote (in preparation for the 2005 national presidential and parliamentary elections); a series of workshops about HIV/AIDs (which MWEDO framed as a women's right issue, as in their right to know how to protect their own bodies and decide who would be their sexual partner); and numerous training sessions with different member groups on land rights, livestock policies, legal rights (including marriage, divorce, and inheritance), and other relevant economic and political issues. Workshop participants were primarily uneducated Maasai women from rural areas, ranging from elderly grandmothers to young, nursing mothers.

Focus group discussions, individual interviews, and informal conversations with MWEDO members in 2005 and 2006 suggest that they enthusiastically support MWEDO's initiatives. One older woman explained to me, "before we stayed home and waited for men, we were dependent on them for everything. But now we go out and support ourselves." "In the past," another woman interjected, "women had no cattle, but now we do." Older women were also avid supporters of providing secondary education to their daughters. "Papers have gotten heavy," noted a delegate to the 2006 MWEDO Annual General Meeting, "we can't understand them. Pastoralist women are far behind. We need education and MWEDO has helped." Or as another commented, "I really want girls to study. In the past they were married/sold off [*kuozwa*] and then some returned home because their husbands had no property. Then they became burdens to their fathers. But now they can support themselves." When one of the male delegates to the Annual General Meeting suggested that MWEDO also fund the education of Maasai boys, "Nanyore," a younger female member of the MWEDO Board of Directors replied:

> MWEDO does not discriminate against boys. But because of the history of discrimination against girls, it has decided to help girls. We women are mothers of both girls and boys. But if a father has cattle, he uses it to educate boys. That is why Munka, Brown and others are here [referring to older Maasai men who were members of the Board of Directors]. Why are there no older educated women here? The money MWEDO is given is for educating Maasai girls. We would encourage men to start their own education fund—you have the money and ability, but we'll work with you.

Nanyore has herself benefited from MWEDO's education initiatives. As the fifth of six wives of an older man, mother of four, with only a primary school education, she decided several years ago that she was finished having children and wanted more education, including learning English, leadership, and computer skills so that she could work with an NGO. Moreover, disgusted with the poor performance of local political leaders, she decided to compete in the election for ward councilor—and won. She is now a respected politician and community leader who carefully navigates the demands of her husband and family and her ambitions for economic security and personal advancement.

In interviews conducted throughout Maasai areas with women (both MWEDO members and nonmembers), they expressed the same urgent needs: hunger, poverty, lack of clean accessible water, and, for many, lack of functioning, affordable health facilities. (Men echoed many of the same needs in my interviews with them.) No one mentioned female genital modification (FGM), polygyny, or even arranged marriage as priorities for change. The issue of "culture" was, however, raised at the Annual General Meeting in a fierce debate about cultural authenticity, exploitation, and protection. One woman described an incident in which a donor group visited, took a lot of pictures, and claimed they would help—but never followed through. Several women and men discussed the issue of Maasai clothing—how other ethnic groups wore it at weddings and such, or even to make claims to donors that they were Maasai. But when, for example, Maasai men wore shirts and pants, they were accused of no longer being Maasai. "I am wearing a t-shirt," proclaimed a younger man, "does that make me not Maasai?" Only one woman raised the issue of FGM: "What about the problem of circumcision [*kutahiri*]? It is part of our culture, but the government says don't do it. What do we do now?" No one responded, but many shook their heads, and several muttered about the recent vehemence of government sponsored anti-FGM campaigns.

Whose Priorities?

Ironically, although MWEDO propounds a fairly typical agenda of political and economic initiatives to support women's empowerment in which cultural issues are in the background, donors and mainstream feminist groups in Tanzania foreground Maasai "culture" in their interactions and assessments of MWEDO's work. Two examples suffice. The first involves MWEDO's relationship with one of their main international donors, which has an office in Dar es Salaam. During my year of research with MWEDO in 2005–6, representatives from the donor group visited the MWEDO offices constantly, usually with little notice and official visitors in tow. MWEDO workers were expected to suddenly drop their work to escort the donors and visitors to visit some of the Maasai women's groups. Ndinini and other MWEDO staff made phone calls to members of the group, begged women like Nanyore to ask the women to gather, purchased gifts for the women to give the visitors, organized transport and food, and so forth. Inevitably, the same groups were visited every time, because they were only an hour from Arusha and easily accessible by a tarmac road. During the visit, the women would dance and sing, give the visitors gifts, and pose patiently for many, many pictures.

Although Ndinini was grateful for the substantial support MWEDO received from the donor, she confided that she sometimes wondered about the "real" reasons for its support:

> I am not sure if we are just cultural tourism for them. I looked at their website the other day, and there is a big picture of one of their visits to Longido. I am worried that they are just interested in MWEDO because of the nice pictures of Maasai. But we want to get something out of them. We gave them a proposal for maternal health, but they

were not interested. They asked us to prepare a proposal on family planning, but we weren't interested. They wanted to encourage Maasai women to take birth control pills! Can you imagine!?! But what women need is food, health services, education and income—not pills! [The donor] is very heavy-handed!

My interviews with some of the donor staff confirmed Ndinini's suspicions. When asked why they worked with MWEDO, one senior expatriate man quipped, "they make good photo-ops!"

But it is not just white expatriates who romanticize and exoticize Maasai women, treating them as photo-ops to be seen and admired, but not to be listened to. Many Tanzanians do the same.

In September 2005, Merry (a MWEDO staff person), Nanyore, and three other MWEDO group members traveled to Dar es Salaam to participate in the biannual Gender Festival organized by the Tanzanian Gender Networking Programme (TGNP) and the Feminism Activist Coalition (FemAct), two prominent Tanzanian feminist organizations, on the topic of "Gender, Democracy and Development: Popular Struggles for an Alternative and Better World." For four days, more than 2,000 women and men from grassroots organizations, civil society organizations, development groups, government, academia, and overseas participated in plenary sessions, workshops, and performances related to the theme. In addition, there was a large exhibition featuring booths of craft vendors, activist organizations, bookstores and more. The MWEDO members ran a small booth on the fringes of the exhibition to sell beaded jewelry and crafts produced by member groups. An older *koko* (grandmother) and younger woman staffed the booth most of the time, in part because they barely spoke or understood Swahili (much less English), the dominant languages of the Gender Festival sessions. A third Maasai woman who had attended secondary school in Kenya, and so was quite fluent in Swahili and English, also stayed with them. Nanyore and Merry, however, browsed the other exhibitions, attended some plenary and workshop sessions, and occasionally helped at the booth. Merry also presented a brief description of MWEDO's efforts to educate pastoralist girls at a workshop on "popular struggles over education." I spent the days sitting with the women in the booth, accompanying Merry and Nanyore to sessions and meals, and helping Merry prepare and type up her presentation.

From the first day, it was clear that the presence of the MWEDO women and booth created quite a stir among other Tanzanians. Many men and women tried on the jewelry, belts, and shirts to see how they looked, modeling to the exclamations and admiration of their friends (far fewer bought anything). (By the last day, several neighboring vendors were visibly upset, complaining about why "the Maasai" received all the attention. "Why don't they take pictures of us?") Nanyore in particular was the focus of much attention, as she aggressively tried to sell the jewelry ("oh, you look terrific!") or proudly strode her slim, almost seven foot frame through the crowds. On the days she dressed in Maasai clothes, she was thronged by men and women who wanted their picture taken with her, to the point where I suggested, only half-jokingly, that she start charging for the photos. "Are you really Maasai?" asked one woman. "Yes, original!" she responded. "See how my ears are pierced?" (pointing to the holes on both the lower lobe and upper ear). When she stood up to ask a question (about why there were not more women members of parliament, ministers, and government officials in attendance) at one of the plenary sessions, she was mobbed by photographers and participants taking pictures with their own cameras.

But the problem of culture was more than just a performance or display of difference. On the third day, Nanyore wore an elegant dress and modest gold jewelry, enjoying a respite from the constant attention of her admirers. Together with Merry, we attended a workshop on "African Feminism: Theories and Discourses of Resistance." At one point in the discussion, a Tanzanian woman reminded everyone to "remember the problem of culture. For example, among Maasai, where I have done research, women have no rights, they are forced to marry instead of go to school, and are forced to undergo female genital mutilation. Men can sleep around, while women can't." Merry and Nanyore just rolled their eyes at me, but neither responded. Afterward, I asked them if they agreed with the woman. "No," Nanyore replied, "it is not that simple. And the problem is that it is always Maasai who are given as the example of cultural oppression, but they never think about their own cultural oppression." Perhaps more important, "challenging polygyny [which was also raised in the discussion as a sign of women's oppression] and female cutting *are not our priorities.*" Instead, she listed land rights, livestock, hunger, poverty, and education as the more important issues to be addressed.

Debating Culture, Development, and Rights

So what does the story of MWEDO and its relationship to donors, Tanzanian society, and mainstream Tanzanian women's organizations tell us about the role of culture and power in current debates about gender and development? Nanyore's comment, "[these] are not our priorities," gets to the crux of the problem. While she, Ndinini, and other Maasai activists may be concerned about female genital modification, polygyny, and other cultural practices, they are far more alarmed by the increasing impoverishment, lack of rights, and marginalization of Maasai women. What they find troubling is that dominant society in Tanzania, including the main feminist organizations, do not seem to listen to, recognize or support their priorities. Instead, these groups continue to condemn and even criminalize Maasai for one specific cultural practice—female genital modification—and use its presence or absence as a measure of Maasai progress and "modernity."[16] Their attacks on Maasai cultural practices echo repeated campaigns (like "Operation Dress Up" in the late 1960s) by colonial and postcolonial governments (and several religious denominations) to forcibly change other seemingly "primitive" aspects of Maasai "culture" such as their attire, jewelry, and use of ochre on their skins (Hodgson 2001a, 2005; Schneider 2006).

Maanda, a Maasai activist who heads the Pastoralist Women's Council (PWC),[17] the other large Maasai women's NGO in Tanzania, told me a story about how the issue of FGM radically changed her relationship with another well-known feminist NGO in Tanzania, Tanzania Media Women's Association (TAMWA).[18] TAMWA had helped support Maanda when she fled her village as a young woman to pursue further education rather than marry against her will. She also worked for them for a few years in community outreach. But when, several years later, TAMWA asked Maanda and PWC to collaborate in its national anti-FGM campaign, Maanda refused. "I told them it was not my priority, it would block my work." In response, "the woman in TAMWA just told me, 'you won't work against it because you are just an uneducated woman.'" Maanda even refused an offer of over 200 million shillings (over $150,000) from a German donor "because I was not willing to work and campaign against the practice." Instead, "I believe that it should be dealt with indirectly, by educating girls so that they can make their own decisions."

Moreover, like Ndinini and other educated Maasai women activists, she argues that any effort should be toward seeking alternatives to the modification, which is only one small part of a long series of ceremonies and celebrations that ritually transform a Maasai girl into a Maasai woman (Hodgson 2001a, 2005; cf. Abusharaf 2001). She argues, "it is about cultural survival. You can change the cutting, but you need to keep the ceremony, it is important." And in fact, in several Maasai communities the cutting of the clitoris is being replaced by a small, "ceremonial" cut on the inside of the thigh (see, for example, Hodgson 2001a: 241–49). But in other communities fierce condemnation and government criminalization of the practice is making it more secretive, and pushing some parents to "cut" their girls at younger and younger ages, before they can be discovered—which creates new problems about the status of these girl-women with regards to marriage, sex and pregnancy.[19]

Maanda, Ndinini, and other educated Maasai women's activists' stance on female genital modification is both pragmatic and political. It is pragmatic in the sense that they recognize that their constituents—rural, largely uneducated Maasai women—have more pressing priorities, such as ensuring the present and future survival and security of their families in increasingly difficult circumstances. Moreover, they believe that the only way the practice will change is indirectly, through the education of girls (and boys). But their position is also political; it is intended to confront and challenge the structural power of TGNP, FemAct, TAMWA, and other Tanzanian and international women's groups who continue to "speak for" Maasai and other indigenous women, rather than listen to, learn from, and work with them.

Conflicting ideas of "culture" and the role of "culture" in "development" are central to these tensions. Most Tanzanians, especially Tanzanian feminists, view "culture" as equivalent to "tradition," a predominantly negative set of static practices that they believe have oppressed women and obstructed their progress toward equality and development. Yet their fascination with Maasai clothes, jewelry, and women suggests an acceptance, even an embrace, of culture as display and performance. Unfortunately for organizations like MWEDO and Maasai women like Nanyore, the result is that they figure more as "photo-ops" than as protagonists struggling for political and economic empowerment.

In contrast, Maasai activists and their constituents view culture as dynamic, contested, and often the site of female power and authority (see Hodgson 2005). As such, they often disaggregate "culture" by applying a gender analysis to foreground "positive" practices (that is, those that are empowering for women) such as spiritual healing and dispute "negative cultural practices" (which they see as disempowering) like domestic violence. Moreover, they make clear that the problems they face today are not inherent to their "cultures" and "traditions," but the product of broader political and economic forces such as colonialism, missionary evangelization, capitalist industry, the privatization of land and other natural resources, population pressures and

HIV/AIDs that are depriving them of their lands and livelihoods and seriously eroding their rights. Even domestic violence and the "culture of patriarchy" are understood as historically produced, linked to and articulated with conflict, violence and patriarchal orders occurring nationally, regionally and internationally.

But the tensions also reveal different ideas about "gender" and "gender equality." Several Maasai women, in conversations with me, explained that while they wanted "equality" vis-à-vis Maasai men and all Tanzanians in terms of rights to control and inherit property and resources and access to health, education and other social services, they were not necessarily seeking "equality" in terms of "women taking men's roles and men taking women's roles." Instead, as Mary Simat, a Kenyan Maasai activist with the Indigenous Peoples of Africa Coordinating Committee (IPACC), stated at the UN Permanent Forum in 2004, "The key principle should be the *complementarity* of gender."[20] Many Maasai women, in other words, are seeking equality in terms of rights but not necessarily roles; most would be content to pursue their historical responsibilities caring from young and sick animals, managing milk processing and distribution, trading, cooking, caring for children, and so on if the related rights and respect that used to accompany these roles were restored. But they also recognize that years of political and economic changes have undermined such possibilities, imposing new regimes of cash, commodities, private property, and wage labor that require new ways of being and surviving.

Thus they confront the mainstream international women's movement with a more radical perspective on individual rights that recognizes how political-economic structures like capitalism, neoliberalism, or what some have called "the New World Order" produce structural obstacles to the free exercise of such rights, so that the promotion of individual rights may at best mask and at worst perpetuate and aggravate these systemic inequalities and imperial relations. They also show how some of these seemingly universal, acultural rights are in fact inherently "culture-bound," with their naturalized assumptions about individual agency, liberal ideas of gender equality, and the inherent values and specific visions of modernity and progress (cf. Hodgson 2001b; Merry 2006: 228). Moreover, several examples in this chapter illustrate how the national and international women's movement itself, in its practices and policies toward Maasai women, has been complicit at times with imperialist "recolonization." If these organizations really cared about the health and well-being of Maasai women, why not support them in addressing the economic and political causes of disease, hunger, and insecurity? And if they really cared about the human rights of Maasai women, why not support the economic and political rights that Maasai women are seeking to obtain? Although they face tremendous struggles in their daily lives, Maasai women are hardly the ignorant "beasts of burden" shackled to tradition or the docile embodiment or exhibitors of culture that some have assumed. Their current struggles should encourage us to consider more nuanced, dynamic understandings of the relation of culture, power and rights in the context of history and socio-economic change (Hodgson and McCurdy 2001).

PART III

Mobilizations and Mediations

Chapter 8

The Rights to Speak and to Be Heard: Women's
Interpretations of Rights Discourses
in the Oaxaca Social Movement

Lynn Stephen

This chapter highlights the process by which several hundred women in Oaxaca City, Mexico, from different types of backgrounds took over state and then
commercial media for a period of several months and in the process came to a
gendered analysis of human rights. Their thinking centered on what they called
the rights "to speak," "to be heard," and "to decide who governs." Through an
event-centered analysis I will argue that the appropriation of human rights discourses became gendered through the process of the media takeover. Through
their experience running state television and radio stations and subsequently
commercial stations, women who held the stations produced a gendered local
vernacular of rights talk that then became accessible to many other women and
men in the city. Women who were previously silenced and characterized themselves as "short, fat, and brown and the face of Oaxaca" allowed new voices to be
heard, new faces to be seen, and permitted silenced models of governance and
democratic participation to move into the cultural and political mainstream.

The Oaxaca Social Movement of 2006: Political Context,
Rights Talk, and Events

Oaxaca has historically been one of the poorest states in Mexico and continues to rank either first or second to Chiapas in extreme poverty, depending

on the year and data source. Home to more than sixteen different indigenous ethnic groups, each with a distinctive identity, language, and self-identified traditions, Oaxaca often seems to belong to a different country than the central and northern parts of Mexico because of its strong indigenous cultures and intense poverty. Some estimates put the number of people living in extreme poverty as high as 78 percent (Thomas 2006). About 33 percent of its 3.5 million inhabitants are indigenous according to the 2005 population counts (INEGI 2006).[1] The capital city of Oaxaca had an estimated population of 256,270 in 2008 (Encarta Encyclopedia MSN 2008). Oaxaca City grew rapidly in the 1980s and 1990s due to immigration from the countryside to the city. Mixtec- and Zapotec-speaking populations make up significant portions of the city today.

Unlike the rest of Mexico, where the Party of the Institutional Revolution (Partido Revolucionario Institucional, PRI) was finally ousted from power after a seventy-year rule in 2000, the state of Oaxaca has remained rooted in an authoritarian political model where the PRI (and other political parties as well) use selective and sometimes more widespread repression, manipulation of the justice system, and political co-optation to retain control. While the Mexican constitution and law provide for freedom of speech, rights for women, and racial equality with specific mention of indigenous peoples, these ideological rights are juxtaposed with a contradictory reality in Oaxaca. There, a political elite has maintained control of politics and economics through a regional political culture that is built on a contradiction between claims to equal citizenship rights for women, indigenous people, and the poor and the lived reality of people who lack the resources, public spaces, and legitimacy to exercise such rights. Awareness of citizenship rights for these silenced sectors is at an all-time high due to ongoing contact with discourses of rights coming from the Mexican National Human Rights Commission, the Oaxacan Commission for the Defense of Human Rights, social movements, and a wide range of NGOs. A repressive state political system has made expression of such rights increasingly dangerous.

Elected amid widespread charges of electoral fraud in 2004, Oaxaca Governor Ulises Ruiz Ortiz took office with a pledge that there would be no more social protests in the streets and public spaces of Oaxaca. He moved the seat of the state senate and the governor's palace to the sleepy, pottery-producing town of San Bartolo Coyotepec in an attempt to dissuade the continual occupations of these public governance spaces by relocating them outside the capital city. More recently, the state government was moved again, to a new fortress called the "Administrative City," in another small town about ten miles outside the capital. The governor's removal and reinscribing of state governance spaces as well as his brutal treatment of social protesters and anyone who criticized his government set the stage for a prolonged period of conflict, polarization, and violence.

During the summer and fall of 2006, what began as a large group of teachers exercising their right to bargain for higher salaries through the occupation of Oaxaca City's historic colonial square erupted into a widespread social movement after state police violently attempted to evict the teachers. The movement included "megamarches" of thousands, creation of the Popular Assembly of the Peoples of Oaxaca (Asamblea Popular de los Pueblos de Oaxaca, APPO—a coalition of more than 300 organizations), occupation of state and federal buildings and offices, takeover of the state's television and radio stations, and construction of barricades in many neighborhoods. Regional movements throughout the state questioned the legitimacy of the state government. The main events that are the focus of the analysis here took place during August 2006, two months into a five-month period in which the APPO maintained control over significant parts of the city of Oaxaca. A complex mixture of movements including a teacher's movement, indigenous movements, women's movements, student movements, peasant movements, and urban neighborhood movements coexisted in Oaxaca for several decades and are the political soup out of which the social movement of 2006 emerged (see Magaña 2008; Poole 2007b; Rénique 2007; Esteva 2007; Stephen 2007).

As elsewhere in Mexico, the 1990s saw major growth in the number of organizations in Oaxaca carrying out work they called human rights monitoring and defense. The defense of the human rights of indigenous peoples in Oaxaca is rooted in the experience of organizations such as the Isthmus Coalition of Workers, Peasants, and Students (Coalición Obrera, Campesina, Estudiantil del Istmo, COCEI), Union of Indigenous Communities of the Northern Zone of the Isthmus (Union de Communidades Indigenas de la Zona Norte del Itsmo, UCIZONI), and Services of the Mixe People (Servicios del Pueblo Mixe, SER-MIXE) formed in the 1980s and dedicated to gaining power at the municipal level, defending indigenous land rights, promoting community-based grassroots development, and later linking to national networks and movements for indigenous rights and self-determination (see Stephen 2002: 235–37; Rubin 1997). Initially, organizing focused on human rights at the grassroots level emerged not out of organizations with the label human rights, but out of organizations defending indigenous and peasant rights. Because members of these organizations suffered from harassment, death threats, illegal detention, and imprisonment, their work increasingly came to focus on defense and protection of their members. The independent teachers confederation, National Coordinator of Education Workers (Coordinadora Nacional de Trabajadores de Educación, CNTE) formed within the National Union for Education Workers (Sindicato Nacional de Trabajadores de Educación, SNTE) described below created its own human rights organization in the 1980s called the Teachers Human Rights Commission (Comisión Magisterial de los Derechos Humanos, COMAT), which dealt with disappearances, assassination, and human rights violation of teachers in the independent unions.

In the 1990s, with the militarization of several regions of Oaxaca including the Loxicha region, specific human rights organizations were founded, as was a Regional Center for Human Rights. Many of the organizations that now participate in the Regional Center for Human Rights Bartolomé Carraso (BARCO) are supported by the Catholic Church. Other state groups include the Center for Human Rights Flor y Canto, the Center for Human Rights Siete Principes, and the Oaxaca Network for Human Rights (Red Oaxaqueño de Derechos Humanos, RODH).These groups have undertaken campaigns to defend the rights of communities and individuals in the face of military and paramilitary occupation and harassment as well as individual cases of detention, torture, and illegal incarceration. The Mexican League for the Defense of Human Rights (Liga Mexicana de Defensa de los Derechos Humanos, LIMEDDH) established an office in Oaxaca in 1996.

The State Commission of Human Rights in Oaxaca (Comisión Estatal de Derechos Humanos de Oaxaca) was formed in 1993 in response to a new state law calling for the formation of the commission and outlining how it should work. The website for the commission, now called the Commission for the Defense of Human Rights of Oaxaca (Comisión para Defensa de los Derechos Humanos de Oaxaca, CDDRO), states: "with the creation of this commission the necessity of the people of Oaxaca to have their rights and liberties guaranteed as well as the prompt and impartial procurement of justice is satisfied." The specific human rights CDDRO states that its projects address include "the right to life, to physical integrity, equality, liberty, dignity, and judicial security of all persons, property, as well as the best possible efficiency in the provision of public services" (CDDRO 2008).

In addition to the areas of indigenous rights and human rights, women's rights have also received much institutionalization in communities, NGOs, and branches of the government. All this history is an important backdrop to the current movements in Oaxaca and the kinds of rights claims they are making. The historic feminist organization, Grupo de Estudios sobre la Mujer, Rosario Castellanos A. C. (Rosario Castellanos Group for the Study of Women), began in 1977. In the 1980s, it sponsored weekly radio shows, workshops on health, and worked to bring women's rights to state and city political arenas. In 1991 it opened La Casa de la Mujer Rosario Castellanos, and in 1995 it began a scholarship program for young indigenous women that provides mentoring and support to continue in high school and university.

In the 1980s and 1990s, a wide range of indigenous, peasant, urban, student, and other organizations had "women's" committees within them, functioning as internal human rights committees had in the 1980s. In 2003, women's groups from around the state of Oaxaca, including independent groups such as the Grupo de Estudios sobre la Mujer Rosaio Castellanos, as well as women's committees and caucuses within other groups, formed the Huaxyacac Collective. The purpose of this alliance-building network was to pressure candidates in the 2004 elections (in which Ruiz Ortiz was "elected" governor of Oaxaca) to sign the Oaxaca Agenda for Gender Equity, which would have obligated Oaxaca to adhere to the Convention for the Elimination of All Forms of Discrimination Against Women ratified by the Mexican Senate in 2001 (Dalton 2007; Magaña 2008). The Huaxyacac Collective also pressured the administration of Ruiz Ortiz shortly after his election to take action on the alarming number of femicides in the state.[2] In 2006 and beyond, the Huaxyacac Collective was an active member of the APPO, and some of the women who took over public media in 2006 were from the collective. Some were also a part of the independent teachers movement.

Since 1979, Local 22 has joined other locals in forming a dissident federation within the SNTE, known as CNTE. The CNTE was formed to democratize the larger group, to democratize the process of education, and to democratize the country, according to CNTE activists Alfredo Chiu Velásquez and Rogelio Vargas Garfias.[3] While the CNTE controls about 45 percent of the 1.4 million workers in the SNTE nationally, in the state of Oaxaca CNTE leaders estimate that they have about 60,000 members. In Oaxaca indigenous teachers, particularly bilingual indigenous teachers, are a significant presence in the CNTE. It is estimated that 60 to 80 percent of the teachers in the CNTE are women.

As part of their annual bargaining strategy with the state governor, the teachers of Local 22 occupy the historical town center or *zocalo* of the city of Oaxaca. Usually this occupation lasts one to two weeks, while union officials work out annual agreements about salary, benefits, new schools, classrooms, and programs for children. In 2006, their demands included breakfasts for children, chairs and infrastructure for classrooms, a cost of living increase for teachers, and other matters related to improving the educational experience for children. The governor of Oaxaca refused to negotiate and instead sent in poorly prepared state policemen who attempted to evict the teachers and their families camped in the zocalo. Many were camped out with small children and sleeping in tents, on cardboard, next to improvised kitchens.

On June 14, 2006, the governor launched a massive operation against the teachers with helicopters strewing tear gas canisters, hundreds of armed police beating back unarmed teachers, destruction of the teachers' radio station known as Radio Plantón, and destruction of teachers' personal property. In addition, dozens of people were seriously wounded, leaders were arrested, and the population in the center of the city was massively affected by the presence of tear gas. Small children were intoxicated with gas, as were many other bystanders and neighborhood residents who had nothing to do with the teachers or their occupation of the city center.

The eviction of the teachers was unsuccessful. They regrouped and spread out to a larger area, with more than 30,000 teachers from around the state continuously occupying a large part of the city center. The outraged city residents who had watched the brutal treatment by police against women, men, and small children began to bring the teachers food, blankets, water, and other necessary items. Businesses such as restaurants let them use their bathrooms and kitchens and helped supply food. Entire extended families reorganized their lives to provide support to those in the occupation. The teachers from different regions of the state worked out a rotation system whereby one group would rest and go back to their families for a week and others would take their places. After a week of rest, they would return to the occupation and others would take off a week to rest. Four days after the intended ouster of the teachers, a widespread coalition of more than 300 organizations formed calling itself the Asamblea Popular de los Pueblos de Oaxaca. Many key APPO participants were also members of Local 22 who militated in other organizations outside the teachers' union.

In July the APPO took over many state and some federal buildings, including the state legislature, state offices for collecting taxes, offices for various social services, and some offices of the legal system. Large marches were frequent and the official police forces were seen less and less. The governor was unable to show his face in the capital city. The APPO successfully ran a boycott of a long-running state-sponsored folk festival known as the Guelaguetza, which was a major tourist attraction and revenue generator in the city. In addition to preventing the festival from happening, the APPO and Local 22 sponsored a successful free parallel event that over 30,000 people attended (see Poole 2007a).

By the end of July the social movement had a very solid presence in the city with marches happening every other day, nightly rallies, and cultural activities showcasing young musicians writing songs about the movement. A wide range of independent video producers sold cheap DVDs highlighting footage of the attempt to oust teachers from the zocalo, interviews with the wounded, and "extras" on other social movements in Mexico, such as the Zapatista Army of National Liberation (Ejército Zapatista de Liberación Nacional, EZLN) in Chiapas and the May 2006 confrontation in Atenco where hundreds were arrested, many were wounded, and some prisoners were sexually assaulted by federal police (see Gibler 2009: 71–80).

Women's Takeover of Public Radio and Television Stations

On August 1, 2006, between 2,500 and 5,000 women participated in a march known as La Marcha de las Cacerolas, the march of the pots and pans. They brought cooking pots and utensils to bang with while shouting slogans related to the Oaxaca movement. They called for the ouster of the governor, justice for those who had been arrested and detained, and fulfillment of the teachers' original demands. The idea according to Conchita Nuñez, a longtime feminist and also member of Local 22, was "to make women visible by the banging of pots and to assemble all kinds of women . . . I remember that there were even some sex workers who participated in the march. . . . The idea was to arrive at the zocalo and make a lot of noise. After we got downtown they started to talk about going to the station." Another participant, Mariana Gómez, recalls that the several hundred women from the march who decided to go to the state television and radio stations didn't decide to take over the stations, but merely wanted to have some time on the air. Once they were at the station and were denied air time and not given any forum, they decided to take over the station. Their treatment at the station led many to decide to take over the media. She recalled:

When we got there some women asked for some time on the air to tell the truth about what was happening. First they told us to wait. . . . They didn't make any move toward letting us get on the air so we said, "You know what, we are going to occupy the station." We had a meeting in the patio of the radio and TV stations and decided to take them over.

The women decided to take over what is known as the Oaxacan Radio and Television Corporation (Corporación Oaxaqueña de Radio y Televisión, COR-TV). In the 1990s, COR-TV had a director who was well known for his support for public media and was also a reporter. Under him, people in Oaxaca became accustomed to having the programming content reflect a wide range of concerns from across the state. There was programming in indigenous languages and all the ethnic groups in Oaxaca were represented. According to Roberto Olivares of the MaldeOjo TV Collective and a long-time independent film-maker and journalist I interviewed in 2008, COR-TV would "even go out and record the community's fiestas or broadcast on traditional indigenous medicine. People got used to it being an effective public medium." In the late 1990s and 2000s, COR-TV was taken over by other directors and became like other public broadcast media in Mexico, which "are media in the service of governors and those in power, they are more instruments of propaganda than public media," according to Roberto and many others. Thus by 2006 COR-TV and radio functioned primarily to applaud the actions of the governor and prepare the public for upcoming governmental campaigns.

Another participant in the march, Catalina Ruiz, emphasized the idea that COR-TV was a publicly owned medium, equivalent to public television and radio in the U.S. This was an important part of her argument that women were justified in taking it over. For many women in the march who were a part of the decision, the initial denial of a space to share their perspectives and to speak on the air of a public television station was pivotal in how they came to view their right to hold the station and open up the airwaves. They were familiar with the television and radio stations' past history as more open and this along with their determination to have their perspective aired formed their first conceptual moment of analysis in terms of their rights "to speak" and "be heard."

They didn't even give us permission to talk for even an hour. So the compañeras decided that we were going to stay. We said, "This media is ours. It is paid for by money from our taxes. We pay for it every time we buy something. It is supposed to be public, to be ours. So now since it is ours, we are going to keep it and run it."

Before the first television broadcast a young woman announced that she and a larger group of women had just taken over the TV and radio station. Once they decided to hold the station, the women held the employees in the station and insisted that they put them on the air. The technicians agreed and they had their first broadcast on television.

The Gendered Construction of Rights Inside the Station

Once they had taken possession of COR-TV, the women organized them-selves into a series of work brigades. For the first two days they barely slept and there was a great deal of tension in the air. No one was sure whether the police would try to storm the station, the transmission towers would be shot out, or what else would happen. Shortly after the takeover, the APPO and Local 22 responded by sending groups of people to guard the station and assure the safety of the women inside. The approximately 300 women who ran the stations renamed the TV station Television for the People of Oaxaca (Televisión para el Pueblo Oaxaqueño) ; the radio station was dubbed Radio Cacerola or Pots and Pans Radio in reference to the August march that led to the takeover. Women were organized into work brigades who rotated be-tween security posts in and around the station and the transmission towers, programming of radio and TV, food and cooking, receiving and organizing visiting individuals and delegations that came to the station to get on the air, outreach and contact with movement activists to monitor events, marches, and security concerns. The physical strain of working constantly, getting lit-tle sleep, interacting with hundreds of people who came to the station every day to be on the air, and ongoing discussions of what kind of programming, vision, and ideas should be projected greatly intensified the experience for many women. Running the radio and TV station was a transformative pro-cess for women who had left their normal routines, families, and even chil-dren to do so. Many had called their husbands to tell them that they were not going home and to bring them clothing, food, and something to sleep on. For many women, this was the first time they had left their families for an unspecified period of time.

Rosario Romero,[4] who supported the teacher's occupation in the center of the city and then participated in the TV and radio station occupation, stated:

The day that we took over Channel 9 (COR-TV), I stayed there with other women. I asked one of them to lend me a telephone to call my husband. He said, "Where are you? You went to march and didn't return." I explained to him what I was doing at the station. I said, "Please bring me a sweater and two or three for the other women." I stayed until six in the morning and then went home for a while. He was ok with that. For me, the rebellion has been marvelous. . . . The kind of repression we lived through as women is hard. . . . But it is worth what I have learned.

Patricia Jiménez, who became one of the spokeswomen for the group occupying the station, also recalled the intensity of the occupation and the importance of women being able to speak on the air and have their voices heard—the rights to speak and be heard. "Women who took over the station would say 'we took over this station because we want our voices to be heard and we want to appear on TV'. . . . Those of us in charge of the production responded, 'Go ahead.'"[5] And they did, as did many other people.

From early in the morning until late at night, Radio Cacerola and Televisión para el Pueblo Oaxaqueño became the chief means for people to voice their opinions, receive news, and have debates for most of August 2006. Everyone from the motor-taxi association of six neighborhoods denouncing a corrupt licensing official to Zapotec vegetable farmers fed up with a corrupt local mayor used the station to air their opinions. Regular radio shows cropped up on topics including the murder of women in Ciudad Juárez and Oaxaca, celebrating local musical groups, and hosting discussions of indigenous rights in more than half a dozen of Oaxaca's sixteen indigenous languages.

When local municipal police refused to leave their barracks and Oaxacan head of security and transportation Aristeo López Martínez put together an improvised police force of undercover "municipal" police rumored to include paramilitaries from outside the state, Radio Cacerola announced where they were seen and encouraged people not to lose faith. When APPO leaders were detained without a warrant, Radio Cacerola relayed the kind of vehicle the police used and encouraged people in the neighborhood where the leaders were last seen to search for the car. When APPO needed supporters to reinforce groups of people holding more than twenty state government buildings, the call went out over Radio Caserola. When fifty-year-old Jose Jiménez Col-menares was shot dead in the middle of a peaceful protest march on the way to the TV station, Radio Cacerola broadcast the news and urged people not to be afraid and to continue to protect the station and other buildings that had been taken over by APPO. The women behind the radio station appeared to be not militant fighters, but rather long-time Oaxaca residents who had finally gotten fed up with their invisibility and bad treatment by state govern-ments that had been promising to improve their lives for decades. They were also tired of remaining silent in their homes and in the streets.

Radio Cacerola and Televisión para el Pueblo Oaxaqueño became testi-monial forums where all the disaffected of Oaxaca could share their stories. Day and night people flooded the station with calls and shared their past grievances, as well as calling in warnings about repression, conflict, and sus-picious activities. The right to speak and to be heard was taken up by many and became generalized to a much larger public the longer the women con-trolled the stations. The TV station also became the source of alternative po-litical histories and interpretations of past and present events.

Over the three-week period that women occupied COR-TV and Radio, long and difficult discussions ensued among them about what they were doing, what kind of programming they wanted to produce, and what kinds of rights they were asserting in the process. For many, the first way they experi-enced their rights, as individuals but particularly as women, was through lit-erally speaking on the radio and/or in public. While we don't usually think of "the right to speak" as gendered, many of the women who occupied the radio station were accustomed to being silent or soft-spoken, whether at home or in larger mixed grassroots organizations such as the teacher's movement. While women are a majority of the membership of Local 22, very few are in the public leadership structure of the CNTE. Many teachers complained of sexism and exclusion from leadership positions in the union (see Stephen 2007: 109–11). "The right to speak" was experienced by many women specifi-cally as a gendered right because it was articulated within a group of several hundred women in a space where women held power and delegated respon-sibilities to one another and to men. If "silence" was the norm for many of the women in grassroots movements they participated in and in their marginal political positions as poor, dark, and working class, then "speaking" as and with women was experienced as a "woman's right."

Ruth Guzmán,[6] whose husband Ramiro Aragon was detained, tortured, falsely charged, and jailed for 90 days from August to November 2006, re-called what it was like the first time she spoke in public in a press conference that was broadcast on Radio Cacerola, filmed, and attended by reporters. Her husband Ramiro was still in jail. Her brother and a friend of his who were tortured and detained had been freed. On August 12, when Ruth's brother Elionai was released along with his friend Juan Gabriel (both teachers), they held a press conference. It was the first time Ruth had spoken about what happened in public. She had not been an activist before. It was one of her mo-ments of becoming a political actor. I asked her how she remembered feeling in that moment.

> The first time I spoke in public was on August 12, 2006. . . . Before that we were angry, but in that interview . . . we made Ulíses Ruiz (the governor) directly responsible for what happened. I said that it was he who had beaten Ramiro, my brother Elio, and Juan Gabriel. I said we were holding him accountable for anything that happened to my family. . . . So I accused Ulíses Ruiz directly and that appeared in the press. . . . I had spoken.

Ruth connects "speaking" with the right to hold the state governor responsi-ble. She is asserting not only her right to speak, but also her right as a citizen to hold those who govern accountable.

The identification of many women with being silenced and marginal-ized in multiple arenas of their lives amplified the importance for them of earning the right to speak and be heard through their occupation of COR-TV *and* their ability to facilitate this right for many others—both men and women who also had been silenced. Catalina who was identified above observed:

> We hope that this is a lesson for the larger movement, for women, and for the media. We also hope that it is a lesson for the next governor so that it is clear the governor has to obey the citizens and this includes women. Article 39 of our constitution says—and when you hear this being read in the voice of a working class housewife it is clear—the article says we have the right to decide who will govern us. And if the person who is governing us doesn't work out, then we have the right to change that person.

In this portion of her narrative Catalina makes the move from articulating the right of women to speak and be heard—particularly working-class women, which in Oaxaca invariably means women of indigenous descent—to the right of women as citizens to decide who will govern them. She links the rights to speak and be heard to a more general right of political citizenship for those who reside within a country (she makes reference to the Mexican constitution) to remove from power those who govern ineffectively.

Another key participant in the station occupation and programming, Fidelia Vásquez,[7] picks up on this theme. In her narrative she explicitly frames her identity as a Oaxacan working-class woman of indigenous descent and deliberately genders her description of what is going on. Fidelia is also a teacher, a member of the Local 22, and a self-declared supporter of the APPO. What is most striking about this testimonial is her claim that women who are "brown, short, and fat" are the face of Oaxaca, represent the people, and have a right to a voice through their occupation of the TV and radio stations and also a right to decide who will govern them.

> I am a woman born in Oaxaca of Zapotec and Mixtec blood. We Oaxacan women ask that a woman be treated with the same rights as a man. Our mission as women is to create, educate, communicate, and participate. That is why we are here occupying the state radio and T.V. station. . . , From the countryside to the city, we Oaxacan women are tired of bearing this burden alone of the repression we are experiencing from a long line of people who have governed us and from our current governor, Ulíses Ruiz. . . . We went out into the streets on the first of August to tell Ulíses Ruiz that he had to leave Oaxaca. We are women who don't usually have a voice because we are brown, we are short, we are fat, and they think that we don't represent the people, but we do. WE are the face of Oaxaca. . . . It is too bad that the government doesn't recognize the greatness, the heart, and the valor of the women who are here. We are here because we want a free Mexico, a democratic Mexico, and we have had enough. . . . They will have to take us out of here dead, but we are going to defend the TV station and radio.

Fidelia's narrative is the most dramatic in terms of the stakes she sees for defending the rights she is claiming: the rights to speak and be heard, the right of women who are "brown, short, and fat" to represent the "face" of

Oaxaca, and the right to determine who governs. She is prepared to die to defend these rights. This narrative is a demonstration of the intense process and passion that women who occupied the stations went through.

Broadcasting the Right to Speak, the Right to be Heard, and the Right to Decide Who Governs to a Larger Public

The passion reflected in Fidelia's statement suggests the determination of women who occupied the station to extend the rights they had articulated for themselves to others. As radio and TV broadcasting from the redefined COR-TV moved into its second week, the opposition to the movement grew as did the means to repress it. On August 10, José Jiménez Colmenares (a mechanic whose wife is a teacher) was killed in a peaceful march, several people were disappeared, and in the place of local Oaxaca police, paramilitary police who were not from the area appeared in civilian clothes and began to circulate in the late afternoon and at night in large convoys.

As stated above, Radio Cacerola became a testimonial forum for thousands of disaffected people in the state. Delegations arrived daily to denounce the governor on the air or other corrupt officials (see Stephen 2007: 101–3). At one point the waiting list was so long that people were told to return in several days in order to ensure that their points of view would be heard. The parade of perspectives aired on the radio made a big impression on many in the city. Josefina Reyes, a forty-year-old working-class mother whose husband has been in the U.S. for almost five years, reflected on the testimonial aspect of the radio that she observed.

> The thing that happened with the women taking over the state radio station and TV and then on the other radio stations is that lots of people began to arrive and to go on the air. They would talk about what was going on in Oaxaca. And it wasn't just people from the city. People started to arrive from the towns and the ranchos from all over the state to say that they too were unhappy with things. They would go to the station or call in to say that they were in agreement with the movement, that they supported it.

In addition to facilitating the rights to speak and be heard for those who arrived to go on the air, the women occupying the station also provided a direct communication channel for the movement and provided protection for people who might be in trouble. The massive access the radio provided to many people to speak and be heard provided an open forum for different kinds of ideas—ideas that many people had never heard about before. This point was also emphasized in the narrative of Josefina Reyes:

> There would be young people on Radio Cacerola who talked about neoliberalism and the people started to know more things. Before we never heard about these things and we were not interested. But people started to know more and more, like about the Plan Puebla-Panama and other things that our government was involved in with other nations. People started to hear more and more from lots of people and to know more. They got more and more fed up with our government.

The effects of the movement-controlled radio and TV station became obvious not only to those in the movement who steadily increased their control of the city in August 2006, but also to the governor and the state legislature. Unable to meet in their offices because they were controlled by the APPO and Local 22, state senators were meeting in hotels in the outskirts of the city. The governor made press appearances at resorts on the Oaxacan coast and then appeared on a national television show broadcast from Mexico City to assure everyone that things were under control in the city of Oaxaca. During the dawn hours of August 21, a group of masked men shot out the transmission towers of COR-TV, rendering the stations inoperable. As soon as they began to destroy the transmission towers, a group of APPO members spread out over the city and began to take over 13 other commercial radio stations. The women who remained at the occupied COR-TV and radio stations decided to surrender the station buildings because they were unable to transmit further without the towers. They turned over the COR-TV and radio installations to federal police through a mediated dialogue.

When the dust settled, the federal government had accused the state government of Oaxaca of destroying the transmission towers of COR-TV. On August 22, during a clean-up operation, 400 Ministerial State Police and Municipal Police of Oaxaca designed to retake the 13 commercial radio stations from the APPO. Police opened fire on APPO members guarding one of the newly occupied radio stations in Colonia Reforma. Architect Lorenzo San Pablo Cervantes was shot dead and others were wounded. The APPO ultimately held onto one of the stations, dubbed Radio La Ley, and also took over Radio Universidad, run by students through the Universidad Autónomia Benito Júarez de Oaxaca (UABJO). The students were in favor of using Radio Universidad to support the APPO and the social movement. Through September, October, and most of November, Radio Universidad and Radio La Ley continued the functions that occupied COR-TV had assumed. They served as forums for a wide range of people to speak, be heard, and express their ideas about state government. They also were spaces where new ideas for democratically governing the state and the meaning of citizenship were discussed. The primary voice of Radio Universidad was Berta Elena Muñoz, an M.D. who first set up a first-aid station for people wounded in the increasingly bloody confrontations that emerged in the city. She also became a radio announcer.

At the end of September, Oaxaca was further militarized, with the Marines running an exercise with almost 100 soldiers, helicopters, and armed vehicles in the coastal region. On October 27, independent reporter Bradley Will and four Oaxacans were killed and more than 24 people were wounded in a day of multiple confrontations. On October 30, approximately 4,500 soldiers from the Federal Preventative Police carried out a large operation to push the movement occupation out of the center of the city. Using planes, helicopters, and tanks they massively launched tear gas canisters. They also used high pressure water hoses and batons to move people. Dozens of people were wounded and 23 people detained. At least one person was killed (Aguilar Orihuela 2006). The APPO and Local 22 relocated their encampment in the UABJO and in front of the Santo Domingo Cathedral. Radio Universidad became the primary communication forum for the movement from October 30 until November 25, when Federal Preventative Police carried out a final repressive clean-up operation which resulted in the imprisonment of more than 200 protesters. "Many detainees have reportedly been subject to ill-treatment, torture and denial of access to family and independent legal counsel. Many were also not apparently involved in violence and evidence against them was reportedly fabricated" (Amnesty International 2006: 7).

Analysis and Conclusions: Articulating the Gendered Rights to be Speak, to be Heard, and to Decide Who Governs

While one might suspect that the primary avenue of rights talk for the different kinds of women who came together to take over state television and radio and later commercial radio in Oaxaca would be feminism, in fact that was just one strand of the discourse that entered discussions. More central to the definition of a package of rights that emerged as "the right to speak," "the right to be heard," and "the right to decide who governs," what Sally Merry (2006; this volume) and Richard Wilson (2007) refer to as the vernacularization of human rights discourses. Merry discusses both replication and hybridity in her work on how vernacularization functions in relation to gender violence. Of concern here is her discussion of hybridity in the vernacularization of human rights, which occurs "when institutions and symbolic structures created elsewhere merge with those in a new locality, sometimes uneasily" (2006: 46–48). In Oaxaca, human rights and more specifically indigenous rights, women's rights, and the rights of the poor are expressed as an idea, "as a kind of floating signifier that represents a new form of human dignity and moral worth" (Goodale 2007: 160). Thus human rights "can reinforce—and embolden—existing normativities, even if their provisions or rules or 'laws' do not , strictly speaking, conform to specific human rights instruments" (160). In the context of the Oaxaca social movement, the merging of appropriated notions of general, universal "human rights" with particular, local injustices suggests a kind of denotative rights talk where "actors gesture towards aspects of human rights talk with very little specificity or actual content" (Wilson 2007: 358) in relation to specific human rights laws or treaties.

What interests me here is to unravel how the denotative appropriation of human rights talk in Oaxaca through the process of hybrid vernacularization was gendered. I used an event-based frame of analysis because I believe that it was through the process of their three-week occupation of Oaxacan state TV and radio stations that the women created their analysis. I am suggesting that for many (but not all) of the women involved, their gendered connection to human rights talk came not through their absorption of an initial gendered analysis of human rights influenced by feminist organizing and presence in the social movement circuit of Oaxaca, but through a different process. The case of women who organized to take over public and later commercial media in Oaxaca suggests that human rights discourses became specifically gendered through the exercise of specifically defined local rights—"the right to speak," "the right to be heard," and "the right to decide who governs." Many of the women who participated in the takeover of COR-TV and radio came with long histories of silence. Some were silenced as daughters in their families growing up, some were quiet or silent in their relationships with adult men, and many were the backbone and main support for Local 22 and

grassroots organizing in their communities but silenced when it came to assuming public leadership roles.

This does not mean, however, that they were not leaders, that women did
not speak to one another or have influence in the movements some participated in. Many assumed the role of center-women, a concept articulated by
Karen Brodkin (1988) in her analysis of union organizing at Duke Medical
Center. Center-women, Brodkin writes, gain their positions through their
ability to mediate and resolve conflicts by reconciliation, and to provide
emotional support and advice—skills they learned in their families, but were
able to deploy in organizing. In both the union analyzed by Brodkin at Duke
Medical Center and the Oaxaca social movement, there were gendered styles
of leadership. Most people recognize only one aspect of leadership—that of
public and solo speakers. Women can experience this as silencing but also
can recognize that they provide other kinds of leadership, less visible. Brodkin writes that in her initial analysis of Duke Medical Center workers she
missed the crucial aspect of network centers. She states: "almost all the public
speakers and confrontational negotiators were men . . . women were centers
and sustainers of workplace networks—centerwomen or centerpersons—as
well as the large majority of the union organizing committee" (1988: 132).
Rather than just individuals following a popular orator, "leadership in the
union drive involved already existing hospital-based social networks . . .
around class and race-conscious or at least job-conscious values. . . . Center-
women were key actors in network formation and consciousness-shaping"
(133)

Like the organizing model at Duke Medical Center Brodkin analyzes,
most of the "public" speakers for the APPO and the teachers' movement were
male. In the takeover of the TV and radio stations, the leadership was female.
Thus while women were not the public spokespeople for Local 22 and other
organizations, they did have organizing skills. What was different about their
experience taking over COR-TV was that they also became public leaders
who spoke and were heard "like men." For them, this was a new experience
and was articulated as a new set of gendered rights. In enacting the rights to
speak and be heard, Oaxacan women came to conceptualize what their rights
were, thus creating their own localized culture of rights which became a part
of the larger movement ideology that washed over the city for a period of
several months (see Speed 2007: 184). This gendered, local culture of rights
became accessible to many other women and through radio and came to influence their views as well, at least temporarily.

Whether this new set of gendered rights articulated by women who took over the media in Oaxaca will have a lasting legacy is unclear. The Oaxaca social movement, the APPO, and other organizations such as the Coodinator of Oaxacan Women (Coordinadora de Mujeres Oaxaqueñas, COMO) continue to exist and to struggle for some of the same rights they articulated during 2006. Without a doubt one of the clearest legacies of the 2006 Oaxaca social movement is the proliferation of community radio stations since 2006, which offer alternatives to state-run and commercial media in many parts of Oaxaca. The "right to speak" and "the right to be heard" have been taken up in dozens of communities in Oaxaca. The model provided by the women who took over COR-TV in 2006 has spawned a multitude of on-air forums for people throughout the state to share their perspectives and generate discussions on a wide range of themes. Their effectiveness is perhaps demonstrated by the Oaxaca state government's continued determination to shut them down.

At the end of August 2008, the Assembly of Community and Free Radios of Oaxaca (Asamblea de Radios Comunitarios y Libres de Oaxaca) met in Zaachila. Twenty-two Oaxacan community radio stations along with three international ones and representatives from eight universities and a wide range of NGOs constituted themselves as a permanent assembly. This assembly was formed just one day after federal and local police sacked the community radio station known as La Rabiosa, a Mixtec radio station of the Center of Community Support Working Together (Centro de Apoyo Comunitario Trabajando Unidos, CACTUS). As in Chiapas, the Mexican government has set out to engage in the political, physical, psychological, cybernetic, and broadcast annihilation of individuals and groups that are labeled as criminals and ultimately as terrorist threats (see Leyva Solano 2009). Taking down radio stations and attacking those who work in them was a key strategy of the Oaxacan government in 2006 and continues in the present. What appears to remain however, is that the "right to speak," "the right to be heard," and "the right to decide who governs," are being articulated in ever-wider circles and have become vernacularized in many corners of Oaxaca as basic human rights and critical components of local conceptions of citizenship.

Chapter 9

Muslim Women, Rights Discourse,
and the Media in Kenya

Ousseina D. Alidou

The proliferation of private media broadcasting stations, private newspapers, and magazines resulting from democratization processes in most African countries has created an outlet for the pluralistic voices in various national constituencies, but also ideologically divergent affirmations in Muslim polities. This development in old and new information and communication technologies (ICTs)—radio, audio cassettes, television, satellite, internet, and magazines—plays a key role in shaping the sociopolitical discursive practices in Muslim societies (Alloo 1999; Eickelman and Anderson 1999; Salvatore 1999; Haenni 2002; Schulz 2005). This interplay between democratization and the media phenomenon is especially significant as educated Muslim women become active agents as media producers, hosts, and consumers (Alidou 2005; Nouraie-Simone 2005; Mernissi 2005; Skalli 2006), and offers a platform for advocating for their rights within the nation.

In this chapter, I illustrate this trend with a case study in Kenya: a women's radio program, *Ukumbi Wa Mamama* (Women's Forum) hosted by the Islamic-oriented Radio Rahma (The Voice of Mercy) in Mombasa. I show how secular learning and skills have been mobilized by certain Muslim women for religious and sociopolitical ends on behalf of Muslim women in particular and the Kenyan Muslim community at large, in the political context of the nation in transition. These Islamist women's voices challenge prevailing and deeply entrenched orthodoxies that have defined relations not only between men and women in the Muslim communities, but also between

Muslim women and non-Muslims, including their non-Muslim "sisters." "Islamist" women in the Kenyan context refers to Muslim women whose activism is shaped by an Islamic framework rather than by secular reasoning, which they reject as a constituent of western colonialism. Partly as a result of this they are strong supporters of the continued existence of the Kadhis court but within a reformed framework sensitive to women's rights.[1]

As in other African countries, Kenya's adoption of mass education policy in the post-colonial era produced a great number of educated young women, among them Muslims. This education allowed young Muslim women to develop skills in ICTs. Combined with the introduction of domestic satellite dishes and Islamic electronic commodities from all over the world, these skills have helped Kenyan Muslim women connect with the Umma—the global Muslim community. In the process, this new ICT-based networking and the knowledge arising from it have created a space for an alternative women's understanding of Islam and Islamic discourses regarding gender identity. Furthermore, the mid-1980s onward were also characterized by global Islamic education exchanges at the tertiary level (college and university). Many Kenyan Muslim students, including women, who were interested in Islamic studies benefited from Islamic scholarships to study abroad.

The process of democratization that began in the early 1990s had a dual effect for Muslim women. First, it liberated both print and electronic media from excessive state control, making them more open to use by different constituencies. Several FM radio stations, some ethnic-based, some religious in focus, emerged as a direct expression of the national mood for democratic pluralism. Among Muslims, the first was Radio Iqra (Radio Recite), operating from Nairobi. This was followed with the establishment of Radio Rahma (Radio Mercy) and more recently Radio Salam (Radio Peace), both in Mombasa. Invariably, these radio stations hosted programs catering to women or focused on women's issues. Second, democratization has fostered a pluralism that has included female articulations of political Islam. Whether framed within secularism or Islamism, these new Kenyan Muslim women activists are using their advanced literacy in English, Arabic, and Kiswahili and competency in the old and new ICTs to provide and debate distinct perspectives about Muslim women's lives.

Institutionally, virtually all Muslim organizational structures in Kenya, such as the Supreme Council of Kenya Muslims (SUPKEM) and the National Union of Kenya Muslims (NUKEM), have been entirely male-centered and male-dominated. The founding of the National Muslim Council of Kenya

(NMCK), pioneered and chaired by Nazlin Omar Rajput, a Muslim organization with an overwhelming women's grassroots membership, marked a clear departure from this patriarchal tradition. NMCK sent a clear signal of the determination of Muslim women activists to transform the gendered structures of Kenyan Muslim organizational leadership.

The primary mission of NMCK is to fill the gap of women's underrepresentation created by male-dominated organizations. More important, its goal is to provide an effective mechanism for addressing major societal issues affecting Muslim women and children, including HIV-AIDS, gender disparities, the role of religion in addressing women's rights, and social justice in their own communities and the nation at large. NMCK is also active in providing a Muslim women's perspective on governance. As Nazlin Omar Rajupt points out:

> The situation of Muslim women is made all the more invisible due to the lack of accessible information on their status, their priority needs and the factors that contribute to their marginalization. Without reliable gender sensitive information, awareness raising on persistent gender inequalities is undermined and the development for effective "action for change" program is constrained. Also while a small number of Muslim women community groups exist, they are geographically scattered, not well organized and are not linked through formal networking arrangements. Instead the interests of Muslim women tend to be represented by male dominated and gender blind organizations acting as umbrella bodies for Muslims, which have no interest nor programs targeted specifically for Muslim women nor any representation of women throughout the nation.[2]

Clearly, then, some Kenyan Muslim women are beginning to refuse to be part of the patriarchal vision of the unconditional unity of Muslim polity. To them, Muslim unity must arise not only from confronting the non-Muslim "Other" on questions of distributive justice, but also from the promotion of a more just relation across gender within the Muslim *Umma* itself.

However, because of their limited economic resources, Muslim women activists and producers of magazines or electronic programs centered on women's issues often have to adopt a strategic acceptance of co-optation[3] by (religious or secular) male media sponsors who use religion as a platform for advancing their agenda. A close analysis of Muslim women's media discourses reveal that while on the surface Islamist women identify with the broader Muslim male clergy's denunciation of the state's discrimination against Muslim people, they diverge on questions related to Muslim women's rights in Muslim communities resulting from patriarchal misrendering of the Shari'a. As a result, Muslim women public figures are resorting to new Muslim women's electronic venues to interrogate the patriarchal dimension of political Islam and secularism, especially their failure to adequately address the rights of Kenyan Muslim women in the Muslim communities and the nation at large.

Muslim women's activism uses the electronic media, especially the radio, as a more accessible and more effective mode of engaging Muslim communities in general and Muslim women in particular, the majority of whom lack competency in English and functional literacy in Roman and Arabic scripts. My focus here will be specifically on one episode of *Ukumbi Wa Mamama*, a two-hour weekly program of Radio Rahma aired from 7 to 9 p.m., just after the evening (*maghrib*) prayer when most people are at home.

Ukumbi Wa Mamama demonstrates how Islamist women radio talk-show hosts in Kenya are using their agency to transform the social order of patriarchal Islamist ideologies, and at the same time, are responding to and engaging their non-Muslim sisters on questions related to women from a Muslim perspective. Although this process can generate acrimony within and across communities at its early stages, it has begun to engender a culture of democratic national and intercommunal dialogues on issues fundamental to the inclusion of voices unheard before in the national platform.

While there is no doubt that there is an ideological convergence between the various orientations of patriarchal Islam on the place and status of Muslim women in society, the intervention of Muslim women as radio talk-show hosts, guests, and callers is commonly associated with the rise of the new Salafism.[4] The pluralism resulting from the democratization process has also engendered the development of public and gendered Islamic discourses. Furthermore, even though Muslim women's radio programs are a product of patriarchal patronage, women radio hosts and guests exercise a high degree of autonomy of critical thought. As agents of change, they use this electronic platform to subvert the co-opting/corrupting forms of social control of the (re)presentation of Muslim women by inscribing women's readings of Muslim reality in a manner that differs from traditional male perspectives.

Kenyan Muslim women hosts of radio programs such as *Ukumbi Wa Mamama* are mainly the products of secular education. They draw their knowledge about Islam and the Hadith from an intensive self-engagement with Islamic cyberliteracy through the English medium and their involvement in new community-based Arabic *madrasas* and *darsas* (classes) run by new female and male graduates from Islamic universities with competing schools of thought. Their commitments to Islamic radio talk-shows centered on women's issues stems from two concerns. First, in spite of the secularity of their education, they felt that the dominant non-Muslim majority misrepresented and misunderstood Muslim women's reality. Many argued that when references are made about Kenyan women, the nuanced experiences of minority Muslim women are not taken into account, or perceived as "non-indigenous." For these educated Muslim women radio activists, reclaiming their citizenship in a nation-state that discriminates against them as a religious minority becomes a critical mission. Second, they feel it is urgent to confront their own community about the patriarchal interpretation of Islam and its link to Muslim women's oppression. This double marginalization of the Kenyan Muslim woman, it is argued, hinders her optimal participation in national public affairs. Thus, radio talk-shows are used by Muslim women as a channel for unveiling the taboos in their own communities while also contributing to the democratic processes through the plurality of discourses generated by their programs.

These two interrelated missions of women's radio talk-shows were amply demonstrated in the *Ukumbi Wa Mamama* discussion on the Sexual Offense Bill[5] (SOB) on May 22, 2006. This bill was brought before the Parliament through the initiative of a woman legislator and lawyer, Njoki Ndung'u, in an attempt to curb the rising incidence of a variety of sexual crimes in Kenya which had hitherto been treated rather lightly by the penal code. The Bill was later revised and finally enacted into law in 2006 as the Sexual Offenses Act. Among other things, the new law incorporated into the Constitution several hitherto unrecognized sexually related offenses, including pedophilia, child pornography, gang rape, deliberate infection with HIV/AIDS virus, trafficking for sexual exploitation, and sexual harassment, especially in the workplace. It also introduced new harsher minimum sentences for sexual offenses and set up a DNA databank and a registry of convicted pedophiles.

The particular episode discussed here took the form of an interview between Amina Abubakar, host of the show, and Nazlin Omar Rajput as the program guest, with contributions from the listeners via phone or SMS (cellphone text messages). The show opens with a famous Swahili song that praises Mamama, playing on the ambiguity of the word, which can mean both mothers and women. In essence, the song was demanding for mothers and women in general the respect and honor accorded to them in Islam. As the interview reveals, the discussion of the bill unfolds through overlapping themes of serious concerns to the community ranging from rape and incest in the Muslim community to possible actions.

At the time of this radio interview Nazlin was a nationally prominent activist in the Orange Democratic Movement (ODM), a political party that had emerged in the heat of an acrimonious political contestation over the constitutional referendum of 2005. The electoral commission had selected a banana symbol for a YES vote and an orange for a NO vote. ODM acquired its name from its mobilization activities against the new proposed constitution, which it regarded as a dilution of an earlier draft of a proposed revised constitution, the so-called Boma Constitution (which resulted from a series of representative assemblies that met at the Bomas of Kenya). Partly because of the efforts of leaders like Nazlin, the ODM accomplished its objective when the majority of Kenyans voted NO in the referendum. The results of the referendum, in turn, gave Nazlin and other ODM leaders a new political clout in the nation.

In the aftermath of the referendum, Nazlin declared her intention to run for the presidency of Kenya in the country's next general elections, then scheduled for December 2007. Though she probably knew her chances of winning were slim, she saw the elections as a window of opportunity to inscribe the voice of a minority, Kenya Muslims, even as she articulated politico-economic agendas that were both national and transethnic. But did not the doctrinal provisions of Islam bar her from contesting and assuming political leadership at the highest level of public service in Kenya? Certainly many Muslim men raised this argument against Nazlin's candidacy, taking a narrow reading of Verse 34 of Chapter 4 of the Qur'an, "Men are the protectors/representatives of women." Nazlin was not deterred by such attacks. On the contrary, she put the issue in the foreground of her radio interview:

Nazlin: Assalamu alaikum wa rahmatu-llahi wa barakaatuhu. Greetings. My name is Honorable Nazlin Omar Fazaldin Rajput, a Kenyan politician in the Orange Democratic Movement. I am also known as "Mother Orange" and I have made a decision to vie for the Kenya presidency seat. I am also the National Muslim Council of Kenya Chairlady.

In this opening, Nazlin accomplishes four objectives. First she makes it clear to her predominantly Muslim audience in a predominantly Mus-

lim constituency of Mombasa that she is a Muslim, signified by the greet-
ing "Assalamu-alaikum," ("peace be with you") and a secular political leader
of national prominence. She makes her position known that she disagrees
fundamentally, from an Islamic perspective, with Muslim men and leaders
who question her right to vie for the presidency on the ground of her sex.
Moreover, by declaring her political ambitions in an Islamic program, she
also signaled that she was fully prepared to debate the subject. Her introduction also capitalized on her national leadership image—underscored by
self-identification as "Honorable," a term usually used to refer to politicians of
national stature—to lend greater authority and credence to what she would say
in the rest of the interview. Finally, as any astute politician would do, she was
taking advantage of this media moment to campaign for her presidential bid.

By the time Nazlin was invited to be a guest on *Ukumbi Wa Mamama*, she
was nationally known as a critic of the Sexual Offenses Bill as it was originally
put before the Parliament. To avoid any misunderstanding, however, Nazlin
wanted her audience to understand that there were legitimate circumstances
that called for sexual offenses legislation, and that those circumstances prevailed in predominantly (coastal) Muslim communities of Kenya as much as
in the rest of the country. So from the very beginning of the interview she
was very careful to frame her critical comments on the Bill within the context
of the sexual violations that were rampant in Muslim communities, as the
following excerpt of the radio program shows:

> Amina: If you have just tuned in, you are listening to 91.5 Radio
> Rahma, the Voice of Mercy. It is 7:17 and we want to discuss the issue
> of sexual harassment. Bi Nazlin, tell us the content and what this is all
> about because we keep hearing complaints that the bill [Sexual Of-
> fenses Bill, SOB] is too harsh.
> Nazlin: There are various amendments that need to be made to suit
> all religions, be it Islam or Christianity rights. There is gender vio-
> lence in the bill. It favors the woman and oppresses the man a little. As
> we express our opinions we need to strongly support the bill as rape
> cases are on the increase. Even among Muslims rape is high, here in
> Mombasa, the Coast Province, and the North Eastern Province. We
> did a survey at the National Muslim Council of Kenya and it was evi-
> dent that rape is on the increase and almost 60% of women have been
> raped in their homes. . . . [inaudible . . . interjections]. . . . their sisters,
> children or their relatives have been raped.

Amina: We have heard that an 84- or 85-year-old woman has been raped and the youngest rape victim is 5 months old! Nazlin, 85 years! 4 months! And you wonder why?

Nazlin: (Interjects) On issues of gender and rape we have formed a committee in Lamu to look into the rape of young boys, I don't know what word to use to refer to the rape of young boys . . .

Amina: Sodomy.

Nazlin: Sodomy. But I think this Bill does not consider the plight of sodomized boys. A lot of women complained during the Lamu work-shop, cried a lot during the viewing of the survey video. In almost all houses, not all but many houses, you will find a boy who has been sodomized. It is even much better to send a girl to the shop in the eve-ning, not a boy because the boy will be raped. Lamu has a population that is 90% or 95% Muslim and yet Islam is strongly in opposition and very hostile to such acts . . .

Amina: To such an act.

Nazlin: Such sexual acts are on the increase among Muslims. I have a program here in Mombasa known as the Oasis 04 program that helps provide paralegal aid and seek justice for women and children in the legal system. You find a case where a father died and the mother who worked married again and the grandfather was left to care for the child. He raped the seven- or eight-year-old child every night for three years. When people discovered this, the child had all sorts of sexual infections out of the rape. What kind of Islam is this? Is this what the Qur'an teaches us? Instead of being a good example to oth-ers, we Muslims are engaging in shameful acts that one cannot even talk about. We are seeing a father raping his child of four years, three years, two years, who cannot even speak. It is very shocking!

Born in 1967, Nazlin is a woman of modest educational accomplishment. She only completed high school because of her family's decision to marry her off at an early age. In spite of this background, she is clearly a brilliant person who has continued to read widely in both the western and Islamic traditions. In the process, she has acquired a degree of consciousness and skills in criti-cal literacy that seems to be rare for Muslim women of her level of formal education. With a sophisticated mastery of both Kiswahili and English, she came to see herself as a cultural translator and mediator, with the ability to read critically the implications of both secular laws and Muslim doctrines. As a result, Nazlin was able to delineate the areas of the proposed law that were technically problematic, especially for Muslim citizens. The excerpt below, for example, demonstrates her sharp awareness of questions of legal definition, evidentiary procedure and the consequences of law on public resources.

> Nazlin: There is a conflict there. The SOB, for example, brings the [burden of] proof of evidence. I am not well experienced to speak about this, but if you claim someone has raped you, say Mohamed Salim or whoever, when you bring evidence which is based on hearsay to court, the proof of evidence lies on the defendant. If you accuse someone of raping you, he must prove his innocence. This is very different from other law systems in the world, where the proof of evidence lies with you as a complainant. I think this is unfair to the brothers.
>
> There is also a section that shamefully says that if the male or female organ penetrates the other, it is rape. Since when did the female organ penetrate the male one? Nature does not allow that. They are directly referring to the [female] sexual organs or the anus. Our Islamic religion does not restrict such an important discussion because these are acts that are being debated in the whole country.
> Amina: Yes.
> Nazlin: It was dishonest to mention men and women when they simply meant men. They should have simply stated that if "a man penetrates a woman . . . " because it is humanly impossible for a woman to penetrate a man. The other dishonest thing about the SOB is that in page 406 it states that if the bill is passed, it will not add any expenditure of public funds. It will definitely increase public funds [expenditures]. For example in Article 43 it says that sexual offenders will be put under constant supervision and a system will be arranged that will ensure rapists are under constant surveillance. So that is a cost and they should not say that there will be no cost. There will be cost which is ok. We are ready to have our taxes go into this, but they should be a bit more factual. It also talks about rehabilitative programs for rapists. This is cost . . . and we have to be honest about this. We as citizens are ready to increase our taxes to cover the expenses for the rehabilitation. That is, to cater for that, as it comes with additional costs.
>
> There is another section that is not right because a lot of our Mus-

lim brothers and sisters are living with the virus. The virus is all over the country . . .

Amina: Has spread.

Nazlin: It has really spread and our brothers are living with the virus but Article 27, section 7 of the SOB states that if a rapist who is HIV positive infects the complainant, who is the female victim, with the virus or any other sexually transmitted disease like venereal, gonorrhea, whichever, [then] the law will apply to punish the rapist. [However,] If it is established that the government did a test that was inaccurate and probably indicated that you were HIV positive and infected a woman with HIV or you discover later that the rapist has no virus or the woman was raped but was not infected, then the rapist whose tests were inaccurate has no right to defend himself. He cannot bring any claim against the government, against the Minister of Justice, or against the medical practitioners or against legal personalities who contributed to his detention, psychological torment, or shame.

In short, Nazlin leaves no room for doubt that she can speak about legal and legislative matters with the same kind of authority that is normally associated with a trained legal mind. Nazlin's most persistent message, however, was not on the technical weaknesses and problems of the Bill. It was on the fact that, in her opinion, the Bill was not sufficiently multicultural. She believes that in letter and scope it was not responsive to the multicultural tapestry that defines Kenya beyond religious affiliation. Her concern as a woman and a political leader in the country was that the new legal and constitutional dispensation must constantly bear in mind the cultural diversity that prevailed in the nation without allowing room for culturally and community-based violation of the rights and freedoms of every citizen, especially those of women and children. Understanding, however, that her audience at this particular forum was predominantly Muslim, she proceeded to highlight those areas of the Bill that were not compatible with Kenyan Muslim doctrinal beliefs.

One of these is the imperative of fairness. The sentiment expressed in the above excerpt that we must somehow "be fair to our brothers" is one that recurs elsewhere in the radio interview. It is in line with the Islamic tenet of 'adala, fair, just, and equal treatment before the law, in particular, and in society at large. By invoking this conviction, Nazlin seeks to reassure Muslim men that she would not support a Bill that, in the course of trying to protect women and children, ends up unfairly demonizing and victimizing men. Her reassurance, in turn, serves as another strategy for galvanizing the support of men once the Bill has been duly revised. In this way, Nazlin continues to foreground her knowledge of Islam in an authoritative manner to connect with her audience while using it subversively in favor of the primary objectives of the Bill.

The other relevant issue Nazlin takes up in her critical appraisal of the Bill is the definition of marriage, which, in her opinion, automatically excludes both Muslim and non-Muslim African understandings of the institution of marriage. Throughout the colonial period in Kenya, the British imposed a monogamist interpretation of marriage. In the process certain rights and benefits were often denied to spouses and children of spouses other than the first one, both during the lifetime of a husband and on his death. This colonial tradition clearly was carried over to the framing of the Sexual Offenses Bill, inadvertently reversing the gains that "co-wives and their children" had acquired in the postcolonial state. As seen in the excerpt below, this particular provision is one that Nazlin attributes to the influence of "foreign" ideologies.

Nazlin: The problem with this bill is that when it talks of rape it seeks only to prevent rape and to make certain rulings on rape. It does not clearly define rape despite talking about rape issues. The day that the bill was introduced into parliament I went there to listen to what our brothers would support in the bill. The following day the media attacked those who opposed the bill until it is amended, which was unjust. They had strong reasons. SOB section 2 on the matrimonial causes act defines marriage as a "voluntary union of one man and one woman for life to the exclusion of all others."
Amina: Those aside.
Nazlin: What does that clause mean? It will mean two very dangerous things if we allow it to pass as it is. It means that marriage means a voluntary union of one man one woman for life! What I am asking is whether this bill is redefining marriage and that there can be no divorce. Second it is saying to the exclusion of all others what about Muslims, we are supporters of polygamy.
Amina: Islam allows four wives. (inaudible)
Nazlin: Or one to four. It is unfair for the bill to state "to the exclusion of all others," especially for those of us who are in polygamous marriages. If a man has a second wife, then that is a sexual offense. This

is dangerous and against polygamy and it is a way of trying to sneak foreign ideologies through the back door.

Amina: Yes.

Nazlin: And again when it reads "one man and one woman for life to the exclusion of all others" it is trying to criminalize polygamy in its totality and it may make polygamy a sexual offense. It doesn't take into account the consent by the wives in the polygamous marriage, and the SOB has declared polygamy illegal. I am asking my African colleagues what the Muslims should do and why were they not consulted before they introduced such clauses in the bill. I am well known in Kenya and have introduced almost eight bills in my life. Was it so difficult for Njoki Ndung'u to ask me what the Islamic position is or to even ask other groups about the same? Why didn't they ask?

Amina: To include Muslims in the bill.

Nazlin: . . . Njoki Ndung'u, I have complained again, is taking this issue as a feminist agenda, and I don't agree with the feminist agenda. This is an attack on Islamic Shari'a law and the Qur'an's provisions, which is a fundamental issue for us Muslims, and we cannot allow it to be passed. If some Muslim women do not want polygamy that is our own and their own problem. But we cannot conflict what God has decreed. Section 13 subsection II of the African Christian Marriage and Divorce Act should be automatically repealed after the SOB. Yet the provision [the African Christian Marriage and Divorce Act] was in favor of poor women. It was created to protect poor women who had no access to the protection of the law in the face of oppressive and abusive negative traditions and customary practices. It helps the women married under the Marriage and Divorce Act to have automatic guardianship of their children when their husbands die. It was designed to avoid the preying conduct of some in-laws and domineering relatives who took it to themselves to deprive a widow of her children and property and thereby chase her away. Why should you allow these women to repeal a statute that protects poor Christian women?

What we see from above excerpt is, in part, a strategic maneuver on the part of the "political" Nazlin to garner wider support for the Bill once it incorporates certain revisions. She understood that many Kenyans who are still rooted in their indigenous cultures, and many African men—Muslims and non-Muslims alike—who have a vested interest in polygyny would use the provision as a ground for rejecting the entire Bill. The provision also posed the danger of creating division within the ranks of women, alienating even some of those that the Bill is intended to protect.

It is also crucial that Nazlin concludes by addressing directly the initiator of this powerful Bill, Njoki Ndung'u, suggesting in a politically coded language that the feminist agenda that is partly responsible for the formulation of this Bill must be articulated strategically in a way that would not result in the defeat of the Bill. Since the Bill's main objective is to seek redress for gender-based sexual violence against women and children, Njoki Ndung'u and other supporters of the Bill, including Nazlin herself, ought not to allow the definition of marriage at this stage to cost them the support of the religious bodies and other numerically significant constituencies.

Yet another fundamental issue in the Bill of critical concern to Nazlin, and which has a bearing for the Muslim community, is the penalty for rape. As indicated earlier, the Bill recommended stiffer sentences for rape than had existed in Kenya's penal code before. The Bill's new proposed standard of culpability for this sexual crime was definitely not sufficient for Nazlin. As the excerpt below indicates, she called for the ultimate penalty, death, as part of her recommended amendments to the Bill:

Nazlin: The Bill states also that no one will be hanged for raping or injuring a 4-month-old child they have raped. The person will be imprisoned for 15 years. It is a total waste to keep a rapist in bars for 15 years and use our taxes to feed him, protect him, and treat him in hospital. This is an animal, and even an animal is incapable of raping its offspring. Even a pig cannot do that! This person has become a strange being that requires to be wiped out of the community. I support the death penalty. You will even hear women who support the bill and do not support the death penalty with the excuse that it is a Human Right. Why are we taking European customs and making them our own? We cannot be under western ideology, and they should not force us to change our way of life. Look at a 4-month-old or 11-year-old child who has been raped and torn from front to back, the sexual organs have been destroyed, the mouth is filled with dirt, and the child has been left to die. I have seen a 4-year-old child whose mouth has been filled with dirt and the pelvic area has been broken and displaced; she has been torn from front to back as the man tried to penetrate her forcing open the womb and intestines. She is left bleeding even through the eyes, ears, nose, and mouth. Her shoulders are dislocated from the beatings. Her womb had to be removed. (inaudible both speaking) Why should these rapists live? He left the child for dead. It is attempted murder. Whether he used his hands, a knife, a *panga* [machete], or his manhood, it is murder and he deserves to be hanged. This is the harsh punishment I want added to the SOB. Let me give you an example. You see in America there are many states that constitute the United States of America.

Amina: Yes.

Nazlin: It unites them together. There are many states in America that clearly state that it is attempted murder to rape a child between certain months up to age 14. We should also institute harsher punishment for sexual offenders. I am saying that it will help for some to be publicly hanged to set an example to others.

To underscore the issue of harsher penalties for rapists, Nazlin challenges the government to take the issue of rape more seriously than it has done. In the exchange below between a caller and Nazlin, she encourages the Muslim community to be pro-active as a way of putting pressure on the government to assume its responsibility of punishing perpetrators of sexual offenses with utmost vigilance.

Caller: I have forgotten one thing, Ms. Nazlin. In the seven o'clock news today on Nation it has been reported that a teacher in Kisumu has raped more than forty children. I watched as one child after the other narrated their ordeal. As a politician how will you deal with this issue, Ms. Nazlin, because this man may be jailed and released on a bail of 150,000 kshs. My suggestion is that if the teacher is released we women should organize a phenomenal demonstration with Ms. Nazlin as the leader. It will be inhuman to release him and we have no government. (background—inaudible people talking)

Nazlin: That, Allah, is the most worrying thing, and [for] every parent today and even our brothers and sisters who have no children. Forty children! I want to ask the women who have presented this bill and yet do not want to include the death penalty, why should such an animal be allowed to live?

Amina: It is now important to amend the bill as soon as possible.

Nazlin: Very fast! The more they delay the bill the more people continue to suffer. The problem with Kenya is that we do not have strong laws and there are too many loopholes in the system. A penal code is already in place, and yet a man will manage to be bailed out after paying kshs.150,000. I am warning the government that if they release this man on bail we women will look for him everywhere and we shall not let him go. And if the masses lynch him we shall blame the government because it is supposed to . . . keep him out! We need to see fast resolutions on this case.

Here Nazlin is talking the language of a concerned national politician. And from the sentiment expressed by the caller, she has a constituency of Kenyans who have faith in her leadership and mobilization abilities. It is against this backdrop of popular confidence enjoyed by Nazlin that the host of the radio program proceeds to seek Nazlin's policy recommendations to reduce the incidence of rape in the country.

Amina: It's 8:09 East African time. This is the program Women's Forum that comes to you every Saturday from 7 to 9 p.m. Your host Amina Abubakar together with Nazlin Omar Rajput discussing the SOB. Ms. Nazlin, let's imagine that there is nothing to protect us from rape. What are some of the things that contribute to rape? Is it the dressing or what is it? What can you do to reduce or remove such a thing?
Nazlin: If we have no SOB then the penal code should be strengthened and stricter punishment installed when you have a teacher raping forty students like the case today. Even if it means the death penalty. Sexual offenders should be publicly hanged two or three times, and that is when this insanity will come to an end. Secondly, I would like to add is that every district in the country should have an advocacy program. Most of our problems emanate from the police stations and the police. The police receive bribes from rapists; or the family of the girl may pick a bribe from the sexual offender from the police; or in other cases the police threaten the victim's family, case files end up missing, and people I think get a lot of frustration.

First, the police should be warned and trained, any police who take bribes should be charged and their pictures published in the newspapers alongside those of the sexual offenders so that we may know them.

When the sexual offender is released 5, 6, 10 years later, his picture should be published again so that people may know which offender has been released. If he repeats the sexual offense he should be imprisoned for life and his picture put up in public. I would like to see high profile advocacy programs for training the police, men, and women at the community level. Social workers, village actors, paralegals should be trained on issues of rape. Those will be the people who will continue to train the community. We should also have an effective advocacy program for the media, radio, television, newspapers where there is a monthly program on rape cases, so that people are well informed.

We should look at champions, those rape victims who are suffering the stigma. They should be offered some protection and a better life. They should educate others on issues of rape on TV and radio, so that people may stop concealing sexual offences in their homes. That is very important.

The primary Islamic doctrine, the Qur'an and the Hadith, do not overtly address the issue of rape or any kind of coercive sexual act. They only deal with consensual sexual relationship, within or outside the institution of marriage. In line with general practice in Islamic jurisprudence, the principle of analogy was invoked here, with Muslim jurists attempting to construct laws on rape on the strength of legal reasoning involving another relevant crime. The closest of those sexual "crimes" explicitly addressed in Islam is, of course, *zina*, which may include consensual extramarital or premarital sexual unions. Islam considers *zina* to be a very serious sin and its punishment in law could include death. If an "adulterer" could be condemned to death, then legal analogy easily leads jurists to regard a rapist to be even more deserving of a death penalty. This manifestly Islamic position is clearly the one assumed by Nazlin, not only because of the magnitude of the violence inherent in rape, but also because that is the kind of penalty that would be in conformity with at least some readings of Islam.

On the other hand, as the excerpt below demonstrates, Nazlin is careful in how she addresses the issue of "marital rape" that is also treated as a sexual crime in the Bill.

Nazlin: There is also another clause in this bill that does not bring out the distinction between marital sex and sex out of marriage. It is important to differentiate sex in marriage and sex . . .

Amina: Outside marriage.

Nazlin: Outside marriage. I will now bring you to Section 199, 144 Section II and 145 subsection II of the penal code [which] defines clearly the marriage institution and punishment for sexual offenders. The SOB states that you can report your husband for raping you within your marriage relationship. Do you understand?

Amina: Yes.

Nazlin: Do you think that as a legally married woman you can accuse your husband of rape and still go back to the marriage relationship that you had before?

Amina: It is impossible.

Nazlin: If it has reached a time where your husband is forcing himself on to you, then it is wrong. The Islamic law states clearly that do not approach your wives as donkeys, use good . . . (unclear) words and foreplay before the act.

Amina: Excite her.

Nazlin: Excite your wife until she is in a state of enjoying the love making too. If your marriage reaches a point where your husband forces himself on to you like a donkey like the Shari'a quotes, you should seek the counsel of the Kadhi so that he may attend counseling, and if this does not work it is better to divorce. But it is impossible for you to accuse your husband of rape whereby he is jailed for 15 years and you still expect to return to happy and lasting marriage. It is better to divorce and continue relating with others.

In Islam sex is a right of the man, as it is of the woman, and unless there are reasons of health and such, it is never to be denied when requested. Rather than risk alienating the support of men at this critical juncture of the Bill's history, Nazlin skirts around the issue, never really stating explicitly that it is conceivable to have rape within marriage. On the other hand, she counsels men not to just "throw" themselves on women like "donkeys," but, as Islam would require, to work their way around their sexual desires by taking the time, creating the environment, and making the effort to arouse their partners sexually.

It is quite evident from the above excerpts of the radio interview, that the host and guest of *Ukumbi Wa Mamama* used a "tell it like it is" approach to sensitize the Muslim community. Needless to say, this is a bold and potentially dangerous political undertaking for Muslim women. However, the responses to the show by male and female callers indicate great appreciation of how the host and the guest used the radio platform to lift the curtains of silences on pervasive taboo issues in Muslim societies which the 'ulema (the predominantly male scholars of Islam) have not successfully addressed. According to one caller, for example,

> Caller 1[female]: Yes! We are grateful to Ms. Nazlin and Radio Rahama for opening our ears to this debate that has been going on in the papers. We are happy that she has made us aware of the inequalities in the Bill because we, the old [ones] were not understanding what was going on. We were blaming the parliamentarians who were not supporting the bill. But we are now aware that this bill is against Islam and I don't think any Muslim will support it because it is not beneficial to us. We have our own Shari'a laws despite being in a non-Islamic state. That is my contribution. Thank you Bi Nazlin and Amina for today's program.

Other callers, including Muslim men, continued to shower praises on Nazlin and Amina for the enlightening program they conducted on the Sexual Offenses Bill. Thus, through a women's radio talk-show, Muslim women created a space for engaging the community in self-interrogation while also carving an opening for their public participation in national debates.

> Caller 2[male] My Name is Ali of Tudor, I want to praise Sister Rajput. . . .
> and
> Caller 4 [male] I agree with you Ms. Nazlin and wish you all the best. Continue the discussion. Thank you.

An examination of the language used in *Ukumbi Wamama* clearly shows Kenyan Muslim women's exposure to global transnational Muslim women (feminist) activist networks and discourses through virtual travels in cyberspace, SMS, satellite, DVD, magazines, or tourism or business travels throughout the Muslim world in non-Western countries as well as in the West. Nazlin's appearances as one of the most outspoken Kenyan Muslim women public figures on international television networks such as CNN, internet presence and participation in international conferences are clear indications of her commitment to reach out to a constituency beyond the national confinement. Finally, this new trend by some Muslim women in Kenya to use new information technologies to make public intervention on serious issues affecting their human rights within their own communities and in the nation at large is in line with Susan Hirsch's (1998) study of some Swahili women's use of the Kadhis court in the postcolonial dispensation. As Hirsch concludes:

> Whether or not the act of Swahili woman's filing a case in Kadhis Court is called resistance (by the women themselves or by me), it confronts cultural expectations for female behavior by positioning a woman outside the domestic realm and in a public, official context in which she seeks to alter her circumstances. Turning to Kadhis Court affirms her connection to Islam, even as it calls her piety into question and, simultaneously, constitutes her as a supplicant to the State. Perhaps, most importantly . . . Kadhis Courts provide the context for women to narrate problems. (Hirsch 1998: 137)

In conclusion, then, a close reading of the excerpt from the radio talk-show *Ukumbi Wa Mamama* reveals the extent to which the democratization process of the media has provided an opportunity for Muslim women media producers such as Amina Abubakar and Nazlin Omar Rajput to bring to the public forum what has traditionally been considered a matter of private domain. They use their agency to shatter the traditional boundary between the public and the private not only in the Muslim community, but within the Kenyan nation. It also shows the commitment and dedication of Muslim women activists, often of limited education, to acquire skills in critical literacy to read and deconstruct not only religious texts but secular materials like legal documents and scientific literature on diseases that have a bearing on their lives. Muslim women activists are creatively using the media opportunities accorded by the democratization process to galvanize their literacy and intellectual skills and resources towards social justice for all.

This quest for social justice for all is what makes it wrong to suggest that for Muslim women, these technological developments in information exchange and communication are important only insofar as they serve their needs and agendas and those of the Muslim community. Women have also used them repeatedly to link the local with the national (and even global), the Islamic and the secular. If Muslim women activists have used the media to interrogate power relations within the patriarchal Muslim community, they have also galvanized the technology towards challenging the hegemony of the non-Muslim majority. And if the media has enabled them to advocate more effectively their rights within Islam, it has also empowered them to reclaim their citizenship within their own communities and the nation at large. This dynamic is precisely what makes a figure like Nazlin both a *Muslim* leader and a *Kenyan* leader. In this process of re-reading Islam and redefining citizenship, Muslim women are not only "multi-culturalizing" the human rights regime in their country, but also putting to rest the long-held view of Muslim women as passive onlookers. Those behind the NMCK and Radio Rahma's *Ukumbi wa Mamama* program have left no doubt that Muslim women are bold agents of change within their own communities and well beyond.

Chapter 10

Fighting for Fatherhood and Family: Immigrant Detainees' Struggles for Rights

Robyn M. Rodriguez

In his poem, an immigrant detainee from England writes "Oh Lord I Plead, Trying to be part of this nation, For what the wicked done to us, This government is so unjust (WHY), In a jail cell I sit, And ask myself why, Do broken spirit die, The voice of my son cry, Daddy why why, Daddy why (WHY)?" The poem featured prominently in a report by the New Jersey Civil Rights Defense Committee (NJCRDC), *Voices of the Disappeared: An Investigative Report of New Jersey Immigrant Detention* (NJRDC 2007).

Voices of the Disappeared is aimed to counter a late 2006 audit of detention facilities in different parts of the country including New Jersey, conducted by the Office of the Inspector General of the Department of Homeland Security (Office of the Inspector General 2006). In addition to the presence of a federally run detention facility, a number of county jails in the state of New Jersey have contracts with the federal government to incarcerate immigrant detainees. The expressed purpose of the Office of Inspector General's audit was to "identify and investigate deficiencies from Immigration and Customs Enforcement (ICE) detention standards related to facilities used by ICE to house immigration detainees" (Office of the Inspector General 2006). The audit focused on five facilities across the country. Among those audited, two were based in New Jersey, the Hudson County Correction Center and the Passaic County Jail. Activists of the NJCRDC believed that the report completely glossed over the often extreme conditions of hardship and abuse that detainees suffered at these facilities. Indeed, NJCRDC was concerned that by only focusing on a small handful of facilities, the audit had the effect of representing the mistreatment of immigrant detainees as isolated phenomena. Drawing on the hundreds, perhaps thousands of letters, petitions, and other material forwarded to them from immigrant detainees in the state's various county facilities the group, of which I have been a volunteer over the last few years, illustrated that the abuse is in fact quite widespread and indeed endemic to the system of immigrant detention.

The poem makes visible the hidden, or in NJCRDC's words the "disappeared" casualities of the domestic front of the "war on terror." While Republicans and Democrats alike have supported the stepped up policing efforts against what they and jingoistic citizen groups represent as the innately criminal, potentially terroristic, sexually deviant, (often) male foreigner, what is obscured from this discourse are the costs that immigration enforcement has for immigrant detainees themselves as well as their partners, wives, children, parents, siblings, and others close to them.

However, the poem also raises important questions about the limits and possibilities of rights and belonging for immigrant detainees as well as their loved ones. As the poem states, detainees are, "Trying to be part of this nation," but to what extent are they able to make rights claims, tainted as they are by their condition of incarceration (though they may be legal permanent residents), their status as noncitizens (documented or undocumented) or in some cases, their criminal pasts? Even as we know that the criminal justice system and the current immigration apparatus are critically flawed and ultimately create the conditions that lead to these men's incarceration, what space of maneuver is left for detainees and their advocates to make rights claims?

This chapter examines how immigrant detainees (many of them men) craft their claims to rights and belonging in the U.S. I examine the ways detainees' claims may be similar to, but often significantly different from the claims constructed by activists on migrants' behalf. My work here draws and reflects on my activist work advocating for immigrant rights in New Jersey. I and my colleagues at NJCRDC have framed immigrant detention, especially after 9/11, as a constitutional violation. We have also explicitly or implicitly made claims to international human rights conventions or have insisted on immigrants' economic contributions to the country in our struggles against the raids and other enforcement sweeps that put immigrants into detention. We have crafted these rights claims in partnership with and/or on behalf of immigrant detainees and deportees drawing on the framings we believe may resonate with broader publics as well as government officials and thereby elicit their support. Our framings parallel those that have been effectively put forward by other activists, in other places, and in other times.

Yet there is much that falls out and is effectively "disappeared" from these strategic articulations of rights and belonging. Though male immigrant detainees and deportees draw on these discourses to some extent, they also frame their claims in unique and unexpected ways. Many immigrant detainees affiliated with NJCRDC, for instance, construct their demands for release from detention on the basis of their status as fathers and in relation to their families. Certainly, some of these claims are similar to the claims commonly invoked by NJCRDC and other immigrant rights activists who claim that the citizenship rights of U.S.-born are violated because they are denied their parents. Other family-based claims made by detainees, however, are more creative and feature less prominently as part of the repertoire of immigrant activist mobilizations. Detainees mobilizing in New Jersey's jails claim that stepped up immigration enforcement contradicts the spirit of immigration law (specifically the 1965 Immigration Act) as it separates rather than unifies families. Moreover, they point out that detention threatens family stability emotionally, not just financially. Indeed, what we as activists may not anticipate, or perhaps what we may overlook in our reliance on specific kinds of rights frames, is how immigrant men highlight their own longings and desires to be with the ones they love. In other words, feeling and emotion infuse detainees' claims in ways we may ignore. To what extent these claims are actually "successful," that is, whether they will lead to increased public support for the detainees' eventual release and a stay of their deportation orders is unclear. Yet an analysis of the sets of claims detainees attempt to make, as expressed in the poem that opens this chapter, points to some of the limits of more conventional rights frameworks as they pertain to the immigrant detainee and his family, while perhaps identifying different and new possibilities for claims to rights and belonging in the United States. This becomes especially urgent for me, as a scholar-activist, engaged in the fight to advocate for immigrants' rights yet often faced with officials and a broader public unsympathetic to constitutional or even human rights claims being put forward on detainees' behalf.

We continue to know very little about the effects of homeland security policies on immigrants and their families. As my colleague Ethel Brooks puts it, part of the challenge in doing work that examines the consequences of these policies is that it is akin to doing research in conditions of war. This is, indeed, a situation of war for immigrants and their families. After all, "homeland security" is in many ways but the domestic counterpart to the "war on terror." Despite moves by the Obama administration to close the detention facilities of Guantanamo Bay, it is unclear whether detention facilities holding immigrants in different municipalities across the United States, particularly those that have been cited by activists as having committed egregious forms of abuse on detainees, will be closed as well. Indeed, under Department of Homeland Security Secretary Janet Napolitano, the aggressive enforcement of homeland security policies, including immigration enforcement, has continued unabated.

Less still do we know about men (and it is predominantly men) in detention, as so much of what happens in jail can be difficult to access. Moreover, the many who are ultimately deported are often too ashamed and traumatized from their experiences in detention to speak of them (Sheikh 2008). My work with NJCRDC, therefore, offers a unique opportunity to hear these men, and in writing this chapter, to amplify their voices as expressed through the thousands of letters they wrote to the organization over the last few years. While the scholarship on immigration has insisted on attention to the significance of gender, much of the focus has typically been on women. There continues to be less attention on the gendered constructions of masculinity as it figures in public discourse and ultimately in immigration politics. Nor has the scholarship addressed the complexities of immigrant men's subjectivities. This chapter will draw primarily from the *Voices of the Disappeared* report produced by the NJCRDC, as it offers an important vantage point from which to understand the violence of "homeland security" and detainees' resistance to it. The report also offers a glimpse into the complexity of immigrant men's subjectivities, and therefore troubles and counters negative representations of immigrant masculinity that have become increasingly prevalent in public discourse.

Rights and Belonging for Immigrants

Social movements scholars across the social sciences interested in understanding immigrant rights movements have examined the various ways immigrants in the United States, including the undocumented, have framed claims to rights and mobilized to assert them. The research has paid close attention to immigrant rights movements' responses to anti-immigration groups' attempts to introduce legislation at the local, state, and national level that would limit or exclude new immigration flows into the United States as well as negatively impact immigrants already residing in the country.

Much of the scholarship indicates that immigrant rights movements have often drawn on international human rights frameworks in their campaigns. Anthropologist Susan Coutin finds in her research on undocumented Salvadoran immigrants, for instance, that they and their advocates mobilized around the claim that they were in fact "refugees" in their bid to secure legitimate residency in the U.S. Indeed, in struggles against the U.S. government around this claim, Salvadoran undocumented immigrants were eventually successful in securing temporary protected status that would give them legal status and protect them from deportation (Coutin 1998, 2007).

Sociologist Lynn Fujiwara examines immigrant struggles against the 1996 welfare reform laws which aimed to cut all benefits to non-citizens. She finds that immigrants and their advocates similarly relied on international human rights frameworks. In their fight against welfare reform, activists also focused on immigrants' status as refugees as a means of asserting their right to welfare services. In addition, activists advocated on behalf of elderly and disabled immigrants, drawing attention to their vulnerability. In their mobilizations activists depended not only on international human rights frameworks, but indeed on moral claims around the need to protect the vulnerable. They were successful in their efforts as welfare programs for these populations of immigrants were restored (Fujiwara 2008).

Yet the terrorist attacks of 9/11 and undocumented immigration, especially in a time of economic crisis, seems to have foreclosed the possibility of successfully drawing on an international human rights framework in struggles against detention for immigrants and their advocates, as this framework depends on notions of individual "victimhood" or "vulnerability." Furthermore, because many of the immigrants in detention have criminal records (for which they have often already served time), there is little sympathy from officials and the broader public to critically examine their treatment. Changes in immigration law have redefined and widened the scope of what is considered "criminal" activity with respect to immigrants, causing many young, immigrant men of color who have committed minor infractions in the past like drug possession or petty theft to be (re)imprisoned. While it can be argued that these men are victims of an unfair criminal justice and immigration system, the fact that they have engaged in criminal activity, however broadly defined, and are not U.S. citizens makes it virtually impossible for immigrant detainees and their advocates to make the kinds of claims other activists have made in the past. Though immigrant men with criminal pasts may have served out their sentences and should be considered restituted, they continue to be seen as victimizers and never victimized, despite evidence to suggest that they are being unjustly punished by racist and classist laws.

Even undocumented immigrants who do not have criminal records are excluded from being able to claim "vulnerability." Their undocumented status ascribes to them a master status of a law-breaker who is undeserving of support and empathy. This is exacerbated by their incarceration. Indeed, even if their incarceration is the consequence of the noncriminal offense of being without legal status, they are categorically marked as undesirable social deviants. In the next section, I discuss the gendered (and racialized) representations of the immigrant male as threatening to national security and to the more intimate spaces of American citizens' neighborhoods and homes, as well as the immigration policies that have been passed in response to these figurations. Understanding the gendered and racialized logics of immigration policy and politics is necessary to understanding why conventional rights claims are incredibly limited for immigrant detainees.

Gender, Immigration, and National Security Policy After 9/11

The bombings of New York City's World Trade Center on September 11, 2001, gave rise to new immigration legislation, most notably the reorganization of the Immigration and Naturalization Service under the aegis of the newly formed Department of Homeland Security (DHS). While the "war on terror" is being waged in faraway sites like Afghanistan and Iraq, its domestic counterpart is "homeland security," and it is the immigrant who is ultimately figured as the enemy. Since 9/11, two key laws have been passed that dramatically affect immigrants residing in the United States.[1] The USA Patriot Act of October 26, 2001, almost immediately after the terror attacks, included major provisions that enhanced surveillance of immigrants and hastened the process of their detention and ultimate deportation if they were found to be linked to terrorist activities or designated terrorist organizations. Moreover, the act ultimately exempted these cases of detention or removal from processes of judicial review. Almost one year later, on November 25, 2002, the Homeland Security Act was passed, giving rise to the Department of Homeland Security (DHS) and resulting in the reorganization of the Immigration and Naturalization Service (INS) and the creation of new sets of offices to handle the enforcement of immigration law (border patrol, deportation and removals, etc.) and the provision of immigration services (naturalization, asylum, adjustment of status, etc.).

What has therefore emerged is a conflation of the categories of "immigrant," specifically Muslim or what authorities (mis)recognize to be "Muslim-looking" immigrants, with "suspected terrorist." Indeed, with the passage of HR 418, the so-called "Real I.D. Act," in early 2005, it has become increasingly clear that even the categories "refugee" and "asylum seeker" have been conflated with the category "suspected terrorist."[2]

This conflation of the "Muslim-looking" immigrant with "suspected terrorist" is gendered as the "immigrant/suspected terrorist" is figured as male. Indeed, in the immediate wake of the September 11 attacks, accounts from the media and immigrant advocates document how Muslim and Arab immigrant men in particular have been targeted for surveillance, questioning, detention, and deportation (Ahmad 2002; Cainkar 2004; Kaushal et al. 2004). Notably, they are more often than not detained and deported on immigration charges, not terrorist charges. Yet, Irum Sheikh observes, "the state's discourse on national security rationalizes these procedures by implying that these individuals have the potential to become terrorists in the future. Therefore it is safer to either deport or imprison them" (Sheikh 2008: 83).

Though their countries of origin do not necessarily have al Qaeda links, anti-terrorist provisions of post-9/11 immigration legislation have nevertheless affected Latinos (Cornelius 2004; Llorente and Perez 2005; Waslin 2003). Since well before 9/11, however, the Latina immigrant mother has been the focus of calls for immigration policy reform such as those by proponents of Proposition 187 in California in the 1990s. Proposition 187 aimed to deny immigrants social services if they were suspected of being undocumented immigrants. Supporters of the proposition often depicted immigrant mothers as problematic breeders whose unruly reproduction strains already strapped public services. Not only are they feared for their fecundity, they are resented for what is expected to be their failure to adequately cultivate authentic Americans: English-speaking and culturally "assimilated" (Jacobson 2008). Of late, discourses of what Chavez calls the "Latino Threat" have shifted from a fixation on the immigrant mother to the presumably single, immigrant male (Chavez 2008). Indeed, this discourse has often targeted Mexican immigrants (Newton 2008). Single immigrant Mexican men, particularly cohabiting day laborers, are figured as dangerous; they are represented as potentially criminal by virtue of their undocumented status. Newton argues, "The border, now more than a geo-political boundary, looms large in contemporary immigration discourse, and its pathologies (real and imagined) follow the people associated with its transgression" (30). Immigrant men are even represented as having a proclivity to sexual deviance, including pedophilia. This is evidenced in a statement by the sheriff of the Passaic County Jail in New Jersey: "These are people that cross over the border illegally, commit rape, sodomy, peddling drugs to our kids" (Keller 2006). I would suggest that is it precisely immigrant men's (in this case, day laborers') homosociality and their seeming detachment from heteronormative families (even though they may well be married, have children, and financially support their families in Mexico) that make them threatening to the sheriff and others who share his view. These gendered and racialized representations of the dangerous immigrant man have very real consequences for immigration policy.

Numerous immigration scholars link post-9/11 immigration control policies under the Bush Administration, particularly border enforcement, with previous attempts at immigration control initiated by the Clinton Administration (Cornelius 2005; Hing 2006). The Illegal Immigration Reform and Immigrant Responsibility Act of 1996 (IIRIRA), signed into law under the Clinton administration, contained provisions aimed at regulating admissibility to the United States (including bolstering border security) and eligibility to live in the United States. Among the provisions meant to monitor and police immigrants already living in the United States were those that allowed immigration authorities access to FBI criminal databases to identify and ultimately remove specific categories of "criminal aliens." The range of activities that immigrants engage in that could be considered "criminal" was expanded under IIRIRA. Moreover, the law made it much more difficult for undocumented migrants to make appeals to legalize their status before an immigration judge. Since IIRIRA was passed, undocumented migrants are now required to have been present in the United States for ten continuous years, they must prove that their U.S. citizen or permanent resident family members (specifically spouses, parents, or children) would experience "exceptional and extremely unusual hardship" if they are deported, and finally, undocumented immigrants are to exhibit good moral character by not having been convicted of criminal or security offenses (Critical Filipino and Filipina Studies Collective 2004). For the undocumented, it has become increasingly difficult to claim that deportation (let alone detention) would cause "exceptional and extremely unusual hardship" on their families. Undocumented fathers and mothers are being forced to leave their U.S.-born children behind in the United States or to take their citizen children to live in countries they have never known.

IIRIRA, moreover, can be linked to earlier efforts to expand immigration enforcement (and concomitantly detention and deportation) by the Reagan administration in the 1980s (Dow 2004). It was under this administration that the militarization of the U.S.-Mexican border was stepped up. Mexican male immigrants, whose migration to the U.S. can be directly traced to the legacy of the federal Bracero Program through which Mexicans were actively recruited to work in the U.S. by agricultural employers, found themselves suddenly "illegalized."[3] Indeed, agricultural employers (as well as others) could better profit from Mexican migrants' vulnerability as "illegal" workers. The threat of detention and ultimately deportation could guarantee employers of all types a pool of compliant workers. Detention, meanwhile, became a strategy by which the Reagan administration could deny Central Americans who had been displaced by civil wars the opportunity to seek asylum, and thereby deny its culpability in producing those wars. In addition, the escalation of the government "war on drugs" would have significant impacts on immigration enforcement. As Nopper reminds us, the expansion of immigration enforcement is necessarily connected to the expansion of the prison-industrial complex (Nopper 2008). America's drug war targeted men of color, and since immigrant men's undocumented status was linked, however dubiously, to criminality, they were among those who were incarcerated.

IIRIRA and other immigration policies, along with the plethora of administrative and departmental actions taken by the Bush administration and the Department of Justice, have created new conditions of uncertainty for immigrants, regardless of legal status, currently residing in the United States. The consequences for immigrant men, however, have been of a particular sort, as they have been singled out, perhaps more than women, for detention. Indeed, immigrant men can find themselves in detention for any number of reasons under the current legal framework. Legal residents are finding that their status is precarious, as simple administrative violations like a failure to report a change of address to immigration authorities renders one "illegal" and therefore liable to detention and deportation. Of course, legal residents who may have committed and served time for what were once nondeportable crimes as youths are finding themselves in detention as adults because the category of deportable criminal offenses has been expanded and is being applied retroactively. Undocumented immigrants, with or without "criminal" pasts, are being put immediately into detention for deportation when apprehended.

Detainees' Struggle for Rights

Detention Nationally and in New Jersey

Although the federal government has often been reticent about fully divulging the statistics on immigrant detention or deportation, numerous human rights and immigrant rights organizations have managed to press the Department of Homeland Security to release this information.[4] A 2008 report by the National Network of Immigrant and Refugee Rights (NNIRR) indicates that DHS Immigration and Customs Enforcement jails over 30,000 immigrants every day simply because they are undocumented (NNIRR 2008). According to research by Amnesty International, approximately 300,000 immigrants are detained annually (AI 2008). Indeed, this figure includes not only undocumented immigrants, but even immigrants with legal permanent residence status (Human Rights Watch 2009). By its own estimate, DHS detained 378,582 immigrants in 2008, a 22 percent increase from 2007 (DHS 2009). The DHS 2008 annual report details how many people it has apprehended and removed, their country of origin, and the crimes they may have committed while in the United States. Significantly, Human Rights Watch's analysis of deportations from 1997 to 2007 reveals that of those immigrants with criminal records who were deported, 72 percent were deported for nonviolent offenses. Though ICE and groups organizing for increased immigration enforcement and restriction would have the public believe those being targeted for deportation are immigrants with violent criminal histories, the data show otherwise.

It is difficult to find a gendered breakdown of immigrant detainees or deportees. However, as I have already suggested, given the gendered and racial "profiling" that characterizes immigration enforcement (which is necessarily related to police enforcement), it is perhaps not unreasonable to assume that a good majority of those being apprehended are men. Of course, post-9/11 immigrant men are more likely to be apprehended in the name of "national security" even when their only offense is that they lack proper documentation.

The increasing enforcement of immigration laws within the interior of the United States has resulted in a situation whereby the number of detainees has surpassed the capacity of federal immigration detention facilities. The federal government has therefore outsourced immigrant detention to cash-poor county jails like many of the county jails in New Jersey. These jails earn an estimated $90 to $105 per detainee on a daily basis. Though it is difficult to get an exact figure, 2009 reports put the total number of immigrant detainees in New Jersey's county jails at more than 700 (Governor's Blue Ribbon Advisory Panel 2009). Immigrants in detention for administrative or civil infractions find themselves housed with others serving out sentences for criminal offenses. Of course, for immigrants who have already served time for past crimes, detention for criminal offenses now deemed deportable is effectively "double jeopardy." Yet the legal distinctions between detainees and the regular jail population are important ones. As immigration attorney Brian Lonegan explained in an interview with the *North Jersey Herald News*, a New Jersey-based newspaper, "One is in detention for criminal reasons: when someone commits a crime, they plead guilty, they're sentenced. That's punishment. But when immigration takes them into custody, their current detention is not a punishment, their current detention is not a sentence; they're being held so that the United States government knows where they are and can actually deport them" (Henry 2006). These legal distinctions, however, are seldom recognized by county jailers or officials who have signed contracts with immigration authorities to hold immigrant detainees. Until activists and immigrant detainees were successful in forcing the termination of the DHS contract with the Passaic County Jail, detainees were subject to physical abuse by prison guards; in some cases attack dogs were used against them (Keller 2006).

Throughout the state, immigrant detainees have reported that they are being denied medical treatment. Even the federal government was forced to conduct an internal audit of county facilities, which confirmed what detainees had been reporting, as I discuss above. This audit, not surprisingly, insisted that these were merely isolated incidents (Fisher 2007). In 2007, there was a major struggle led by detainees at the Middlesex County jail over a fellow immigrant detainee's death. The detainees signed a petition attesting to the medical neglect suffered by him and other detainees. Immigrant rights activists on the outside called for an independent investigation of jail conditions as well as an end to the county's contract with the DHS. In my observations of meetings of the Middlesex County Freeholders I found that officials generally failed to acknowledge the legal distinctions between the jail's criminal and immigrant populations. When asked to provide the public with an actual breakdown of the jail's inmates, they refused and insisted that immigrant detainees were rapists, murderers, and other sorts of hardened criminals. How, then, do immigrant detainees, who are virtually rendered rightless by virtue of their imprisonment make claims for the right to be released from detention, let alone for better treatment while in detention?

The Right to Humanity

As for other immigrant rights groups before them, NJCRDC has attempted to invoke international human rights laws in their advocacy for immigrant detainees. Notably, however, assertions of human rights conventions have mainly focused on Geneva Conventions governing the rights of prisoners. Indeed, the group likens the treatment of immigrant detainees to that of Guantanamo detainees (NJCRDC 2007).

The frame that dominates NJCRDC's advocacy for immigrant detainees, however, has been one that highlights the constitutional violations of immigrant detention. Moreover, the group suggests that these violations against immigrants ultimately impinge on the rights of U.S. citizens. In a 2004 newsletter put out by the group it states "These assaults on the immigrant communities are immoral and unjust. They are also unconstitutional. We are now living in a two-tier, apartheid-style society where citizens have legal protections but immigrants do not. If we accept this treatment of our nation's immigrants, the next target will be the constitutional rights of U.S. citizens" (NJCRDC 2004).

NJCRDC has especially focused on the right of habeas corpus, insisting that if immigrants are, in effect, being treated like criminals, they are entitled to the same sorts of rights that the U.S. justice system accords to criminals, that is, access to legal representation and trial by jury. As it stands, immigrants who are accused of violating immigration law are subject to the immigration courts where they may or may not have access to lawyers and where decisions about their deportations are made at the discretion of immigration judges. New Jersey immigration judges have been censured by the 3rd Circuit Court of Appeals for "a disturbing pattern of immigration judge misconduct" (Donahue 2005). In spite of repeated warnings from appellate courts across the nation, immigration judges in New Jersey engage in either neglectful or outright biased conduct in court. Hence, those immigrants who actually get a day in court face judges already positioned against them. Even if immigration judges may be sympathetic to immigrants' plights, immigrants are hard-pressed to meet the strict criteria now required for a stay of deportation. I recall that one of NJCRDC's activists half-seriously joked that if the Sensen-brenner bill, which would have formally made undocumented immigration a criminal offense and provoked the widespread immigrant rights protests of 2006, had actually passed, immigrants might actually enjoy some modicum of legal relief through the criminal justice system (though itself quite prob-lematic) since the immigration system is so terribly flawed.

Immigrant detainees have often invoked their constitutional rights in their petitions for release from detention. For instance, in a petition signed by 35 detainees at the Passaic County jail, they write, "The immigration de-tainees are treated as criminals but don't have the same rights as criminals to attorneys and a jury trial, and [are] put in jail for months now. NOW where is our constitutional rights" (NJCRDC 2006). Here, immigrant detainees speak to the legal distinctions that attorney Brian Lonegan referred to above. Yet, their point is these distinctions give them no legal recourse because in the final analysis they are immigrants. In other words, they believe that if they were being held as actual suspected criminals, they would at least be entitled to the legal protections afforded to criminal suspects.

Immigrant detainees have also made appeals for their human rights. Iden-tified only as B.G., one immigrant detainee claimed, "They treat us like animals because we are immigrants, they think we have no human rights in the world." Actually, detainees' claims to "human rights" were less to insist on "human rights," which, as invoked by B.G. ultimately refers to the Universal Declaration of Human Rights adopted and proclaimed by the United Nations in 1948.

Rather, detainees insist on their desire to be treated like human beings. Their appeals are less to "human rights" as such but instead are declarations of their humanity. Ba Madani, for instance, explains his participation in pro-test actions inside the jail as motivated by a desire "to prove to myself that I am still a human being." Saleh Ajaj speaks to how "they did not treat us like human being, they treated us like animals." In a March 2006 petition by 55 detainees, they demand "to be served our food in a human fashion." De-tainees' demands to be treated "like human beings" points to the ways they are treated in detention—as something less than "human" and thus as beings completely without entitlements or "rights." Some groups of undocumented immigrants have been able to assert their "human rights" by insisting on their status as asylum seekers, a category expressly protected under UDHR Article 14, which states, "Everyone has the right to seek and to enjoy in other coun-tries asylum from persecution," but detainees must first insist on their very humanity before being able to invoke "human rights." Immigrant detainees' condition of imprisonment, even if merely for administrative violations, marks them as "criminal" or in some cases "terroristic." As Dow observes, "The backward logic of corrections was part of contemporary INS detention from the start: if someone is locked up, then by definition he must be a security threat" (Dow 2004: 162). In all cases immigrant detainees are rendered dangerous, representing all things inimical to humanity and therefore treated as nonhumans.

Fighting for Fatherhood; Fighting for Family

Detainees insist on being treated "like human beings" but further examination of the petition cited above reveals that they make this appeal on the basis of their being embedded in families: "We immigration detainees are held in legal limbo with [sic] department of Homeland Security . . . [DHS] place the detainees behind bars without having criminal charges against them. It's unconstitutional to deprived [sic] human being [sic] of there [sic] life and liberty and most of all there families." Here, detainees cite the most often quoted provision of the U.S. constitution, on the protection of "life, liberty and the pursuit of happiness." Yet "happiness" is replaced with "families" as detainees reframe their constitutional rights as one that includes their right to their families.

The detainees further make a case that their detention means that they "never [get] a chance to reunite with there [sic] families, parents are being taken away from there [sic] children. Where are the family ties laws?" Here, detainees appear to be referring to the family reunification provisions of the Immigration Act of 1965 as a means of making claims to their families and ultimately for release from detention. Family reunification was a key feature of the Immigration Act of 1965 along with the rescission of what were ultimately racist national-origins quotas that restricted immigration from non-Western (Third World) countries. The Immigration Act of 1965 extended entrance priority to relatives of lawful permanent residents, a privilege that was already being enjoyed by U.S. citizens. The family reunification "preference" system ranked who among a citizen's or legal permanent resident's family members would be eligible for entry to the United States. Among the top preferences were spouses and unmarried adult children (Hing 2006). In their petition, detainees attempt to put this earlier act forward as a means of questioning more recent immigration policies being used against them.

Often, detainees speak to the economic hardships that detention places on their family members in their appeals to government officials and the broader public for support of their release. A detainee from the Dominican Republic writes, "Please don't let them break [my] family apart. My wife is left all alone to work and care for three small children. It is very hard for her. She is suffering the loss of her husband very much and the children miss their father very much . . . I am totally devoted to my family and trying to raise my children the best way possible, but now I am about to lost [sic] my family." In speaking to his role as economic provider to his family members, this detainee draws on a dominant discourse deployed by immigrant rights activists and others supportive of less restrictive and punitive immigration policies. Immigrants have often been depicted as being a drain on public resources and thereby depriving taxpaying U.S. citizens of their full enjoyment of social services (Calavita 1996). Highlighting immigrants' economic self-sufficiency and indeed their economic contributions to the nation as a whole has therefore been an important strategy for those fighting for immigrant rights.

However, what is interesting is that detainees as well as their family members attempt to illustrate that detainees are in fact embedded in a much broader web of family relations beyond the nuclear family. Detention economically affects detainees' siblings and elderly parents as much as it affects their wives/partners and children. The sister of one detainee from Haiti speaks of the way her brother is a "main source of help for our aging parents, both of whom are limited in their abilities to live independently" (NJCRDC 2007). It could be argued from this letter, then, that detention produces conditions that might lead to conditions of economic dependency among detainees' extended family members—the very conditions pundits opposed to immigration do not want in the first place. While U.S. immigration policy has tended to privilege the nuclear family, this letter reveals that for immigrants, ties beyond the traditional nuclear family are important. Not merely immediate family members suffer from the economic and emotional trauma of separation.

It is notable, too, that detainees point out that the economic hardships suffered by their families have transnational effects. Ba Madani, for instance, was concerned about the hardship placed on the family he left behind in Mali. Indeed, Ba made his way to the United States to ultimately find ways of bringing them to the United States. In an interview he says, "I have lived in this beautiful country for 15 years with the dream of bringing my family here. Now they want to send me back with one shirt, one pen, one (pair of) shoes, to my kids. What I'm gonna tell them: 'I made you wait 15 years, and here

I am, with nothing?'" (Henry 2005). Ba's case offers a different perspective on the transnational family from what is typically discussed in the migration scholarship. Much scholarship has examined the ways migrant women (particularly those employed as domestic workers) have struggled to care for the children they leave behind even as they engage in the work of care in Western households (Parrenas 2003). Less prominent has been the degree to which male migrants engage in care work for the families they leave behind. The literature typically figures male migrants as if they are merely breadwinners, not fathers or husbands with affective ties to their children and wives. Ba's sense of failure in this letter is not merely a failure to provide economically for his family, but indeed, an emotional failure in having subjected his family to years of separation. The importance of immigrant men's emotional labor for their families is further illustrated in a quote from an immigrant from Sierra Leone, who asks, "who will be their [his children's] role model?" (NJCRDC 2007: 18). In the case of the Haitian detainee mentioned above, his sister notes that, "Both of our parents' medical and general living conditions have been deteriorating. In particular, our mother has been battling a severe state of depression over the absence of her son who was—and continues to be—her main reason for living. Our mother is now totally deaf and has no comfort of hearing her son's voice on the phone" (20).

If detainees expressed concerns about their family members outside detention facilities, they also demanded better opportunities to communicate with their family members from within the jails. Petitions signed by detainees in different county facilities cited inadequate access to their families as among their key grievances. A 2005 petition signed by detainees in Hudson notes that "Pictures that come in your mail from our family is not given to us when it should be in our mail when it come to this facility." A letter to NJCRDC from a Barbados immigrant details that "The visiting schedule is too short and our families are traveling long distance and we only get to talk to them for about 15 minutes in front of a big glass and unable to touch our kids, nieces, nephews." This detainee speaks to his desires for physical contact with his children, to be able to display love and affection to relatives outside his immediate family who are also important to him. One detainee deported back to the United States writes, "The Department of Homeland Security unjustly continues to deny me the right to see my children and family who reside in the United States. Your truth in justice is simply a one way street. I have demonstrated you have lost what you once called the Land of the Free. The United States has become a prison." These letters speak to the sorts of suffering men experience in detention just as much as to the agony of their family members; it places men in a complex set of familial relationships that are generally obfuscated in public debates about undocumented immigration and immigrant detention.

Though women are not being detained in the same percentages as men, they are also being put into detention facilities. In some cases, however, women's status as mothers allows them to stay out of detention, though it does not necessarily avert their deportation. Marta Ramos, a Camden resident and native of Guatemala who was identified during a raid of her residence, did not accompany her brothers to detention because she is the mother of four U.S.-born children. She was, however, required to report to immigration officers on a daily basis (Archambeault and Laughlin 2006). Although her detention may have been averted, her deportation has not. Most immigrants are simply forced to leave the U.S. with their children as their children have no real claims of citizenship on their behalf. Yet, this mother's case does reveal the gendered ways immigration enforcement works as mothers, more than fathers, can assert their status as parents to avert detention.

Concluding Thoughts

After 9/11, the U.S. government has expanded its immigration apparatus to target a wide range of immigrant communities for removal from American society, especially men who are figured at once as "suspected terrorists" and "criminals." These men are detained for sometimes indefinite periods of time, and often deported.

The research presented here explores alternative frames by which immigrant detainees attempt to assert their rights to be released from detention. Detainees and their advocates draw on conventional frames like international human rights discourse, or U.S. constitutional rights discourse, but many are also making claims to and on behalf of their families. The family unification laws of past immigration policies are invoked against more recent policy changes. The right to family is reframed as a constitutional right, as the right to "happiness" is interpreted as a right to the family. Economic arguments are made on behalf of the family, as detainees insist on their vital role as key breadwinners to their families. Finally, the emotional toll on families, as well as on detainees themselves, is made in pleas to officials and the broader public to address the issue of detention. Families are construed in very broad terms; they include the typical nuclear family, but also the extended family including elderly parents and in some cases, nieces and nephews.

Of course, there are potential limits to detainees' claims to and of behalf of their families. First, the family claim rests on heteronormative logic, as it relies on particular normative family forms. This claim necessarily excludes same-sex partners and their children, but can also exclude unmarried partners with children. Moreover, what does it mean for the children of detainees, many of whom are citizens and yet cannot assert the same sorts of claims as their adult counterparts? The undocumented children of immigrants offer an especially compelling case because many are raised and educated in the U.S., but may not know of their undocumented status until they are young adults. For example, Sharon Nyantekyi, a Ghanaian-born woman, was detained during a green card interview. Her husband had sponsored her for legal residency, but at the interview, old records revealed that Sharon had had deportation orders issued against her as a child because she and her parents were undocumented.

Interestingly, older children of immigrants are taking a more active role in activism around immigrant rights. According to a *Newark Star-Ledger* report, as of 2002, census data put roughly 300,000 babies in the U.S. per year as born to undocumented parents. The same article describes that in some cases, the U.S.-born children of immigrants act as stand-ins for their parents who are afraid to mobilize (Donahue 2006).

The struggles of immigrant detainees and their children pose challenges for the scholarship on immigration and citizenship and indeed, for immigrant rights movements. Studies of immigrant rights movements and the movements themselves need to interrogate other modalities by which immigrants can and do articulate their claims to rights. While international and domestic legal frameworks offer some redress to immigrants, under current conditions they may reach their limits. To what extent can emotional claims, like those made by detainees here, be made by immigrants more broadly? In what ways can a sort of "affective citizenship" become a successful means of mobilization? Can individuals make claims to and on behalf of the people with whom they have economic and affective relationships? What are the limits and possibilities of children's citizenship? As a "vulnerable" category of people, what sorts of claims can they make to or on behalf of their parents as well as for themselves as increasingly the rights and entitlements of their citizenship is mitigated by the legal status of their parents?

Chapter 11

Defending Women, Defending Rights: Transnational Organizing in a Culture of Human Rights

Mary Jane N. Real

This is a self-reflexive essay to introduce the Women Human Rights Defenders International Coalition (WHRD IC), for which I serve as coordinator. Using the Coalition as a point of reference, the chapter examines the complexities of transnational organizing for women's human rights. It provides an overview of the global-local articulation of human rights within which the Coalition operates, and points to the power of mobilizing under the appeal of a culture of "universality" of human rights while exposing the difficulties and dangers of advancing a women's human rights agenda within a fundamentally androcentric framework and a pervasive culture of patriarchy.

In spite of the resounding acceptance of "women's rights as human rights" following the World Conference on Human Rights in Vienna, Austria in 1993, the culture of human rights has not fully integrated women's human rights. A closer reading of the prevailing interpretation of the United Nations Declaration on Human Rights Defenders reveals that attempts to infuse human rights with a gender perspective have highlighted the specificities of gender needs, but earnest efforts to address these gender-specific concerns tend to reify a special category of "women human rights defenders" instead. This has further reinforced the persistent "ghettoization" of women's human rights.

Mobilizing around human rights and adopting it as a framework for advocacy have given visibility and legitimacy to women's concerns. The framework has recognized the validity of women's issues and translated these into rights, for which the state can be made accountable. Activists demanding their enforceability are beginning to be recognized as "human rights defenders." However, the danger of employing a human rights framework becomes apparent as women human rights defenders exercise their activism within a formidable culture of patriarchy. Advocacy for women's human rights and its defense is taking place not only in a situation of selective enforcement of rights by the state, but more alarmingly in a context of violent backlash against defenders of women's rights insidiously deployed by the state, as well as by ultraconservative forces in the family and community in the interest of "upholding religion" or "preserving culture and tradition."

Forging a Coalition in Defense of Women's Human Rights

The term "defender" comes from the United Nations Declaration on Human Rights Defenders, adopted by the General Assembly in 1998, after thirteen years of negotiations between member-states and human rights advocates. The Declaration does not create new rights, but recognizes that the act of defending human rights is a right in itself. It affirms that human rights also apply to activists, acknowledging them as rights-holders vis-à-vis the state as an accountable duty-bearer. Although not legally binding, the Declaration draws authority from the rights already protected in the Universal Declaration of Human Rights, the International Covenant on Civil and Political Rights, and the International Covenant on Economic, Social and Cultural Rights—otherwise collectively referred to as the International Bill of Human Rights (OHCHR 2004: 19).

Article 1 of the Declaration identifies a "defender" as any person "who promotes and strives for the protection and realization of human rights and fundamental freedoms." Unlike other instruments that confer human rights only to individuals, the Declaration clarifies that a defender could refer not only to a person or a group of persons, but also to a collective or any organization working for human rights. Careful not to adopt a fixed definition, United Nations Special Representative on Human Rights Defenders Hina Jilani explained that what characterizes a defender is the *activity* of promoting and protecting human rights (2004: 6–7, emphasis mine).

There was not much debate within the WHRD IC around adopting the term "defender." The framework presented a strategic opportunity to convene the International Campaign on Women Human Rights Defenders as a platform to push women's human rights from the margins to the center in a collaboration among representatives of women's rights, human rights, and lesbian, gay, bisexual, and transgender (LGBT) groups. A follow-up on the recommendation to organize an international initiative on women's human rights defenders made at an Asia-Pacific consultation convened by the Asia Pacific Forum on Women, Law and Development (APWLD), Amnesty International (AI), and International Women's Rights Action Watch Asia Pacific (IWRAW-AP) in Bangkok in 2003, the Campaign was launched in 2005. It centered on four thematic pillars: (1) to call for the recognition of women human rights defenders; (2) to direct attention to new forms of state violence in the context of the criminalization of political dissent; (3) to demand accountability of non-state actors as violators of human rights; and (4) to promote the issue of sexuality as a cross-cutting human rights concern.

The campaign ran for a year and culminated in an International Consultation on Women Human Rights Defenders that brought together more than 200 women human rights defenders from 70 countries in Sri Lanka, November 29–December 2, 2005 (Real and Chai 2006). While the International Coordinating Committee that ran the campaign was dissolved in 2006, participating organizations followed up recommendations from the consultation. In 2008, the Women Human Rights Defenders International Coalition was formally constituted as an international resource and advocacy network for the protection and support of women human rights defenders. As of 2010, it has 23 member organizations[1] committed to a three-year collaboration to carry out the following strategic objectives:

- to build and advance a knowledge base on women human rights defenders through analysis, documentation, research, monitoring and training;
- to influence policy frameworks and institutions at all levels to advance adequate support and protection for women human rights defenders;
- to develop timely response and systematic interventions for women human rights defenders;

- to support women defenders as individuals as well as building the sustainability of their organizations and movements.

The Coalition coined the term "women human rights defenders" to refer "both to women active in human rights defense who are targeted for who they are as well as all those active in the defense of women's rights who are targeted for what they do" (Real and Chai 2006: 6). It refers to human rights activists who are women, as well as all activists who also defend the rights of women and LGBT persons. But the definition of women human rights defenders is far from settled, as members of the Coalition have continually questioned this term and the boundaries of inclusion/exclusion it signifies.

The 's was dropped because the majority of women's rights organizations prevailed in keeping the emphasis not on defenders of women's rights in general, but on human rights defenders who are women in particular, and the specific manifestations and consequences of the violations they experience because of their gender. The deliberate choice of focusing on women and dropping the possessive subsequently became a cause of concern, not only in relation to the confusion that ensued in translating the full meaning of the term into other languages, but, more important, in acknowledging the LGBT defenders involved in the Coalition.

In formations primarily based on identity politics, articulating a collective entity as a political subject is fraught with difficulties since any act of constituting it bears the threat of essentializing identities and effacing differences. Establishing a collective can easily be made to foreground what is considered common and downplay differences that may threaten the collective. In this instance, the category "gender" has been construed to refer to the majority who are women, eclipsing the differing identities of LGBT members even as the Coalition aspires to construct a collective through which it could advocate for the rights of both women and LGBT activists.

According to Jill Steans (2007: 16–20), a politically constituted subject is not a permanent configuration. It marks only a moment of collective creation and pragmatic strategizing in which members cohere around a common bond and a sense of shared purpose in spite of existing differences. As a collective, it is disconcertingly open to interrogation, not permanently stable but subject to a discursive process in which this politicized identity is affirmed yet continually negotiated, and possibly revised through periodic interventions from those excluded. A process of reflexivity, allowing room for reflection and intersubjective negotiation, creates this possibility of constructing collective identities provisionally based on shared but evolving understanding of unifying interests.

Claiming a Culture of "Universality" of Human Rights

The end of the Cold War galvanized global interest in human rights as central to a vision of postwar world order. Initially working with Western European notions of rights derived from natural law and the concept of legal rights in positive law, advocates of the universality of human rights maintain that the adoption of the Universal Declaration of Human Rights by the UN General Assembly in 1948 represents a broader international consensus on these rights. Their subsequent translation into legal obligations through international covenants and adoption of human rights norms and standards in domestic systems of law demonstrate the widespread acceptance of this claim. Michael Ignatief states: "we are scarcely aware of the extent to which our moral imagination has been transformed since 1945 by the growth of a language and practice of moral universalism, expressed above all in a shared human rights culture" (1997: 8).

Women, organizing in varied, multiple, and concurrent locations and recognizing the power of the discourse on universal human rights, mobilized around the 1993 Vienna World Conference on Human Rights demanding that the universality of human rights apply to every single person by virtue of his or her humanity and that it apply to everyone equally (Bunch and Frost 2000: 4). As the first post-Cold War international gathering on human rights, the Conference came at the heels of the United Nations Decade for Women (1975–1985). By then, many women had participated in three world conferences—Mexico 1975, Copenhagen 1980, and Nairobi 1985. Substantial funding to participate in these processes led by the United Nations, and the "NGO-ization" that began earlier in the decade, hastened the global-local integration of women's organizations into these transnational spaces and raised their critical awareness of the international advocacy around human rights.

When the proposed agenda at the Vienna Conference did not mention women nor include any gender perspective on human rights, there was a ready audience for a worldwide Global Campaign for Women's Human Rights. A broad and loose international collaborative effort, the campaign launched a petition with a simple yet potent slogan, "women's rights are human rights," and called for the Conference "to comprehensively address women's human rights at every level of its proceedings." The petition was translated into 23 languages, with more than 1,000 sponsoring groups that gathered half a million signatures from 124 countries. The campaign generated a groundswell of advocacy within the women's movement and effectively influenced the conference proceedings, with Article 1, Paragraph 18 of the Vienna Declaration and Programme of Action unequivocally stating that "The human rights of women and of the girl-child are an inalienable, integral and indivisible part of universal human rights" (Bunch and Frost 2000: 6).

The WHRD IC is an example of collaboration among activists to advocate for the "universality" of human rights, in principle and practice, fifteen years after Vienna. The Coalition tagline, "defending women, defending rights," is a play on the earlier slogan, "women's rights are human rights." As the victory in Vienna illustrates, the Coalition uses what Steans explains as "the political art of taking an existing discourse that has currency in the current practice of international politics and infusing it with new meanings" (2007: 22).

Claiming a culture of "universality" of human rights, despite continuing contestations, has been a strategic point of convergence in transnational organizing for women's rights. The language of human rights has provided the Coalition with a platform for a shared articulation of rights on which to build alliances across movements. Adopting a human rights framework has allowed it to contribute toward expanding arenas for women's rights advocacy, from local to global. It has extended the legitimacy of human rights to LGBT and women's issues and generated visibility and support for these concerns. In spite of these advances, however, women's rights have not been fully integrated within the universal application of human rights.

With a mandate to monitor the implementation of the Declaration on Human Rights Defenders, the WHRD IC engaged with the office of the UN Special Representative/Special Rapporteur on the situation of human rights defenders. In one of her reports to the Commission on Human Rights in 2002, the Special Representative acknowledged that women human rights defenders face violence or threats, which are "gender-specific and sexual in nature, with consequences that are, in and of themselves, gender-specific" (Jilani 2008: 21–22). This report provided an entry point for succeeding attempts to engender the interpretation of the Declaration on Human Rights Defenders.

Partly due to constant lobbying by the WHRD IC and other advocates, women human rights defenders continue to be mentioned in subsequent annual reports and interventions by the Special Rapporteur before the General Assembly and the Human Rights Council. But the approach has been to confine a specific category to women and sexual minorities—a sector that is particularly vulnerable to violations. In the 2009 report of the Special Rapporteur to the Human Rights Council on the security and protection of human rights defenders, three paragraphs were dedicated particularly to the "security challenges faced by women defenders and defenders of sexual minorities" while the rest of the report, in gender-neutral terms, assessed trends in security and protection of human rights defenders in general (Sekaggya 2009: 16–17).

Highlighting the gender-specific violations against women human rights defenders, without employing gender as an analytical lens to reveal the gendered implications of the causes, forms, circumstances, and consequences of all violations of the rights guaranteed under the Declaration reinforces the persistent dichotomy between human rights and women's rights. It reifies the category of women and sexual minorities, which could point to the need for women or LGBT-specific interventions, but falls short of integrating a gender perspective in the interpretation of the rights of defenders. Failing to apply a gender analysis and treating women or sexual minorities only as an isolated subject of inquiry reinforces the "ghettoization" of women's human rights, with advocates continuing to bear the burden of identifying and meeting the gender-specific needs of women human rights defenders.

Becoming a Women's Human Rights Defender:
Rights Versus "Culture"

Urgent appeals from activists at risk requesting emergency assistance or petitioning for protection have been circulated in the international human rights community in increasing numbers. From the establishment of the mandate of the Special Representative on Human Rights Defenders in 2000 until 2007, the office acted on more than 3,376 urgent appeals from human rights defenders, 22 percent of which involved women (Jilani 2008: 8). In 2008 alone, the Special Rapporteur on Human Rights Defenders acted on about 121 communications involving women human rights defenders, an average of two cases per week (Sekaggya 2009). In 2008–2009, urgent appeals were circulated among members of the WHRD IC at an average of once a week. The figures pertain only to cases reported in these channels, as there is a serious dearth in documentation and reporting. In many instances, violations are not reported because women's rights activism is not considered defense of human rights or women's human rights activists are not recognized as defenders.

Women human rights defenders face increasing threats as part of a backlash brought about by the confluence of the "war against terror" post-9/11 and the global intensification of militarization; the rise of right-wing politics, religious fundamentalisms, and other forms of extremism; increasing conservatism among governments; and the persistence of elitist politics, among other factors. Based on an in-depth survey tracking government counter-terrorism policies for more than 40 countries, the International Commission of Jurists concluded that the framework of international human rights is being actively undermined, not only by regimes that are notorious for doing so, but also by liberal democracies that in the past have subscribed to the importance of human rights (ICJ 2009: 13). Legitimized under the cloak of the "war against terror," authoritarian governments, whether engaged in counter-terrorism measures or in furtherance of their own political interests, have twisted the legal system to criminalize political dissent. Women human rights defenders have been among those punished by the state, as in the case of Imrana Jalal:

14 January 2010
The Women Human Rights Defenders International Coalition (WHRD IC) calls on Fiji's military regime to end its harassment of Imrana Jalal and all women human rights defenders.

The Coalition condemns the politically motivated charges brought against human rights lawyer, Imrana Jalal, by the Fiji Independent Commission Against Corruption (FICAC) on 1 January 2010. A former Fiji Human Rights Commissioner and founding member of the Fiji Women's Rights Movement, who has worked with Coalition members on law reform and human rights issues, Ms. Jalal has a long record of public opposition to all unlawful, undemocratic regimes.

FICAC, headed by a military officer, was established after Fiji's 2006 military takeover to investigate and prosecute corruption, but instead has also been used to persecute persons not supportive of the military regime. Ms. Jalal was publicly served with seven charges alleging breaches of the Public Health (Hotels, Restaurant and Refreshment Bars) Regulations, the Food Safety Act and the Penal Code. The charges relate to a business operated by Bottomline Investments. Ms. Jalal is a director of this company, but has not been involved in its day-to-day operations. These alleged regulatory infractions normally carry a penalty of FJD20.00 (USD10.00) and are Suva City Council offences. A large number of businesses in Fiji's capital, Suva, operate without a licence whilst their applications are being processed.

Similar charges were previously brought against Ms. Jalal's husband, Ratu Sakiusa Tuisolia. These charges were heard in the Magistrates Court, three days prior to the current charges being laid. The Magistrate, Mary Muir, who heard the matters against Mr. Tuisolia questioned the basis for the charges and noted that they fell outside of the jurisdiction of the commission. In a further erosion of the independence of the judiciary in Fiji, the contract of Magistrate Muir was terminated shortly after the matter was raised.

Despite the administrative nature of the charges, Ms. Jalal has now been ordered to surrender her passport. Similar travel restrictions against Ms. Jalal and other women human rights defenders have been part of the continual harassment by the current military regime, headed by Commander Frank Bainimarama. Ms. Jalal has been previously threatened with rape and other human rights defenders have been harassed through abusive use of laws and legal process, threats and deportation.

On 5 January 2010, Fiji's Military Forces Land Force Commander, Brigadier Pita Driti, warned Fiji citizens that they should remember "who is in control." He went on to threaten any dissenters "there are only a few people who [we] could term as adversaries, but I would discourage them from doing anything and I would like to tell them to keep low and try to cooperate with us in trying to maintain peace otherwise they will be in for something really hard in terms of how we will treat them this year." (Fiji Broadcasting Corporation interview)[2]

Imrana could have been easily charged under the Public Emergency Regulations or the Public Order Act, thirty-year old legislation revived by the ruling military regime to crack down on opposition under the pretext of preventing "incitement to violence or disobedience of the law." Instead, as a form of harassment, spurious lawsuits were filed against her under City Council regulations and the Penal Code. Not charging her for human rights-related offenses had the intended the effect of trivializing the value and significance of her political stance against the authoritarian rule and her stature as a prominent human rights lawyer and women's rights defender in Fiji.

The more repressive the sociopolitical environment, the greater the risk for human rights defenders in general. But as the multiple arrests and detention of women activists from the One Million Signatures Campaign in Iran illustrate in the case below, women human rights defenders are made more vulnerable in relation to their advocacy for rights deemed controversial in the increasingly conservative or repressive contexts in which they operate. The attacks are directly linked to their specific advocacy on women's human rights (i.e., the One Million Signatures Campaign call to change gender discriminatory laws in Iran). In other countries, such advocacy for gender equality is legitimate and even initiated by the government, but in the context of Iran where the government prioritizes empowering the state rather than women, it is forcibly suppressed in the interest of ensuring the reproduction of cultural and national identities by retaining state control over women and their bodies.

April 9, 2009
President Dr. Mahmoud Ahmadinejad
The Presidency
Palestine Avenue, Azerbaijan Intersection
Tehran, Islamic Republic of Iran
Your Excellency:
We, the undersigned members of the Women Human Rights Defenders International Coalition, submit this statement to express our deepest concerns regarding the imprisonment of Alieh Eghdamdoost, as well as the recent arrest of 12 other human rights defenders in Iran.

Alieh Eghdamdoost, together with other activists, was arrested at a women's rights demonstration in Tehran in June 2006. On July 6, 2007, she was sentenced to a prison term of three years and four months, and 20 lashes. On appeal, the prison term was reduced by four months, and the judge overturned the lashings. Her sentence of three years is now being implemented, making her the first woman to have a sentence related to women's rights activism.

Eghdamdoost was taken from her home on 31 January 2009 to serve her prison sentence, and has been held in Evin prison since. The fact that Eghdamdoost has been sentenced to a three-year sentence that she is now forced to serve, while some others arrested on the same day faced no charges, were acquitted, or received suspended sentences, demonstrates the completely arbitrary nature of these judicial proceedings. Her imprisonment also sets a dangerous precedent for all women engaged in human rights activism in Iran.

Eghdamdoost is serving her sentence against a backdrop of increased repression targeting human rights defenders, including women's rights activists. On March 26 Iranian security forces detained another 12 members of the One Million Signatures Campaign and Mothers for Peace, as they were sitting in their cars on a street corner in Tehran, preparing for New Year's visits to the family members of some prisoners of conscience.

The twelve individuals arrested on March 26 were Ali Abdi, Delaram Ali, Bahara Behravan, Farkhondeh Ehtesabian, Shahla Forouzanfar, Arash Nasiri Eghbali, Mahboubeh Karami, Khadijeh Moghaddam, Leila Nazari, Amir Rashidi, Mohammad Shoorab, and Soraya Yousefi.

After three days, ten of them were released on bail. The two activists, Mahboubeh Karami and Khadijeh Moghaddam, were kept in detention, [but subsequently released on April 7 and April 8 respectively]. . . .

[These] persons arrested on March 26 were not engaged in a public activity, but were planning visits to private residences at the start of the New Year, as is customary amongst Iranians. The circumstances of their arrest do not even remotely support the charges of "disrupting public order," or "disturbing public opinion," rather appear as deliberate efforts to silence and intimidate these activists. We note, with great concern, that since the One Million Signatures Campaign has been launched, dozens of its members have been arrested, summoned for interrogation, monitored, banned from travel and prosecuted. . . .

Asia Pacific Forum on Women Law and Development
Asian Forum for Human Rights and Development
    (FORUM-ASIA)
Baobab for Women's Human Rights
Front Line, The International Foundation for Human Rights
    Defenders
Human Rights First
International Women's Rights Action Watch Asia Pacific
Observatory for the Protection of Human Rights Defenders[3]

The perpetrators of violence against women human rights defenders are not just the state or its agents. An alarming trend is the increasing allegations of abuses committed by non-state actors. Since the women human rights defenders international campaign began in 2005, women human rights defenders have identified the debilitating impacts of abuse at the hands of their own family and community, who act as gatekeepers of dominant interpretations of "culture," "tradition," or "religion" and impose their own notions of punishment against the transgressors. One such case is the appeal below from a network in Nepal supported by the WHRD IC:

14 January 2009
AN APPEAL FOR SOLIDARITY AND SUPPORT
The National Alliance of Women Human Rights Defenders requests your urgent intervention regarding the death of Ms. Laxmi Bohara, 28, a member of Women Human Rights Defender Network and a resident of Champapur, Ward No. 8, Daji Village Development Committee in Kanchanpur district, Nepal. It was reported that Laxmi was severely beaten and then forced to take poison (Selfos) by her husband. There are evidence of blue marks and severe bruises all over her body. Her 6-year old daughter also made a statement that her mother was severely beaten the whole night by her father (although as a minor, her statement cannot be used as evidence). Laxmi passed away while being treated in the hospital at 10:30 am on 6 June 2008.

Laxmi was a health volunteer and Secretary of Women's Empowerment Centre. She was an active defender of women's rights engaged in advocating for health rights of women. She was married to Tek Raj Bohara for the past 12 years and lived with him and her mother in law, Dhana Devi Bohara in the same house. She was a mother of three children; her daughter is 6 years old and sons are 12 and 4 respectively.

She has been severely criticized and harassed by her husband and mother in law for committing herself to social work. Suspicious if she talked with anyone on the road, she was regularly beaten up by her husband who even threatened to throw her out of the house. There have been instances that he battered the children as well, Laxmi told her friends.

Sharda Chand, the Secretary of Women Human Rights Defenders Network shared that ten days before Laxmi's death, Laxmi was thrown out of the house by her husband. She took safe shelter in the house of her three friends, but went back to her husband after he promised he would not beat her up again.

The father of Laxmi filed a First Hand Information (FIR) to the District Police Office (DPO) stating that his daughter was murdered by the son-in-law and his mother. The police informed the father that his case has been registered under number 224. However, as a part of the Hindu culture, the dead has to be cremated by a man of the family and follow a ritual of 13 days known as the mourning period. Since the religion demands that the man in the family has to initiate this, the Police informed the family members that if a FIR is registered, then the husband would not be able to perform the ritual. Hence, the FIR was not be registered until after 13 days, the husband was freed with the agreement that he will be present at the police station after 13 days.

Kanchanpur district is known for the highest number of cases on violence against women with domestic violence (especially dowry-related violence), at least 2–3 cases per day. Likewise, there are issues regarding women's access to land, concerns of Badi women and neglect of widows in the district.[4]

Laxmi's case shows how women's bodies have become the site of contestation between culture and rights. By becoming an active defender of women's rights, Laxmi made herself visible and vulnerable to attack for defying cultural, religious, or social norms about femininity and the role of women in her society. Her death conveys the danger of defending women's human rights and exercising women's agency in a patriarchal context where individuals who are in positions of power, as a means of maintaining that power, punish those who are perceived to act against the preservation of "culture," "tradition," or "religion" as they have defined it.

As demonstrated in the case of LGBT activists in Uganda below, hegemonic articulations of culture or religion are passed off as the only authentic interpretations that must be defended from any interference from the "West" or foreign influence, in this case, the invocation of human rights. The same rhetoric of rights is being deployed by the state to validate cultural and religious impositions that are discriminatory and considered harmful to the marginalized population, such as enforcing a dominant heteronormative culture through criminalization of homosexuality. In Uganda, legislation was proposed to criminalize deviant sexual identities and relationships, which stirred widespread antagonism against LGBT persons and defenders of sexual rights:

March 2009
Members of the Women Human Rights Defenders International Coalition deplore the systematic discrimination against lesbian, gay, bisexual and transgender (LGBT) people and activists in Uganda. Such abuses violate fundamental human rights and endanger the lives of human rights defenders, including sexual rights defenders, in the country.

In several acts since March 2009, right-wing religious and antigay groups have verbally attacked LGBT persons, by charging them with recruiting children into homosexuality; issuing slanderous remarks; and exposing in the media the names, places of employment and photos of more than 100 people suspected to be LGBT, including several LGBT rights defenders. An article in the leading tabloid The Red Pepper claimed to be exposing "Uganda's shameless men and unabashed women that have deliberately exported the western evils to our dear and sacred society." The strategic manipulation of prejudices about sexuality, known as sexuality baiting, is a dangerous practice that promotes negative stereotyping of LGBT persons and activists, increasing their vulnerability to acts of violence motivated by sexual orientation and gender identity in Uganda.

Moreover, it is alarming that government officials have adopted similar rhetoric. The New Vision, a Ugandan newspaper, reported that Chief Parliamentarian David Migereko stated that gays had exposed themselves, and the government would go after them. "Homosexuality is illegal. The Minister of Ethics, Dr. Nsabu Butoro, has been clear on the matter. Those involved will face the long arm of the law."

The state's discriminatory actions go beyond rhetoric. The police arrested at least five men on charges related to homosexual conduct. Most have been charged with having "carnal knowledge against the order of nature," and one of the detainees has been charged with assaulting a minor and aggravated defilement, subject to the death penalty.

Such discriminatory acts against LGBT and sexual rights defenders committed by state and private actors violate the freedom from discrimination enshrined in the Universal Declaration of Human Rights. Additionally, the criminalization of homosexuality is contrary to Uganda's obligations under the International Covenant on Civil and Political Rights, which protects the rights to freedom from discrimination (art. 2 and 26), freedom of expression (art. 19), freedom from arbitrary interference with the right to privacy (art. 17) and freedom of conscience (article 18). These acts are also contrary to the UN Declaration on Human Rights Defenders, which protects the human rights and freedoms of human rights defenders.[5]

Defense of the rights of women and sexual minorities made within a claim of "universality" of human rights repeatedly runs into the argument of "cultural relativism"—that all cultures are particular and there is no such thing as universality; that human rights could be interpreted differently in different cultural, ethnic, or religious traditions. By questioning the claim to universality, this perspective underscores the importance that the realization of human rights is not a uniform process, but requires culturally appropriate strategies and sensitizes transnational organizing to pay attention to difference and the ensuing contestations as openings to reconceptualize or reconfigure initiatives to be more inclusive and locally relevant. However, discarding the appeal to "universality" of human rights in favor of cultural relativist views is not a straightforward option. Frequently invoked by governments who resist the claim to universality to ward off international scrutiny and escape accountability, absolute adherence to cultural relativist arguments that put a premium on difference unwittingly end up solidifying a counter form of "universalism"—a singular, static, ahistorical concept of culture.

The language of human rights is a highly contested terrain and is susceptible to influence at different levels. Within the Coalition itself, changes in the interpretation of human rights are evident. For example, LGBT groups have been successful in influencing the members to take up sexual rights issues and jointly respond to cases involving LGBT defenders. Moreover, as the Coalition interacts with its members and other defenders on the ground, local struggles infuse its women human rights defenders' framework with new meanings and symbolic resources, which are subsequently translated and redeployed locally. In Nepal, it translated as a strategy for political mobilization, becoming a rallying point among women from diverse ethnicities, castes, and classes to converge and demand political participation in the post-conflict reconstruction processes. In 2008, a network of women human rights defenders was organized as the National Alliance of Women Human Rights Defenders with members in 65 districts in the country.

While the language of human rights can potentially serve as a tool for mobilization, it may also be a source of vulnerability for women human rights defenders. In the contestations between culture and rights, the state as well as powerful stakeholders invested in maintaining a culture of patriarchy have appropriated human rights to justify their own political or personal interests. In the face of these vested interests, women human rights defenders have risked their lives. But rather than remaining victims, the defenders' framework presents them with an opportunity to traverse the trajectory from victims to survivors to defenders and allows them to explore their agency within the shifting terrain of power and politics.

The WHRD IC embodies the complexities of transnational organizing for women's human rights. Its constitution as a political subject is more tentative than permanent, reflecting the fragile compromises across the different movements represented in its membership. It is a collective that is inevitably exclusive, but one that is continually open to contestations in the light of the challenges from those who are excluded. Its strength lies in navigating intersections of differences among its members through a continual process of reflexivity to offer a critique of or develop alternative interpretations of human rights.

Notes

Introduction: Gender and Culture at the Limit of Rights

1. There is a vast literature exploring the history and consequences of the women's rights as human rights movement. Key works include Agosín (2001); Cook (1994); Fraser (1999); Hesford and Kozol (2005); Lockwood (2006); and Peters and Wolper (1995). For a recent overview of the history of human rights, see Cmiel (2004).

2. The title of this section is drawn from a phrase in Abu-Lughod's chapter in this volume.

3. Two current examples of the influence of Christian conservatives in the United States in shaping which rights get recognized, implemented, and enforced are the legal denial of funds to health facilities and organizations that provide information about or access to abortion services as part of the President's Emergency Plan for AIDS Relief (PEPFAR), and the documented involvement of American evangelical groups in inflaming anti-homosexual sentiment and promoting anti-homosexual laws (including the death penalty) in Kenya, Uganda, and several other African countries.

Chapter 1. Gender, History, and Human Rights

I am grateful to Dorothy Hodgson and Richard Roberts for their support of this project. Audiences at the African Studies Association annual meetings in 2008 and 2009, and at seminars and workshops at Emory University and Rutgers University helped me hone my arguments. My colleagues and students at Emory have offered a most stimulating and congenial working environment and I am very grateful to them.

1. For a cautionary if inflated analysis of rapes in the DRC and the complicity of the international community, see Snow (2007). In 2009, Eve Ensler almost singlehandedly put rapes in the DRC on the international agenda, a campaign that resulted in a landmark visit by Secretary Hillary Clinton to the eastern DRC. For examples of this activism see http://www.vday.org/drcongo/background.

2. For how male perspectives structure post-conflict reconstruction see Handrahan (2004).

3. UN Security Council Resolution 1325 on Women, Peace and Security (October 31, 2000), http://www.peacewomen.org/un/sc/1325.html; Resolution 1820 (June 19,

2008), at http://daccessdds.un.org/doc/UNDOC/GEN/N08/391/44/PDF/N0839144.
pdf?OpenElement, both accessed December 8, 2009.

4. African Charter on Human and Peoples' Rights, Protocol on the Rights of
Women in Africa, July 11, 2003.

5. In activism and theory, feminists have sought to make international law more
accountable to women's rights, and have sought ways of putting violence against women
on the agenda. Rhonda Copelon (1994), for example, has suggested that we understand
domestic violence as torture, which thus brings it under international conventions that
outlaw torture.

6. For a helpful review of historical work on human rights see Cmiel (2004).

7. The book can be seen as following in the tradition of David Brion Davis's (1984,
1999) celebrated texts on the emergence of the humanitarian sentiment also in the eighteenth century. He argues that such empathetic imagination led finally to the abolition
of the British and American trans-Atlantic slave trades in the early nineteenth century.

8. With regard to the latter, see Baxi (2006).

9. Of course here I echo Gayatri Spivak's (1988) famous point about how the British
in India sought to rescue brown women from brown men.

10. Lauren (1998) discusses colonialism and international human rights.

11. Ferguson (1992: chap. 2) argues that the figure of Imoinda helps launch an ico-
nography of the suffering black woman.

12. Sally Engle Merry, comment at Rutgers conference.

13. For compelling work on these points in relation to African feminism see
Oyewumi (2002, 2003)

14. For an article that reproduces this perspective see Kinsman (1983); for a critique
see Oyewumi (2003).

15. For discussion of these aspects see Scully and McCandless (2010).

16. See Merry (2006: chap. 6) for the challenges involved in using human rights at
the local level, precisely because of the ways it can render an individual without traditional support structures. I am grateful to the audience at the Culture of Rights workshop, and particularly to Indrani Chatterjee for opening up further discussion on the
issue of the place of women elders.

17. UNHCR, n.d, "Women Rights in Liberia," http://www.unhcr.org/refworld/
pdfid/46f146810.pdf.

18. I know this can be overstated. As Redfield (2006) shows, the concern with rape
and with women's sexual health only emerged fairly recently in MSF, for example.

Chapter 2. Between Law and Culture: Contemplating
Rights for Women in Zanzibar

1. Since Zanzibar is composed of two main islands—Unguja and Penba—and
several islets, I use "island" and "islands" interchangeably to refer to Zanzibar in this
chapter.

2. Modern Zanzibar here refers to the period that accompanied the governance

transition in the early nineteenth century along with increased contact with western imperial powers, events that ultimately defined the island's present political and social landscape.

3. The Zanzibar National Archives cited in this chapter include *Records on Education and Schools*, FILE AB 33/7; *Records on Girls' Education and Schools*, FILE 7AD 21; *Records on the Royal Family* FILE AB/10/89, 116, 128, 134, 135; Zanzibar Protectorate Department of Education, *Annual Report on Education for the Year 1915*, BA5/1, 4, 5.

4. She is featured in the Eastern region volume of the Women Writing Africa Project (Lihamba et al. 2007: 190–91).

5. Widows and Orphans Pensions (Amendment) Decree No. 43 of 1921, amended by Decree No. 1 of 1963.

6. The passage of the Asiatic Widows and Orphans Pensions Decree No. 48 of 1931 is a case in point.

7. According to Pearce (1967), Imam means among other things one whose leadership and example is to be followed; a pattern; a model. In its fuller sense it means (1) the Imam or Khalifa of the Muslim people; (2) the Imam or leader of any body of theology; and (3) the Imam or leader of prayers in any mosque. See Pearce (1967: 99 n).

8. Amina Wadud in *Qur'an and Women* (1999) and Fatima Mernissi in *Beyond the Veil* (1975) speak to the notion of women and *fitna* which is used to justify restriction on mobility and dress in some Muslim societies.

9. Personal Interview with Bibi Mariam Abbass, September 15, 2008, at her home in Zanzibar.

10. While Zanzibar is a multicultural society and hosts one of the oldest Christian communities in East Africa, Sayyida Salme's social position defined the bounds of permissibility of her actions.

11. Ironically, Sayeed Khalifa was the grandson of Thuwein, the eldest living son of Sayeed Said of the Omani branch of the Bu-Said, whom the British had previously stopped from claiming the Zanzibar dominion after his father's death in favor of partitioning the kingdom into two separate dominions. This is but part of the British machination in the affairs of Zanzibar.

12. This explains why she is addressed as Bi or Bibi and rarely as Sayeeda.

13. This period represents the first two phases of the Zanzibar Revolutionary Government, characterized by authoritarian rule.

14. The Legislative Council, later the House of Representatives, was first established in 1926 with both official and unofficial benches. The Official Bench tended to be pro-government while the Unofficial Bench tended to be more critical. The 1926 Council did not contain unofficial African members.

15. For detailed accounts see Fairooz (1995); Al-Ismaily (1999); Juma (2007).

16. Definitions of natives changed over time. The Public Lands Decree of 1921 excluded the Swahili and persons of Asiatic descent (including Comoro and Madagascar) from the definition of indigenous; this definition was deleted in Decree No. 10 of 1954.

17. There are still claims that the first president, Abeid Karume, was not born in

Zanzibar. Similar claims were raised about the third president, Ali Hassan Mwinyi, to disqualify his suitability to lead Zanzibar.

18. Technically the Kadhi, a state appointee, would act as her guardian and arrange for her marriage, thereby meeting the religious requirement for a legal guardian.

19. President Karume took four additional wives, all considerably younger than himself.

20. Some of these laws persist and are being revived in public institutions.

21. The Education Act of 1982 changed the practice, expelling girls who became pregnant, even if married. The law was amended in 2006, allowing pregnant girls to continue with their education once they delivered.

22. Her candidature was defeated on a technicality: she had stood as a candidate under one political party and defected to another without formally resigning from the first. She was a National Parliament MP and among three women standing as for the Vice Presidency.

23. *S.M.Z v. Machano Khamis Ali and 17 other Zanzibaris*, Criminal Appeal No. 7 of 1999 (unreported).

24. Presently the Ministry of Labour, Youth, Women and Children's Development.

25. See Section 156. This includes surrogacy.

26. Section 145(C)(1) is significant in light of the low conviction rates for rape.

27. As part of the main legislation, the expectation is that it is more readily accessible to law enforcement agencies.

28. The fine is about US$700 for men and US$500 for women; prison terms are 14–25 years.

29. To date not a single case has been filed since the law's enactment, convincing many that its passage was politically motivated.

30. Defined as between sixteen and twenty-one in the old law and eighteen and twenty-one in the 2005 law.

31. This is changing; senior government figures are more inclined to speak out against early marriages and urge law enforcement agencies to act against parents and grooms guilty of the practice.

Chapter 3. A Clash of Cultures: Women, Domestic Violence, and Law in the United States

Portions of this chapter are drawn from previous publications by the author. In my former position as Senior Staff Attorney at the NOW Legal Defense and Education Fund (now known as Legal Momentum), I was involved in the effort to draft and enact the Violence Against Women Act of 1994; however, the views expressed herein are my own.

1. Since no single term adequately describes women who have experienced domestic violence, this chapter uses the terms battered woman, victim, and survivor interchangeably. The terms domestic violence, battering, and abuse are also used interchangeably, for similar reasons.

2. *Abbott v. Abbott*, 67 Me. 304 (1877); *State v. Oliver*, 70 N.C. 60 (1874); *State v. Black*, 60 N.C. (Win.) 262 (1864). The idea of a self-contained, private domestic sphere isolated from the larger, public world is highly unrealistic. Legal intervention in the family is inevitable; the law either provides redress to battered women, or else it refuses to do so and thereby condones domestic violence. Furthermore, respect for domestic privacy has never been conferred equally on all families. People of color, the poor, and gays and lesbians have long been subject to unwanted government oversight of their family lives (Roberts 1991). Similarly, for most of American history, when laws against domestic violence were enforced at all, they were often implemented selectively against men belonging to disfavored racial, ethnic, and class groups (Siegel 1996).

3. Violence Against Women Act of 1994, P.L. 103–322, 108 Stat. 1902. Before VAWA, federal statutes addressing domestic violence were limited to a sparse patchwork of criminal laws and relatively modest funding programs, such as the Family Violence Prevention and Services Act (1984, 42 U.S.C. §§10401–15). Both federal and state laws are important components of the legal response to domestic violence. State civil and criminal laws provide the bulk of the legal remedies commonly available to domestic violence victims. A federal law like VAWA differs from state laws in its national coverage, greater prominence in the eyes of the public, access to the superior resources of the federal government, ability to address issues that are controlled exclusively by federal law (such as immigration), and symbolic power as a statement of national ideals.

4. Among other things, VAWA required states to recognize and enforce protection orders issued by other states; authorized federal grants to increase the effectiveness of police, prosecutors, judges, and victim services agencies; provided funding for a national toll-free domestic violence hotline; increased federal financial support for battered women's shelters; reformed immigration law to protect battered immigrant women; made it a federal crime to cross state lines in order to commit domestic violence or to violate a protection order; and provided federal leadership to improve research and record-keeping on violence against women.

5. *United States v. Morrison*, 529 U.S. 598 (2000).

6. Violence Against Women Act of 2000, P.L. 106–386, 114 Stat. 1491; Violence Against Women and Department of Justice Reauthorization Act of 2005, P.L. 109–62, 119 Stat. 2960 (2006).

7. The concept that violence against women operates as a denial of equality was not original to VAWA. Nevertheless, VAWA's civil rights provision infused that concept with a level of legal and social influence within the United States that it had never previously enjoyed. Simultaneous developments in the international human rights arena during the early 1990s, including the 1993 United Nations Declaration on the Elimination of Violence Against Women, combined with VAWA to raise awareness of this issue within the United States.

8. Jessica Gonzales filed a lawsuit in federal court alleging that the police depart-

ment's failure to enforce the protection order violated her constitutional right to due process. The trial court dismissed the case, and the U.S. Supreme Court ruled that the dismissal was proper (*Town of Castle Rock v. Gonzales*, 545 U.S. 748 (2005)). In an opinion authored by Justice Scalia, the Court's seven-member majority held that the state statute concerning arrest for protection order violations did not impose a mandatory duty on the police, and that the statute did not give Gonzales a personal property interest in having the order enforced. Based on different facts and different legal theories, a few other lawsuits brought against police departments for failure to enforce domestic violence laws have been successful (Bartlett and Rhode 2006: 497–99).

9. Battered women's shelters, although not technically a legal remedy, receive government funds and therefore represent another example of government support for separation as a solution to domestic violence.

10. In a study of women in violent relationships, Campbell et al. (1994) found that approximately 25 percent of the women were in the same relationship two years later but reported that they were no longer being beaten or otherwise abused. Bowker (1983, 1986) studied one thousand battered women who successfully put an end to domestic violence, many of whom remained with their partners; he found that legal intervention was among the factors that women identified most frequently as helping to stop abuse.

11. Reports on the duration of protection order hearings include Tracy, Fromson, and Miller (2006), indicating that 75 percent of protection from abuse cases in Philadelphia took less than ten minutes; Ballou et al. (2007), reporting that restraining order decisions were often made within five to fifteen minutes in courts in Cambridge, Massachusetts; and DuFresne and Greene (1995), finding that protective order proceedings in Maryland were typically less than fifteen minutes long.

12. General Recommendation No. 19 on Violence Against Women, 1992, Committee on the Elimination of Discrimination Against Women, U.N. Doc. A/47/38; UN General Assembly Declaration on the Elimination of Violence Against Women, 1993, UN General Assembly Resolution 48/104, U.N. Doc. A/RES/48/104; Vienna Declaration and Programme of Action, 1993, Report of the United Nations World Conference on Human Rights, U.N. Doc. A/CONF.157/24.

13. Since Gonzales's federal case was dismissed without a trial (see note 8 above), she was never able to testify in a U.S. courtroom. Her hearing before the Inter-American Commission on Human Rights was the first time she was able to speak in a legal forum about her ordeal.

Chapter 4. Making Women's Human Rights in the Vernacular: Navigating the Culture/Rights Divide

This research was generously supported by a grant from the National Science Foundation, Law and Social Sciences Program, #SES-0417730. It was originally prepared for a distinguished lecture at the Institute for Research on Women at Rutgers University. It has benefited from comments from the audience at Rutgers and at the Washington College of Law at American University.

Chapter 5. The Active Social Life of "Muslim Women's Rights"

This chapter is abridged from an article published in the *Journal of Middle East Women's Studies* 6, 1 (2009). I am grateful to Indiana University Press for permission to reprint this version here. I want to thank Nancy Gallagher, Sondra Hale, Dorothy Hodgson, and Diane James for helping turn this into an article; audiences at the University of California at Santa Barbara and Yale's faculty seminar on Women, Religion, and Globalization for sharpening the arguments; colleagues and students at Columbia University, particularly Anupama Rao and Dina Siddiqi for helping me think about "rights"; colleagues who guided my exploration of the world of feminist NGOs in Cairo and in the Palestinian context, especially Soraya Altorki, Rabab al-Mahdi, Reem Saad, May Kassab, Naela Refaat, Nadera Shalhoub-Kevorkian, Penny Johnson, and Islah Jad; fantastic research assistants Ali Atef, Amina Ayad, Sara Layton, Leah Riviere, and John Warner; and friends in the village in Egypt who shared their thoughts with me, but whose names I can't reveal to protect their privacy. Both the research and the writing were made possible by fellowships in 2007–2009 from the American Council of Learned Societies and the Carnegie Foundation. I am solely responsible for the statements and views presented.

1. For perceptive analyses of the popular literature on the oppressed Muslim woman, see Bahramitash (2005); Lalami (2006); and D. Ahmad (2009).

2. For another ethnographic approach to rights, see Slyomovics (2005).

3. It goes without saying that I use the term "Muslim women's rights" here not because I believe there is something that unites all Muslim women or makes their lives and access to rights unique, but because the notion that there is such a thing and the work and debates framed in terms of this concept are becoming common sense. And though my examples are drawn from the Arab world, because that is where I have done my research, I am keenly aware of how this skewing perpetuates the association of Islam with the Arab world when in fact Muslims are found around the world. For a good critical analysis of the Muslim woman idea, which she cleverly calls the "Muslimwoman," see cooke (2007). For counterweights to the focus on the Arab world, see the special issue of the *International Feminist Journal of Politics* 10 (2008), Elora Chowdhury, Leila Farsakh, and Rajini Srikanth (2008).

4. Nationalist campaigns to discredit the smaller NGOs for their foreign links must be seen, as Sakr argues, as "a diversionary tactic." Given that Egypt is the second largest recipient of U.S. aid, Sakr concludes that it "seems perverse to suggest that NGOs were more to blame than the government for prolonging dependency on foreign powers" (Sakr 2004:172). For more on NGOs, INGOs, GO-NGOs, and DO-NGOs, see Carapico (2000).

5. See critiques of the *Arab Human Development Report 2005* (Jad/UNDP 2006) by Abu-Lughod (2009b), Adely (2009), and Hasso (2009).

6. Similarly, the annual report on the European Neighbourhood Policy by the Commission of the European Communities notes that a total of 17 million euros was earmarked in 2008 for human rights, women's rights, and children's rights projects in Egypt (CEC 2009: 22).

7. This strategy of setting up a government body to advance rights that were formerly the bailiwick of more critical NGOs, while trying to discredit them by presenting them as part of a foreign plot, was copied, it seems, in the case of human rights. Three years after the creation of the NCW, a National Council for Human Rights was established. As Maha Abdelrahman has argued, with serious restrictions on NGOs and a campaign to misrepresent "human rights and the organisations that attempt to promote these rights as mouthpieces of Western imperialist powers," the regime tarred human rights organizations as a threat to Egypt's national security and reputation. Meanwhile, the regime "has gained a degree of legitimacy in the eyes of the public by representing itself as the protector of national interests. More recently . . . since the debate on and the foundation of the National Council for Human Rights in 2003, the state has refined its discourse on the role of civil society and human rights organisations by promoting an image of itself as the true patron of civil society organisations and the 'official agent' of a more nationalistically defined human rights movement" (Abdelrahman 2007: 287).

8. http://www.adew.org/en/?action=10000&sub=1, accessed September 20, 2009.

9. As part of a required course called Workshop in Development Practice, some masters students were invited to review ADEW's programs and make recommendations.

10. Funders include one Egyptian (Sawiris Foundation for Development) and one Arab (Arab Gulf Program for United Nations Development Organization [AG Fund]); the rest are a who's who of foreign or UN foundations or agencies: the European Commission Delegation of the European Commission to Egypt, Swiss Development Fund, Ford Foundation, Embassy of Japan, Royal Netherlands Embassy, Dutch Organization for International Development Cooperation (NOVIB), German Technical Cooperation (GTZ), Italian Debt Swap Program, United Nations Development Program (UNDP), Australian Embassy, and Embassy of Finland.

11. Naela Refaat, personal communication.

12. CEWLA is sought after as a partner by many, including the School of Oriental and African Studies at the University of London, as when it had a multiyear project on honor crimes. CEWLA commissioned its own study.

13. CEWLA director Azza Sleiman is also part of a transnational network of Muslim feminists who in February 2009 in Kuala Lumpur launched an organization called Musawah, dedicated to seeking justice and equality within Islamic family law. See Abu-Lughod (2009a).

14. For more on the alliance of the state and Al-Azhar in Egypt, see Zeghal (1999) and Moustafa (2000).

15. Bibars was interviewed on Al-Jazeera by Riz Khan on September 22, 2008; http://www.ashoka.org/video/5007, accessed September 20, 2009.

16. http://stopsexualharassment.net/about, accessed September 26, 2009.

17. http://www.netsquared.org/projects/harassmap-reporting-mapping-sexual-harass ment-sms, accessed September 26, 2009.

18. http://www.oneinthreewomen.com, accessed September 21, 2009.

19. http://www.iamapeacekeeper.com/womenshealthadvocacy.htm, accessed September 21, 2009.

20. http://stop-stoning.org , accessed September 21, 2009.

21. See Moghadam (2005: 142–72) for an excellent description of WLUML's positions and history.

22. New evidence of this has emerged in the report of the United Nation Fact Finding Mission on the Gaza Conflict, submitted in September 2009. For the "Goldstone Report" see http://www2.ohchr.org/english/bodies/hrcouncil/specialsession/9/FactFind ingMission.htm, accessed September 27, 2009.

23. Khawla Abu-Baker, ed., *Women, Armed Conflict and Loss* (2004) was published through the Women's Studies Centre in Jerusalem with Swedish funding (Kvinna Till Kvinna [Woman to Woman] and Sida [Swedish International Development Cooperation Agency]).

24. For a subtle analysis of the impact of human rights on Palestinian politics, representations, and subjectivity, see Allen (2009).

25. See Abu-Lughod (2009b), Adely (2009), and Hasso (2009).

26. She explained this element of Islamic law: the man takes two portions and the woman one.

27. This is confirmed by Rachida Chih's study of this and other Sufis of the Khalwatiyya Brotherhood in Upper Egypt. Based on research in the 1990s, she argues, "Women, like men, want to meet the Shaykh for his baraka, for spiritual counseling but also for his mediation and protection against a ruthless husband or to escape a forced marriage. . . . The Shaykh's mediation is so popular that the population of the village has called it *hukm hasani* meaning for them a fair and quick justice that compensates the victims and prevents vendettas" (Chih 2004:162).

Chapter 6. How Not to be a *Machu Qari* (Old Man): Human Rights, Machismo and Military Nostalgia in Peru's Andes

For comments and advice on previous drafts I am indebted to Orin Starn, Diane Nelson, Anne Allison, Wendy Coxshall, Ponciano del Pino, Micaela di Leonardo, Dorothy Hodgson, Daniel Goldstein, as well as by participants at: the Rutgers Symposium on Gender and Human Rights, the American Anthropological Association Panel on Gender at the Limits of Rights (2009), and the Colloquium at the School for Advanced Research in Santa Fe. My colleagues at the Department of Sociology and Anthropology and Peace and Conflict Studies at the College of the Holy Cross provided me with invaluable advice on revision; any errors are my own. This research was generously supported by the Wenner Gren Foundation, the Harry Frank Guggenheim Foundation, the United States Institute of Peace, the Ford Foundation, the College of the Holy Cross and the Department of Cultural Anthropology and Latin American Studies at Duke University.

1. "Wiracocha" is a pseudonym used to protect the safety of my interviewees; the personal names of all non-public figures have also been changed for this reason. The names of all other places and public figures are unchanged.

2. Unless otherwise noted all translations from Quechua and Spanish are my own. I chose to translate the Quechua phrase *machu qari* which means, literally, "old man," to "old men"; the plural form better reflects the figurative way the phrase was used in interviews: "we are all old *men*" (my emphasis).

3. This phrase is the title of an article and a quote from a fieldwork interview by ethnohistorian Ponciano Del Pino. Del Pino interviewed Ayacucho peasant patrollers during the war and found that they expressed pride in their military service by referencing their masculinity (Del Pino 1991).

4. I am indebted here to Kimberly Theidon's earlier analysis of gendered claims to military citizenship in rural Ayacucho, in which she connects the Ayacucho example to Gill's research. See Theidon (2003) as well as note 12.

5. As I will explain farther on, however, forced conscription is also a part of Latin American militaries. Until military reforms in the late 1990s, Peruvian law required young men and women to inscribe themselves in a draft for military service when they turned seventeen. In practice, however, poorer young men were targeted for forcible recruitment through ambushes (called the *leva*) that I describe later in this chapter. According to the Peruvian Coordinator for Human Rights, a common practice to avoid these ambushes was extortion, in which young people or their parents paid $300–400, perhaps a year's salary in the countryside, to be excused from service. Because of the amount of this sum the upper middle classes and elites were more likely than the lower classes to be able to escape military service (Coordinadora Nacional de Derechos Humanos 1997)

6. At the beginning of the war Wiracocha was attacked by the very first rondas in the area—those in the neighboring *puna* (high mountain plateau) villages. These villages had some history of antagonism with Wiracocha, based on hacienda land disputes that pre-dated the dirty war (Yezer 2007). Previous political struggles and land control conflicts determined wartime schisms elsewhere in Ayacucho as well (Del Pino 2008, Heilman 2010).

7. The patrols were modeled in part on the original rondas of Peru's northern provinces. Northern peasants formed rondas before the war to catch cattle thieves; the patrols later became a part of the village justice system (Starn 1999).

8. It is difficult to declare the war absolutely over, as two Shining Path factions are still active in the remote jungles of Ayacucho, Cusco, and Junín at the time of publication. Elsewhere I have shown how Peru's state atrocities against peasant civilians continue into the drug wars (Yezer 2008).

9. *Varayoq* duties and power vary across the Andes, but in Ayacucho these officers were usually in charge of distributing and controlling resources and duties, such as access to pasture land, crop rotations, water and irrigation, and organizing the Catholic festival cycle (Coronel 2000).

10. Studies indicate that there is a strong connection between crime and rising vigilantism on the one hand, and the violence histories of impoverished or post-conflict societies. For Bolivia and Guatemala see Goldstein (2004) and Godoy (2006) respectively.

11. Because it has been used for nutritional and religious purposes for thousands of years, Peru does not classify coca leaf, from which cocaine is extracted, as a drug (Allen 2002). Nevertheless, the state allows only a limited number of producers to grow coca in large quantities, so that most farmers who grow traditional markets have to transport and sell their harvest illicitly (Yezer 2005, 2007).

12. A useful counterpoint to my findings here is Kimberly Theidon's ethnographic research elsewhere in Ayacucho. Theidon found there that village men's heroic narrative of patrol service worked well to establish them as patriots to some of Peruvian society. However, she discovered that inside the village the aftereffects of militarization combined with a narrowly masculine war narrative undermined women's ability to claim their own rights, and paved the way for a more patriarchal system that had already begun during the militarization (Theidon 2003). Our results may show how two areas may have had very different postwar responses, yet I believe that the timing of our research in relationship to the Peruvian Truth Commission (Theidon's original fieldwork happened before the Commission and mine during its mandate) may be influential. Because the Commission reported rondas involved in war abuses in some areas, and paid special attention to women's narratives, especially war widows, giving them space in the most publicized public hearings, it may have undermined the masculine narrative of the war, and changed the patterns that were in place before its inception (see Yezer 2007).

13. During the late 1980s, Juan Luis Cipriani was the Ayacucho archbishop. Now a cardinal, Cipriani's opposition to Peru's human rights movement has been well documented: he famously referred to human rights defenders as "thinly veiled political movements that are almost always Marxist and Maoist" (Comisión de la Verdad y Reconciliación 2003: 399–416).

14. During Peru's state of emergency, human rights and non-governmental aid organizations could be charged with the ambiguous *apologia al terrorismo* law, which criminalized supporting, praising, or "apologizing for" rebel groups. Jo-Marie Burt (2006) reports that fear of being labeled a terrorist subdued much of civil society until 2000, and anthropologist Maria Elena Garcia found that Cusco-based activists limited themselves to nonpolitical projects for fear of state retaliation in 1996 (Garcia 2005: 37). The law was repealed in 2000 after the fall of President Alberto Fujiimori; however, it has been reinstated as this publication goes to press.

15. In Wiracocha these institutions included a variety of state and transnational institutions as well as domestic projects that received funding from abroad. These ranged from the state Repopulation of the Emergency Zone Program (Programa de Apoyo al Repoblamiento de Zonas de Emergencia, PAR), the transnational child sponsorship-based Vision Mundial (World Vision), and the Peruvian Truth and Reconciliation Commission, whose funding was from the Ford and Soros Foundations.

16. With the exception of short periods of planting and harvesting, married wom-

en's duties included child care, laundry, and cooking, all close to home and the village plaza, while herding was often left to children or widows.

17. These *jueces de paz* form a network of local justices in official peasant communities. They have the power to punish misdemeanors and resolve local disputes, including discretionary control over what is passed on to higher magistrates. Deborah Poole (2004) has analyzed changes in the relationship between *jueces de paz* and state power in Ayacucho communities before and after the war.

18. Although notoriously difficult to survey, studies rank Peru as having one of the highest incidences of domestic abuse (Movimiento 2003), cited in (Boesten 2006)

19. Jelke Boesten shows that this belief in keeping the family together at all costs is widespread in Peru, where it often undermines new laws abolishing wife beating (Boesten 2006: 357). See also Cecilia Blondet's critique of Fujimori's superficial domestic abuse policies, which, she notes, were more about creating a stable, democratic image to international lenders (after the president's strong-arm martial law tactics in the war zone) than any real concern or intention to curb domestic violence (Blondet 2002).

20. These data reflect my conversations with women who were willing to talk about domestic violence, which tended to be women who were not in an abusive relationship, or who had been in one but had left (usually women who had left were married to men in other villages and had come back to their childhood home). Only one woman I spoke with testified that she was at that time in an abusive relationship, with a cousin. These conclusions are thus limited by the fact that women in abusive situations were not likely to talk about these topics or participate in open discussions if they were already trying to hide the abuse to avoid social stigmatization.

21. Survey by the NGO IPAZ, Ayacucho. According to the survey the most common communal conflicts in highland villages are domestic, including physical abuse, abandonment, and adultery; after which come conflicts over inheritance of lands. Second and third to domestic conflicts were those between neighbors (over destroyed crops, for example), and intercommunal (over territory, borders, cattle rustling) (Coronel 2000).

22. In one case the defendant was a woman; in the other a man.

Chapter 7. "These Are Not Our Priorities": Maasai Women, Human Rights, and the Problem of Culture

This chapter is based on more than 25 years of ethnohistorical research on the cultural politics of development among Maasai, including a year (2005–6) of intensive field work with several Maasai NGOs. Research and writing have been supported by the John Simon Guggenheim Foundation, American Council of Learned Societies, Fulbright-Hays, National Endowment for the Humanities, Center for Advanced Study in the Behavioral Sciences, and Rutgers University Competitive Fellowship Leave Program. For a discussion of some of the ethical and political dilemmas entailed in this research, see Hodgson (1999).

1. As anyone familiar with the scholarly and activist debates over female genital modification knows, there is a politics to the very naming of the practice. Following

Kratz (2007), I choose to use the politically neutral term "modification" instead of "mutilation" or "cutting." As a scholar seeking to understand how and why the practice occurs, its role within the social and ritual lives of men and women, and the meaning of the practice to all involved, I believe that the term "modification" enables understanding rather than immediate condemnation. Moreover, the phrase "female genital modification" complicates the too easy north-south divide by including consideration of such increasingly common cosmetic surgical procedures in the global north as labiaplasty (reduction of "large" labias), vaginoplasty ("tightening" and "rejuvenating" of vaginas), and clitoral unhooding. For more information on these procedures, see, for example, www.labiaplastysurgeon.com, accessed September 22, 2008.

2. The titles of recent headlines include "Communities Urged to Shun FGM," "Dangers of FGM in Childbirth," "The Crime That Is FGM," "Anti-FGM Rally to Mark Zero Tolerance Day," "How Secure Are Tanzanian girls from FGM today?"

3. The most recent victory is the Protocol to the African Charter on Human and Peoples' Rights on the Rights of Women, which was approved in July 2003, ratified by the minimum of 15 countries by October 2005, and came into force in November 2005. The Protocol details the many rights of women, including "elimination of harmful practices" such as "female genital mutilation" (Art. 5).

4. The First African Indigenous Women's Conference was held in 1998 in Agadir, Morocco, with the support of the Netherlands Centre for Indigenous Peoples (NCIV) and Tamaynut, an organization for indigenous people in Morocco, after two years of consultations with African indigenous organizations through visits, meetings and letters (Mulenkei 1999a: 42; Van Achterberg 1998: 11). Of the original 43 indigenous women invited from North, South, East, and West Africa, 36 were able to participate, representing over 13 African countries (IWGIA 1998: 319; Mulenkei 1999a: 42).

5. The 1995 Beijing Declaration was discussed, written, approved, and signed by 110 indigenous women from 26 countries in the "Indigenous Women's tent" at the NGO Forum that accompanied the UN Decade Conference for Women in Beijing. The Declaration condemned the "New World Order" of transnational corporations and multilateral financial institutions, criticized the Beijing Platform for Action for ignoring how the New World Order was intensifying poverty, challenged the failure of the Platform to question the basic Western orientation of prevailing education and health systems, and called for all governments and other institutions to recognize and respect the rights of indigenous peoples to self-determination, rights to their territories; rights to development, education, and health; rights to intellectual and cultural heritage; rights to control biodiversity and prevent bioprospecting in their territories; cessation of human rights violations and violence against women; increased political participation of indigenous women; and strengthening of their organizational capabilities and access to resources (Beijing Declaration). None of these women were African (IWGIA 1998: 319). According to IWGIA (320), no African representatives are listed as attending two previous international indigenous women's conferences held in 1988 in Adelaide, Australia, and 1990 in Karasjohka, Norway.

6. This description is drawn from Hodgson (2001a: 234–35).

7. At the 1995 UN Working Group, the ratio of women to men in the African delegations was 3 to 30 (IWGIA 1998: 319).

8. For example, at the 2004 annual meeting of the UN Working Group, I was asked to help translate in a meeting between the co-president of AIWO, a woman from Congo who spoke only French and Swahili (in addition to her primary language), and a representative from NCIV (still the primary funder of AIWO) who spoke English, but not French or Swahili.

9. In the brochure, "cultural citizenship" is described as follows: "The program presents overwhelming evidence, carefully documented and organized events of Maasai culture, and shows its potential validity and usefulness; example that of indigenous knowledge and its utility to human development. Likewise, the 'Arts' that is going beyond the Opera house or gallery. It is meant to encourage cultural mapping in development and provision of opportunities without hindering the good traditions and people of their culture."

10. For detailed historical and ethnographic analysis of these processes, see Hodgson (2001a, 2005).

11. The previous two paragraphs are drawn from Sikar and Hodgson (2006: 31–32).

12. Since disaggregated data is notoriously unreliable and difficult to obtain in Tanzania, I have drawn from those statistics that were available at the time.

13. From "At a Glance: Tanzania, United Republic of," UNICEF table of statistics, http://www.unicef.org/infobycountry/Tanzania_statistics.html, accessed January 19, 2006.

14. Although the potential of such micro-lending, petty trade, and small business projects to produce long-term structural improvements in women's economic security and autonomy is much debated by scholars, development practitioners, and even some Maasai women, most rural Maasai women have eagerly embraced these initiatives as at least short-term remedies to their increasingly dire situations. Moreover, MWEDO, like a number of organizations, has tried to counter the implicitly neoliberal "by-your-bootstraps" assumptions of these projects by requiring women to form groups to borrow, trade, and work, rather than receive loans and goods as individuals.

15. Pre-Form I training is a year of intensive remedial instruction in English, Swahili, math, and other subjects to prepare for the secondary school placement exams that determine which students can attend the much less expensive government secondary schools.

16. Among Western feminists, of course, polygyny is also damned, but such debates have little public space in a country like Tanzania where Muslims constitute over a third of the population.

17. The Pastoralist Women's Council (PWC) was founded in 1997 "to promote sound cultural, political, environment and education development of pastoralist women and children to facilitate their access to essential social services and economic empowerment." It works in the Loliondo area of northern Tanzania providing awareness-raising workshops on critical political, policy and rights issues and small loans for income-generating project through a network of over 25 community-based "women's action

groups." In addition, it also supports the education of pastoralist girls and established the "Women's Solidarity Boma" to house and support poor and abandoned women through a revolving livestock project.

18. For an overview of current TAMWA programs, see its website: www.tamwa.org.

19. Similar dynamics seem to be happening in Kenya, according to Olekina (2005), Kipuri (2004), and other sources.

20. Mary Simat comments on behalf of Indigenous Peoples' of Africa Coordinating Committee, May 11, 2004 (author's notes).

Chapter 8. The Rights to Speak and to be Heard: Women's Interpretations of Rights Discourses in the Oaxaca Social Movement

The research for this chapter was conducted in the city of Oaxaca during July and August 2006 and 2007 and August 2008. The research was funded in part by a grant from the Center for the Study of Women in Society to the Americas Research Interest Group, of which I am a part. Other summer research was funded by the Center for the Study of Women in Society at the University of Oregon through research funds granted to me as an Associate Director during 2007–8. This chapter is based on a series of in-depth interviews and personal histories with more than 40 people active in the Oaxaca movement as well as more than 15 others who were observers. Some are public activists who explicitly want their real names used. Others want to protect their identities and have requested pseudonyms. Pseudonyms are used everywhere unless noted.

1. That number is higher if the criteria used to designate indigeneity include self-identification.

2. According to the collective and data from the Instituto Nacional de Estadística y Geografía (Natonal Institute for Statistics and Geography, INEGI 2006) crimes against girls and women between 1999 and 2003 include 351 homicides of girls and women in the state of Oaxaca. The local press reported 267 homicides between 1999 and 2005 and the Procurator-General of Justices Office reported 52 assassinations between January 2004 and June 2005. This information was repeated in a formal denunciation governor Ulíses Ruiz Ortiz sent to the Mexican Congress in July 2006 (Davies 2006).

3. I interviewed Alfredo Chui Velásquez in July 2006 and Rogelio Vargas Garfias in August 2008.

4. She was interviewed August 1, 2007, one year after the occupation of the station.

5. Statement by Patricia Jiménez, August 1, 2007, at a conference commemorating the first anniversary of the takeover of the station. I recorded the conference speeches.

6. Ruth Guzmán was interviewed in July 2007.

7. This interview took place on August 5, 2006, inside the occupied station.

Chapter 9. Muslim Women, Rights Discourse, and the Media in Kenya

I am grateful to my colleagues at the Rutgers Institute for Research on Women, especially to Dorothy Hodgson and Catherine Sameh and the participants at the symposium on The Culture of Rights/The Rights of Culture, who provided me with constructive feedback for earlier versions of this paper. I also would like to thank the anonymous reviewer for her helpful feedback. The research for this study was supported by the Ford Foundation Award for Women's Rights and Social Justice

1. Kenya has a tripartite system of law: the Common Law inherited from the British colonial system; Shari'a, administrated by the court of Kadhis (Muslim jurists) and whose scope is limited to personal law; and Customary Law, designed to be sensitive to ethnocultural differences, again in limited matters of personal laws like marriage, inheritance, and divorce.

2. Rajupt (2004–5).

3. Deniz Kandiyoti (1988, 1997) discussed the strategies that Muslim women used to negotiate with (Islamist) patriarchy. Brink (1991) calls co-optation the ways in which Egyptian women endear themselves to their mothers-in-law in order to reduce the authority of their husband.

4. Salafism is a brand of ultra-conservative Islam relying on Tawhid, the uniqueness of one God, the Qur'an, and the Hadith. The new salafists call for the return to Islam as lived during the time of the Prophet Muhammad.

5. See more information on the Sexual Offense Bill currently passed as Sexual Offences Act, Kenya Police website, http://www.kenyapolice.go.ke/resources/Sexual_Offences_Act_No_3_of_2006.

Chapter 10. Fighting for Fatherhood and Family: Immigrant Detainees' Struggles for Rights

This chapter is based on an issue I have been long involved in politically, but which I have only recently been able to work through in a scholarly way through the amazing intellectual community that is the Institute of Research on Women (IRW) at Rutgers University. My thinking has benefited tremendously from the insights of my colleagues who participated in the IRW 2008–9 The Culture of Rights/The Rights of Culture Seminar. Special thanks are due to Dorothy Hodgson for giving me the opportunity to share my work at The Culture of Rights/The Rights of Culture Symposium, where I had the wonderful privilege of engaging with feminist scholars who have been a source of inspiration for me. In the end, however, this chapter would not be possible without the tireless work of key members of the New Jersey Civil Rights Defense Committee, especially Flavia Alaya, Jeanette Gabriel, Marion Munk and Nicky Newby. Their commitment and courage in standing up and speaking out for the "voiceless" is extraordinary. I only hope that I have done justice to their work in this chapter.

1. I realize that post-9/11 immigration-related legislation has restricted the entry of prospective immigrants and other noncitizens seeking temporary residence in the United States (students, tourists, etc.) through more stringent standards in visa issuance policies and the increased militarization of U.S. borders. My aim, however, is to focus exclusively on how immigration legislation after 9/11 is affecting immigrants already settled and living in the United States.

2. This was the source of discussion at the Forced Migration and Human Rights in San Diego: What the Public Needs to Know Conference held on February 15, 2005, at the Center for Comparative Immigration Studies, University of California, San Diego.

3. For a discussion of the production of "illegality" see De Genova (2000).

4. Human Rights Watch describes how not only was the ICE uncooperative about supplying information on deportations, but ICE keeps inaccurate data on deportations, especially deportation of immigrants with legal permanent residence status in the United States.

Chapter 11. Defending Women, Defending Rights: Transnational Organizing in a Culture of Human Rights

1. As of October 30, 2010, the members of the WHRD IC are Amnesty International (AI); Asia Pacific Forum on Women, Law and Development (APWLD); Coalition of African Lesbians (CAL); Asian Forum for Human Rights and Development (Forum Asia); Association for Women's Rights in Development (AWID); Baobab for Women's Human Rights; Center for Women's Global Leadership (CWGL); Center for Reproductive Rights; Front Line International Foundation for the Protection of Human Rights Defenders (Front Line); Human Rights First; Information Monitor (Inform); International Federation of Human Rights (FIDH); International Service for Human Rights (ISHR); Isis International; ISIS-Women's International Cross-Cultural Exchange (ISIS-WICCE); Latin American and Caribbean Committee for the Defense of Women's Rights (CLADEM); International Women's Rights Organization (MADRE); Peace Brigades International (PBI); Urgent Action Fund for Women's Rights (UAF); Women's Human Rights Action Watch Asia Pacific (IWRAW AP); Women's Initiative for Gender Justice (WIGJ); Women Living Under Muslim Laws (WLUML); and World Organization Ogainst Torture (Organisation Mondiale contre la Torture, OMCT).

2. http://www.defendingwomen-defendingrights.org/fiji_end_harassment.php. Members of the WHRD IC joined a team of observers for Imrana's trial, which took place on July 19, 2010. The High Court in Suva, Fiji "permanently stayed" all the seven charges against Imrana Jalal while one City Council charge against her husband Ratu Sakiusa Tuisolia for "giving false information to a public officer" is still pending in court..

3. http://www.defendingwomen-defendingrights.org/president_mahmoud.php. In spite of the letter and petitions sent to the Iranian authorities, Eghdamdoost remains at the Evin Prison serving her three-year sentence. She was sent to solitary confinement for a week in March 2010 after she recited the events of March 8 (International Women's Day) in the women's ward and was charged with "reciting an article and speech among the women and creating incitement about women's activities, negative propaganda against the regime, insulting the President and the Supreme Leader, and spreading the propaganda of socialism."

4. http://www.defendingwomen-defendingrights.org/nepal_whrd_murdered.php. Laxmi's husband was arrested, but released on bail as the case is being heard in court. Following a 24-day hunger strike and protest on the one-year anniversary of Laxmi's

death on June 7, 2009, a High Level Task Force was formed at the Office of the Prime Minister in Nepal to develop the terms of reference for the formation of a High Level Commission that deals with all forms of violence against women.

5. http://www.defendingwomen-defendingrights.org/members_of_women_human _right.php. Intense international criticism of the anti-homosexuality bill caused Ugandan President Yoweri Museveni to form a commission to investigate the implications of passing the bill. In May 2010, the committee recommended withdrawing it so it has not been debated in the Parliament.

Bibliography

Abaza, Mona. 2006. *Changing Consumer Cultures of Modern Egypt: Cairo's Urban Reshaping*. Leiden: Brill.

'Abd al-Salam, Siham. 2005. *Al-munazzamat al-ahliyya al-saghira al-'amila fi majal al-mar'a* (Small Civil Society Organizations Working on Women's Issues). Cairo: Dar al-'ayn lil-nashr, nur-jam'iyyat al-mar'a al-'arabiyya.

Abdelrahman, Maha. 2004. *Civil Society Exposed: The Politics of NGOs in Egypt*. London: Tauris Academic.

———. 2007. "The Nationalisation of the Human Rights Debate in Egypt." *Nations and Nationalism* 13 (2): 285–300.

Abrams, Kathryn. 1999. "From Autonomy to Agency: Feminist Perspectives on Self-Direction." *William and Mary Law Review* 40: 805–46.

Abu-Lughod, Lila, ed. 1998. *Remaking Women: Feminism and Modernity in the Middle East*. Princeton, N.J.: Princeton University Press.

———. 2002. "Do Muslim Women Really Need Saving? Anthropological Reflections on Cultural Relativism and Its Others." *American Anthropologist* 104 (3): 783–90.

———. 2005. *Dramas of Nationhood: The Politics of Television in Egypt*. Chicago: University of Chicago Press.

———. 2009a. "Anthropology in the Territory of Rights, Human and Otherwise." Radcliffe-Brown Lecture, British Academy, November 17.

———. 2009b. "Dialects of Women's Empowerment: The International Circuitry of the *Arab Human Development Report 2005*." *International Journal of Middle East Studies* 41 (1): 83–103.

———. n.d. "Seductions of the Honor Crime." *Differences: A Journal of Feminist Cultural Studies*. In press.

Abu-Lughod, Lila, Fida J. Adely, and Frances S. Hasso. 2009. "Overview: Engaging the *Arab Human Development Report 2005* on Women." *International Journal of Middle East Studies* 42 (1): 59–60.

Abusharaf, M. Rogaia. 2001a. "Revisiting Feminist Discourses on Infibulation: Responses from Sudanese Feminists." In Bettina Shell-Duncan and Ylva Hernlund, eds., *Female "Circumcision" in Africa: Culture, Controversy and Change*. Boulder, Colo.: Lynne Rienner.

———. 2001b. "Virtuous Cuts: Female Genital Circumcision in an African Ontology." *Differences: A Journal of Feminist Cultural Studies* 12 (1): 112–40.

———, ed. 2006. *Female Circumcision: Multicultural Perspectives*. Philadelphia: University of Pennsylvania Press.

Ackerly, Brooke A. 2008. *Universal Human Rights in a World of Difference*. Cambridge: Cambridge University Press.

Adely, Fida. 2009. "Educating Women for Development: The *Arab Human Development Report 2005* and the Problem with Women's Choices." *International Journal of Middle East Studies* 41 (1): 105–22.

Agosín, Marjorie, ed. 2001. *Women, Gender and Human Rights: A Global Perspective*. New Brunswick, N.J.: Rutgers University Press.

Aguilar Orihuela, Alonso. 2006. *El recuento de los daños*. Oaxaca: Tiempo Nublado. *PRO-OAX* 17: 3–29.

Ahmad, Dohra. 2009. "Not Yet Beyond the Veil: Muslim Women in American Popular Literature." *Social Text* 27 (2/99): 105–31.

Ahmad, Muneer. 2002. "Homeland Insecurity: Racial Violence the Day After September 11." *Social Text* 20 (3): 101–15.

Ahmadu, Fuambai. 2000. "Rites and Wrongs: An Insider/Outsider Reflects on Power and Excision." In Bettina Shell-Duncan and Ylva Hernlund, eds., *Female "Circumcision" in Africa: Culture, Controversy, and Change*. Boulder, Colo.: Lynne Rienner.

Ahmed, Leila. 1992. *Women and Gender in Islam: Historical Roots of a Modern Debate*. New Haven, Conn.: Yale University Press.

Aina, Olabisi. 1998. "African Women at the Grassroots: The Silent Partners of the Women's Movement." In Obioma Nnaemeka, ed., *Sisterhood: Feminisms, and Power: From Africa to the Diaspora*. Trenton, N.J.: Africa World Press.

Al-Ali, Nadje. 2000. *Secularism, Gender and the State in the Middle East: The Egyptian Women's Movement*. Cambridge: Cambridge University Press.

Al-Ismaily, Issa bin Nasser. 1999. *Zanzibar Kinyang'anyiro na Utumwa* (Slavery and the Struggle for Zanzibar). Dubai: United Arab Emirates.

Al-Mahdi, Rabab. n.d. "A Women's Movement in Egypt? Feminism, Post-Colonial, Feminism in Practice." Manuscript

Aley, Juma. 1994. *Enduring Links*. Zanzibar: Zanzibar Series.

Ali, Seham. 2008. Interview with author, Cairo, April 2.

Alidou, Ousseina D. 2005. *Engaging Modernity: Muslim Women and the Politics of Agency in Postcolonial Niger*. Madison: University of Wisconsin Press.

Allard, Sharon Angella. 1996. "Rethinking Battered Women's Syndrome: A Black Feminist Perspective." *UCLA Women's Law Journal* 1: 191–207.

Allen, Catherine. 2002. *The Hold Life Has: Coca and Cultural Identity in an Andean Community*. Washington, D.C.: Smithsonian Institution Press.

Allen, Lori. 2009. "Martyr Bodies in the Media: Human Rights, Aesthetics, and the Politics of Immediation in the Palestinian Intifada." *American Ethnologist* 36 (1): 161–80.

Alloo, Fatma. 1999. "Information Technology and Cyberculture: The Case of Zanzibar." In Wendy Harcourt, ed., *Women@Internet: Creating New Cultures in Cyberspace*. London: Zed Books.

Amadiume, Ifi. 1987. *Male Daughters, Female Husbands: Gender and Sex in African Society*. London: Zed Books.

Amin, Qasim. 1992. *The Liberation of Women*. Trans. Samiha Sidhom Peterson. Cairo: American University in Cairo Press.

Ammons, Linda L. 1995. "Mules, Madonnas, Babies, Bathwater: Racial Imagery, and Stereotypes: The African-American Woman and the Battered Woman Syndrome." *Wisconsin Law Review* 1995: 1003–80.

Amnesty International (AI). 2008. "Jailed Without Justice: Immigrant Detention in the USA." http://www.amnestyusa.org/immigrants/, accessed 21 December 2009.

——. 2009. "Israeli Army Used Flechettes Against Civilians," 27 January. http://www .amnesty.org/en/news-and-updates/news/israeli-army-used-flechettes-against-gaza-civilians-20090127, accessed 19 September 2009.

Amnesty International Mexico. 2006. "Mexico: Laws Without Justice." http://www.am nestyusa.org/document.php?lang=e&id=ENGAMR410152007, accessed August 12, 2009.

Andrews, Penelope. 2007. "Learning to Love After Learning to Harm: Post-Conflict Reconstruction, Gender Equality and Cultural Values." *Michigan State Journal of International Law* 15: 41–62.

Appadurai, Arjun, ed. 1986. *The Social Life of Things: Commodities in Cultural Perspective*. Cambridge: Cambridge University Press.

Archambeault, Teresa Sicard, and Jason Laughlin. 2006. "Camden Family in Alien Muddle." *Courier Post*, March 29.

Ardito Vega, Wilfredo. 2004. "Por que cada vez hay menos ciudadanos peruanos?" *Ideelemail* 365 (June 26).

Arendt, Hannah. 1968 [1951]. *The Origins of Totalitarianism*. New York: Harcourt, Brace.

Arizona Coalition Against Domestic Violence. 2003. *Battered Mothers' Testimony Project: A Human Rights Approach to Child Custody and Domestic Violence*. Phoenix: Arizona Coalition Against Domestic Violence.

Asia Pacific Forum on Women, Law and Development (APWLD). 2006. *Claiming Justice, Claiming Rights: A Guidebook on Women Human Rights Defenders*. Chaingmai: APWLD.

Aweidah, Sama. 2004. "A Glimpse into the Women's Stories." In Khawla Abu-Baker, ed., *Women, Armed Conflict and Loss: The Mental Health of Palestinian Women in the Occupied Territories*. Jerusalem: Women's Studies Centre

Bacchetta, Paola. 2002. "Rescaling Transnational 'Queerdom': Lesbian and 'Lesbian' Identitary-Positionalities in Delhi in the 1980s." *Antipode* 34 (5): 937–73.

Bader, Zinnat. 1985. "The Social Conditions and Consequences of the 1964 Revolution on Land Reforms in Zanzibar." Ph.D. dissertation, Birbeck College, University of London.

Badran, Margot. 1995. *Feminists, Islam, and Nation: Gender and the Making of Modern Egypt*. Princeton, N.J.: Princeton University Press.

Bahramitash, Roksana. 2005. "The War on Terror, Feminist Orientalism, and Orientalist Feminism: Case Studies of Two North American Bestsellers." *Critique: Critical Middle Eastern Studies* 14 (2): 221–35.

Ballou, Mary, Charity Tabol, Dorcas Liriano, Kim Vasquez-Nuttall, Christine Butler, Beverly W. Boorstein, and Sheila McGovern. 2007. "Initial Development of a Psychological Model for Judicial Decision Making in Continuing Restraining Orders." *Family Court Review* 45 (2): 274–86.

Baron, Beth. 2005. *Egypt as a Woman: Nationalism, Gender, and Politics.* Berkeley: University of California Press.

Bartlett, Katharine T. 1990. "Feminist Legal Methods." *Harvard Law Review* 103: 829–88.

Bartlett, Katharine T., and Deborah L. Rhode. 2006. *Gender and Law.* 4th ed. New York: Aspen.

Basu, Amrita, with C. Elizabeth McGrory. 1995. *The Challenge of Local Feminisms: Women's Movements in Global Perspective.* Boulder, Colo.: Westview Press.

———. 2000. "Globalization of the Local/Localization of the Global: Mapping Transnational Women's Movements." *Meridians* 1 (1): 68–84.

Baxi, Upendra. 2006. *The Future of Human Rights.* 2nd ed. New Delhi: Oxford University Press.

———. 2007. *Human Rights in a Posthuman World: Critical Essays.* Oxford University Press.

Benedek, Wolfgang, Esther M. Kisaayake, and Gerd Oberleitner, eds. 2002. *Human Rights of Women: International Instruments and African Experiences.* London: Zed Books.

Beoku-Betts, Josephine. 2005. "Western Perceptions of African Women in the 19th and Early 20th Centuries." In Andrea Cornwall, ed., *Readings in Gender in Africa.* Bloomington: Indiana University Press.

Bettinger-López, Caroline. 2008. "*Jessica Gonzales v. United States*: An Emerging Model for Domestic Violence and Human Rights Advocacy in the United States." *Harvard Human Rights Journal* 21: 183–95.

Bibars, Iman. 2001. *Victims and Heroines: Women, Welfare and the Egyptian State.* London: Zed Press.

Bledsoe, Caroline H. 1980. *Women and Marriage in Kpelle Society.* Stanford, Calif.: Stanford University Press.

———. 1984. "The Political Use of Sande Ideology and Symbolism." *American Ethnologist* 11 (3): 455–72.

Blondet, Cecilia. 1991. *Mujeres y el poder: una historia de Villa El Salvador.* Lima: Instituto de Estúdios Peruanos.

———. 1995. *Hoy, menú popular: comedores en Lima.* Lima: Instituto de Estúdios Peruanos and UNICEF.

———. 2002. *El encanto del dictador.* Lima: Instituto de Estúdios Peruanos.

Boddy, Janice. 1982. "Womb as Oasis: The Symbolic Context of Pharaonic Circumcision in Rural Northern Sudan." *American Ethnologist* 9: 682–98.

———. 2007. *Civilizing Women: British Crusaders in Colonial Sudan.* Princeton, N.J.: Princeton University Press.

Boesten, Jelke. 2006. "Pushing Back the Boundaries: Social Policy, Domestic Violence and Women's Organisations in Peru." *Journal of Latin American Studies* 38: 355–78.

Booth, Marilyn. 2001. *May Her Likes Be Multiplied: Biography and Gender Politics in Egypt.* Berkeley: University of California Press.

Bowker, Lee H. 1983. *Beating Wife-Beating.* Lexington, Mass.: D.C. Heath.

———. 1986. *Ending the Violence.* Holmes Beach, Fl.: Learning Publications.

Boyle, Elizabeth Hegel. 2002. *Female Genital Cutting: Cultural Conflict in the Global Community.* Baltimore: Johns Hopkins University Press.

Bozzoli, Belinda. 1991. *Women of Phokeng: Consciousness, Life Strategy and Migrancy in South Africa, 1900–1983.* Portsmouth: Heinemann.

Brink, Judy H. 1991. "The Effect of Immigration of Husbands on the Status of their Wives: An Egyptian Case." *International Journal of Middle Eastern Studies* 1 (23): 201–11.

Brodkin, Karen. 1988. *Caring by the Hour: Women, Work, and Organizing at Duke Medical Center.* Urbana: University of Illinois Press.

Brown, Christopher. 2006. *Moral Capital: Foundations of British Abolitionism.* Chapel Hill: University of North Carolina Press.

Brown, Wendy. 1995. "Rights and Losses." In Brown, *States of Injury: Power and Freedom in Late Modernity.* Princeton, N.J.: Princeton University Press.

Brysk, Alison. 2000. *From Tribal Village to Global Village: Indian Rights and International Relations in Latin America.* Stanford, Calif.: Stanford University Press.

Bunch, Charlotte. 1990. "Women's Rights as Human Rights: Toward a Re-Vision of Human Rights." *Human Rights Quarterly* 12: 486–98.

———. 1995. "Transforming Human Rights from a Feminist Perspective." In Julie Peters and Andrea Wolper, eds., *Women's Rights, Human Rights: International Feminist Perspectives.* New York: Routledge.

Bunch, Charlotte and Frost Samatha. 2000. "Women's Human Rights: An Introduction." In Cheris Kramarae and Dale Spender, eds. *Routledge International Encyclopedia of Women: Global Women's Issues and Knowledge.* New York: Routledge.

Burrill, Emily and Richard Roberts. 2010. "Domestic Violence and the End of Slavery in the French Soudan, 1905–1912." In Emily Burrill, Richard Roberts, and Elizabeth Thornberry, eds., *Domestic Violence and the Law in Africa.* Athens: Ohio University Press.

Burt, Jo-Marie. 2006. "'Quien Habla es Terrorista' The Political Use of Fear in Fujimori's Peru." *Latin American Research Review* 41 (3): 32–62.

Bush, Barbara. 1990. *Slave Women in Caribbean Society.* Bloomington: Indiana University Press.

Cainkar, Louise. 2004. "Post 9/11 Domestic Policies Affecting U.S. Arabs and Muslims: A Brief Review." *Comparative Studies of South Asia, Africa and the Middle East* 24 (1): 245–48.

Calavita, Kitty. 1996. "The New Politics of Immigration: 'Balanced Budget Conservatism' and the Symbolism of Proposition 187." *Social Problems* 43 (4): 284–305.

Campbell, Jacquelyn C., Paul Miller, Mary M. Cardwell, and Ruth Ann Belknap. 1994. "Relationship Status of Battered Women over Time." *Journal of Family Violence* 9: 99–111.

Carapico, Sheila. 2000. "NGOs, INGOs, GO-NGOs and DO-NGOs: Making Sense of Non-Governmental Organizations." *Middle East Report* 214 (Spring): 12–15.

Casey, Timothy, Soraya Fata, Leslye Orloff, and Maya Raghu. 2009. "TANF Reauthorization Round II: An Opportunity to Improve the Safety Net for Women and Children." *Domestic Violence Report* 14: 65–80.

Charlesworth, Hilary. 1994. "What Are 'Women's International Human Rights'?" In Rebecca J. Cook, ed., *Human Rights of Women: National and International Perspectives.* Philadelphia: University of Pennsylvania Press.

———. 1995. "Human Rights Are Men's Rights." In Julie Peters and Andrea Wolper, eds., *Women's Rights, Human Rights: International Feminist Perspectives.* New York: Routledge.

Chavez, Leo. 2008. *The Latino Threat: Constructing Immigrants, Citizens, and the Nation.* Stanford, Calif.: Stanford University Press.

Chih, Rachida. 2004. "The Khalwatiyya Brotherhood in Rural Upper Egypt and in Cairo." In Nicholas Hopkins and Reem Saad, eds., *Upper Egypt: Identity and Change.* Cairo: American University in Cairo Press.

Chowdhury, Elora Halim, Leila Farsakh, and Rajini Srikanth. 2008. "Introduction: Engaging Islam." Special issue, Chowhury, Halim, and Srikanth, eds., *International Feminist Journal of Politics* 10 (4): 439–54.

Christiansen, Eric C. 2007. "Adjudicating Non-Justiciable Rights: Socio-Economic Rights and the South African Constitutional Court." *Columbia Human Rights Law Review* 38: 321–86.

Clayton, Anthony. 1981. *The Zanzibar Revolution and Its Aftermath,* London: C. Hurst.

Cmiel, Kenneth. 2004. "The Recent History of Human Rights." *American Historical Review* 109 (10): 117–35.

Cock, Jacklyn. 1980. *Maids and Madams: A Study in the Politics of Exploitation.* Johannesburg: Ravan.

Coe, Cati. 2010. "Domestic Violence, Child Pawns, and Sexual Abuse in the Colonial Gold Coast, 1900–1928." In Emily Burrill, Richard Roberts, and Elizabeth Thornberry, eds., *Domestic Violence and the Law in Africa.* Athens: Ohio University Press.

Coker, Donna. 1999. "Enhancing Autonomy for Battered Women: Lessons from Navajo Peacemaking." *UCLA Law Review* 47: 1–111.

———. 2000. "Shifting Power for Battered Women: Law, Material Resources, and Poor Women of Color." *U.C. Davis Law Review* 33: 1009–55.

———. 2001. "Crime Control and Feminist Law Reform in Domestic Violence Law: A Critical Review." *Buffalo Criminal Law Review* 4: 801–60.

Columbia Law School Human Rights Institute, National Economic and Social Rights

Initiative, and Northeastern University School of Law. 2008. *Human Rights, Social Justice and State Law: A Manual for Creative Lawyering.* New York: Columbia Law School Human Rights Institute.

Comisión de la Verdad y Reconciliación. 2003. *Informe final.* Lima.

Comisión para Defensa de los Derechos Humanos de Oaxaca (CDDRO). 2008. "Que es la Comisión para Defensa de lo Derechos Humanos de Oaxaca?" http://www.cedhoax.org/home/cedho.html, accessed January 5, 2009.

Cook, Rebecca J., ed. 1994. *Human Rights of Women: National and International Perspectives.* Philadelphia: University of Pennsylvania Press.

Cook, Sam. 2008. "Advancing the Consensus." Presentation, Emory Human Rights Conference, Emory University, October 18.

cooke, miriam. 2007. "The Muslimwoman." *Contemporary Islam* 1: 139–54.

Coomaraswamy, Radhika. 2002. "Cultural Practices in the Family That Are Violent to Women." Report of the Special Rapporteur on Violence Against Women, Its Causes and Consequences, Ms. Radhika Coomaraswamy, submitted in accordance with Commission on Human Rights resolution 2001/49. New York: United Nations Economic and Social Council, E/CN.4/2002/83, www.unhchr.ch/Huridocda/Huridoca.nsf/0/.

Cooper, Barbara. 1997. *Marriage in Maradi: Gender and Culture in a Hausa Society in Niger, 1900–1989.* Portsmouth: Heinemann.

Cooper, Frederick. 1989. "From Free Labor to Family Allowances: Labor and African Society in Colonial Discourses." *American Ethnologist* 16 (4): 745–65.

Coordinadora Nacional de Derechos Humanos. 1997. "El problema de las 'levas' y maltratos durante el servicio militar obligatorio." Informe.

Copelon, Rhonda. 1994. "Intimate Terror: Understanding Domestic Violence as Torture." In Rebecca Cook, ed., *Human Rights of Women: National and International Perspectives.* Philadelphia: University of Pennsylvania Press.

Coral Cordero, Isabel. 1998. "Women in War: Impact and Responses." In Steve J. Stern, ed., *Shining and Other Paths: War and Society in Peru, 1980–1995.* Durham, N.C.: Duke University Press.

Cornelius, Wayne A. 2004. "Controlling Immigration and Fighting Terrorism: The Uncertain Connection." Paper at Migration and Terrorism: U.S. and European Perspectives, University of California at Davis.

———. 2005. "Controlling 'Unwanted' Immigration: Lessons from the United States, 1993–2004." *Journal of Ethnic and Migration Studies* 31 (4): 775–94.

Cornwall, Andrea and Maxine Molyneux, eds. 2008. *The Politics of Rights: Dilemmas for Feminist Praxis.* London: Routledge.

Coronel, José. 2000. "Núcleos Rurales de Administración de Justicia (NURAJ) sistematización de experiencias." Project Report. Ayacucho, Peru: IPAZ.

Coutin, Susan Bibler. 1998. "From Refugees to Immigrants: The Legalization Strategies of Salvadorean Immigrants and Activists." *International Migration Review* 32 (4): 901–25.

———. 2007. *Nations of Emigrants: Shifting Boundaries of Citizenship in El Salvador and the United States*. Ithaca, N.Y.: Cornell University Press.

Cowan, Jane K., Marie-Bénédicte Dembour, and Richard Wilson, eds. 2001. *Culture and Rights: Anthropological Perspectives*. Cambridge: Cambridge University Press.

Crenshaw, Kimberlé. 1991. "Mapping the Margins: Intersectionality, Identity Politics, and Violence Against Women of Color." *Stanford Law Review* 43: 1241–99.

Critical Filipino and Filipina Studies Collective. 2004. *Resisting Homeland Security: Organizing Against Unjust Removals of U.S. Filipinos*. San Jose, Calif.: Critical Filipino and Filipina Studies Collective.

Cuthbert, Carrie, Kim Slote, Monica Ghosh Driggers, Cynthia J. Mesh, Lundy Bancroft, and Jay Silverman. 2002. *Battered Mothers Speak Out: A Human Rights Report on Domestic Violence and Child Custody in the Massachusetts Family Courts*. Wellesley, Mass.: Wellesley Centers for Women.

Dalton, Margarita. 2007. Los organismos civiles en Oaxaca y el movimiento ciudadano: causas y consecuencias. *Cuadernos del Sur* 11 (24/25): 63–79.

Daly, Mary. 1978. "African Genital Mutilation: The Unspeakable Atrocities." In Daly, *Gyn/Ecology: The Metaethics of Radical Feminism*. Boston: Beacon Press.

Darby, Robert. 2005. *A Surgical Temptation: The Demonization of the Foreskin and the Rise of Circumcision in Britain*. Chicago: University of Chicago Press.

Dasgupta, Shamita Das, and Patricia Eng. 2003. *Safety and Justice for All*. New York: Ms. Foundation for Women.

Davies, Jill, Eleanor Lyon, and Diane Monti-Catania. 1998. *Safety Planning with Battered Women*. Thousand Oaks, Calif.: Sage.

Davies, Nancy. 2006. Denuncia formal de juicio político y revocación de mandato al Gobernador Constitucional del estado libre y soberano de Oaxaca, C. Ulisis Ernesto Ruiz Ortíz. July 22. http://narcosphere.narconews.com/node/186, accessed July 8, 2008.

Davis, David Brion. 1984. *Slavery and Human Progress*. New York: Oxford University Press.

———. 1999 [1975]. *The Problem of Slavery in the Age of Revolution, 1770–1823*. New York: Oxford University Press.

Deane, David J. 1880. *Robert Moffat: The Missionary Hero of Kuruman*. New York: Revell.

De Genova, Nicholas P. 2002. "Migrant 'Illegality' and Deportability in Everyday Life." *Annual Review of Anthropology* 31: 419–47.

Degregori, Carlos Iván. 1990. *Tiempos de ira y amor: nuevos actores para viejos problemas*. Lima: DESCO, Centro de Estudios y Promoción del Desarrollo.

Degregori, Carlos Iván, José Coronel, Ponciano Del Pino, and Orin Starn, eds. 1996. *Las rondas campesinas y la derrota de Sendero Luminoso*. Estudios de la Sociedad Rural 15. Lima: IEP.

Del Pino, Ponciano. 1991. "Los campesinos en la guerra: o de cómo la gente comienza a ponerse macho." In *Perú: el problema agrario en debate*. Lima: SEPIA, Seminario Permanente de Investigacion Agraria.

———. 1998. "Family, Culture, and 'Revolution': Everyday Life with Sendero Luminoso." In Steve J. Stern, ed., *Shining and Other Paths: War and Society in Peru: 1980–1995*. Durham, N.C.: Duke University Press.

———. 2008. "Looking to the Government: Community, Politics and the Production of Memory and Silences in Twentieth-Century Peru, Ayacucho." Ph.D. dissertation, University of Wisconsin, Madison.

Department of Homeland Security (DHS). 2009. Immigration Enforcement Actions: 2008. http://www.dhs.gov/files/statistics/immigration.shtm, accessed December 21.

Donahue, Brian. 2005. "Deportation Judges Faulted for Pattern of Misbehavior." *Newhouse News Service*, December 2.

———. 2006. "Kids of Illegal Immigrants Take Up Cause: Second-Generation Americans Give Voice to Parents Afraid to Speak Out." *Newark Star-Ledger*, April 16.

Dow, Mark. 2004. *American Gulag: Inside U.S. Immigration Prisons*. Berkeley: University of California Press.

DuFresne, Regina, and Jonathan S. Greene. 1995. "Increasing Remedies for Domestic Violence: A Study of Maryland's 1992 Domestic Violence Act in the Courtroom." *Maryland Journal of Contemporary Legal Issues* 6: 155–77.

Dugan, Laura. 2003. "Domestic Violence Legislation: Exploring Its Impact on the Likelihood of Domestic Violence, Police Involvement, and Arrest." *Criminology and Public Policy* 2: 283–312.

Dutton, Mary Ann. 1993. "Understanding Women's Responses to Domestic Violence: A Redefinition of Battered Women Syndrome." *Hofstra Law Review* 21: 1191–1242.

Egyptian Center for Women's Rights (ECWR). 2008. "Our Vision for the Future." June 7. http://ecwronline.org/index.php?option=com_content&task=view&id=188&Itemid=94, accessed September 21, 2009.

Eickelman, Dale, and Jon W. Anderson. 1999. "Redefining Muslim Publics." In Dale Eickelman and Jon W. Anderson, eds., *New Media in the Muslim World*. Bloomington: Indiana University Press.

El Guindi, Fadwa. 2005. "Confronting Hegemony, Resisting Occupation." In Faye V. Harrison, ed., *Resisting Racism and Xenophobia: Global Perspectives on Race, Gender and Human Rights*. Lanham, Md.: Alta Mira Press.

El-Kholy, Heba Aziz. 2002. *Defiance and Compliance: Negotiating Gender in Low-Income Cairo*. New York: Berghahn.

Elsadda, Hoda. 2001. *Significant Moments in Egyptian Women's History*. Trans. Hala Kamal. Cairo: National Council for Women.

Elyachar, Julia. 2007. *Markets of Dispossession: NGOs, Economic Development, and the State in Cairo*. Durham, N.C.: Duke University Press.

Encarta Encyclopedia MSN. 2009. Oaxaca. http://encarta.msn.com/encyclopedia_761589).html, accessed January 15.

Englund, Harri, 2006. *Human Rights and the African Poor*. Berkeley: University of California Press.

Enloe, Cynthia H. 1983. *Does Khaki Become You? The Militarization of Women's Lives.* Boston: South End Press.

Escobar, Arturo and Sonia E. Alvarez. 1992. *The Making of Social Movements in Latin America: Identity, Strategy, and Democracy.* Boulder, Colo.: Westview Press.

Esteva, Gustavo. 2007. "Oaxaca: The Path of Radical Democracy." *Socialism and Democracy* 21 (2): 74–96.

Fairooz, Amani Thani. 1995. *Ukweli ni Huu: Kuusuta Uongo.* (The Truth Is This: Challenging the Lie) Dubai: United Arab Emirates.

Farmer, Amy and Jill Tiefenthaler. 2003. "Explaining the Recent Decline in Domestic Violence." *Contemporary Economic Policy* 21 (2): 158–72.

Feder, Lynette, and David B. Wilson. 2005. "A Meta-Analytic Review of Court-Mandated Batterer Intervention Programs: Can Courts Affect Abusers' Behavior?" *Journal of Experimental Criminology* 1: 239–62.

Ferguson, Moira. 1992. *Subject to Others: British Women Writers and Colonial Slavery, 1670–1834.* New York: Routledge.

Fiore, Christine and Kristen O'Shea. 2007. "Women in Violent Relationships: Experiences with the Legal and Medical Systems." In Kathleen A. Kendall-Tackett and Sarah M. Giacomoni, eds., *Intimate Partner Violence.* Kingston, N.J.: Civic Research Institute.

Fischer, Karla and Mary Rose. 1995. "When 'Enough Is Enough': Battered Women's Decision Making Around Court Orders of Protection." *Crime and Delinquency* 41: 414–29.

Fisher, William. 2007. "Audit Finds Multiple Abuses in Immigration Jails." Inter Press Service News Agency, February 9.

Fraser, Arvonne. 1999. "Becoming Human: The Origins and Development of Women's Human Rights." *Human Rights Quarterly* 21: 853–906.

Friedman, Marilyn. 2003. *Autonomy, Gender, Politics.* Oxford: Oxford University Press.

Fujiwara, Lynn. 2008. *Mothers Without Citizenship.* Minneapolis: University of Minnesota Press.

Garcia, Maria Elena. 2005. *Making Indigenous Citizens: Identities, Development, and Multicultural Activism in Peru.* Stanford, Calif.: Stanford University Press.

Gardella, Adriana. 2007. "Domestic Violence Case Makes International Claim." www.womensenews.org, March 1, 2007.

Geertz, Clifford. 1983. "Local Knowledge: Fact and Law in Comparative Perspective." In Geertz, *Local Knowledge: Further Essays in Interpretive Anthropology.* New York: Basic Books.

Gibler, John. 2009. *Mexico Unconquered: Chronicles of Power and Revolt.* San Francisco: City Lights Books.

Gill, Lesley. 2000. *Teetering on the Rim: Global Restructuring, Daily Life, and the Armed Retreat of the Bolivian State.* New York: Columbia University Press.

———. 2004. *The School of the Americas: Military Training and Political Violence in the Americas.* Durham, NC: Duke University Press.

Glassman, Jonathon. 2000. "Sorting Out the Tribes: The Creation of Racial Identities in Colonial Zanzibar's Newspaper Wars." *Journal of African History* 41: 395–428.

Godoy, Angelina Snodgrass. 2006. *Popular Injustice: Violence, Community, and Law in Latin America*. Stanford, Calif.: Stanford University Press.

Goldfarb, Phyllis. 1996. "Describing Without Circumscribing: Questioning the Construction of Gender in the Discourse of Intimate Violence." *George Washington Law Review* 64: 582–631.

Goldfarb, Sally F. 2000a. "'No Civilized System of Justice': The Fate of the Violence Against Women Act." *West Virginia Law Review* 102: 499–546.

———. 2000b. "Violence Against Women and the Persistence of Privacy." *Ohio State Law Journal* 61: 1–87.

———. 2008. "Reconceiving Civil Protection Orders for Domestic Violence: Can Law Help End the Abuse Without Ending the Relationship?" *Cardozo Law Review* 29: 1487–1551.

Goldman, Ronald. 1997. *Circumcision: The Hidden Trauma*. New York: Vanguard.

Goldscheid, Julie. 2000. "*United States v. Morrison* and the Civil Rights Remedy of the Violence Against Women Act." *Cornell Law Review* 86: 109–39.

———. 2004. "Crime Victim Compensation in a Post-9/11 World." *Tulane Law Review* 79: 167–233.

———. 2005. "The Civil Rights Remedy of the 1994 Violence Against Women Act: Struck Down But Not Ruled Out." *Family Law Quarterly* 39: 157–80.

———. 2006. "Domestic and Sexual Violence as Sex Discrimination: Comparing American and International Approaches." *Thomas Jefferson Law Review* 28: 355–97.

———. 2007. "Elusive Equality in Domestic and Sexual Violence Law Reform." *Florida State Law Review* 34: 731–77.

Goldstein, Daniel M. 2004. *The Spectacular City: Violence and Performance in Urban Bolivia*. Durham, N.C.: Duke University Press.

Gollaher, David L. 1994. "From Ritual to Science: The Medical Transformation of Circumcision in America." *Journal of Social History* 28 (1): 5–36.

———. 2000. *Circumcision: A History of the World's Most Controversial Surgery*. New York: Basic Books.

Gondolf, Edward W. and Ellen R. Fisher. 1988. *Battered Women as Survivors: An Alternative to Treating Learned Helplessness*. Lexington, Mass.: D.C. Heath.

González-Cueva, Eduardo 2000. "Conscription and Violence in Peru." *Latin American Perspectives* 27 (112): 88–102.

Goodale, Mark. 2006. Introduction to "Anthropology and Human Rights in a New Key." *American Anthropologist* 108 (1): 1–8.

———. 2007. "The Power of Right(s): Tracking Empires of Law and New Modes of Social Resistance in Bolivia (and Elsewhere)." In Mark Goodale and Sally Engle Merry, eds., *The Practice of Human Rights: Tracking Law Between the Global and the Local*. Cambridge: Cambridge University Press.

Goodman, Lisa A. and Deborah Epstein. 2008. *Listening to Battered Women*. Washington, D.C.: American Psychological Association.

Goodmark, Leigh. 2005. "Telling Stories, Saving Lives: The Battered Mothers' Testimony Project, Women's Narratives, and Court Reform." *Arizona State Law Journal* 37: 709–57.

———. 2008. "When Is a Battered Woman Not a Battered Woman? When She Fights Back." *Yale Journal of Law and Feminism* 20: 75–129.

Gorriti, Gustavo. 1999. *The Shining Path: A History of the Millenarian War in Peru*. Trans. Robin Kirk. Chapel Hill: University of North Carolina Press.

Governor's Blue Ribbon Advisory Panel on Immigrant Policy. 2009. "Recommendations for a Comprehensive and Strategic Statewide Approach to Successfully Integrate the Rapidly Growing Immigrant Population in New Jersey." http://www.state.nj.us/publicadvocate/home/pdf/ipp_report_march.pdf.

Grewal, Inderpal. 1998. "On the New Global Feminism and the Family of Nations: Dilemmas of Transnational Feminist Practice." In Ella Shohat, ed., *Talking Visions: Multicultural Feminism in a Transnational Age*. New York: New Museum of Contemporary Art.

———. 2008. "Postcoloniality, Globalization, and Feminist Critique." Special Book Review Forum on Human Rights and Gender Violence. *American Anthropologist* 110: 517–20.

Gronlykke, Silole Mpoke. 1998. "The Role of Women in Maasai Culture." In Angeline Van Achterberg, ed., *Out of the Shadows: The First African Indigenous Women's Conference*. Amsterdam: Netherlands Centre for Indigenous Peoples.

Gupta, Akhil and James Ferguson. 2002. "Spatializing States: Toward an Ethnography of Neoliberal Govermentality." *American Ethnologist* 29 (4): 981–1002.

Haenni, Patrick. 2002. "Au-delà du repli identitaire . . . les nouveaux prêcheurs égyptiens et la modernisation paradoxale de l'islam." Religio-Scope, *Analyse*, November. http://www.cedej.org.eg, accessed September 30, 2005.

Hajjar, Lisa. 2001. *Domestic Violence and Shari'a: A Comparative Study of Muslim Societies in the Middle East, Africa and Asia*. In Lynn Welchman, ed., *Women's Rights and Islamic Family Law: Perspectives on Reform*. London: Zed Books.

Hale, Charles. 2006. *Mas que un indio (More Than an Indian): Racial Ambivalence and the Paradox of Neoliberal Multiculturalism in Guatemala*. Santa Fe, N.M.: School of American Research Press.

Halley, Janet. 2006. *Split Decisions: How and Why to Take a Break from Feminism*. Princeton, N.J.: Princeton University Press.

Halley, Janet, Prabha Kotiswaran, Hila Shamir, and Chantal Thomas. 2006. "From the International to the Local in Feminist Legal Responses to Rape, Prostitution/Sex Work, and Sex Trafficking: Four Studies in Contemporary Governance Feminism." *Harvard Journal of Law and Gender* 29: 335–22.

Hampton, Robert L., Ricardo Carrillo, and Joan Kim. 2005. "Domestic Violence in African American Communities." In Natalie J. Sokoloff and Christina Pratt, eds., *Domestic Violence at the Margins*. New Brunswick, N.J.: Rutgers University Press.

Hanafi, Sari, and Linda Tabar. 2005. *The Emergence of a Palestinian Globalized Elite: Donors, International Organizations and Local NGOs*. Jerusalem: Institute of Jerusalem Studies, and Ramallah: Muwatin, the Palestinian Institute for the Study of Democracy.

Handrahan, Lori. 2004. "Conflict, Gender, Ethnicity and Post-Conflict Reconstruction." *Security Dialogue* 35 (4): 429–45.

Hanna, Cheryl. 1996. "No Right to Choose: Mandated Victim Participation in Domestic Violence Prosecutions." *Harvard Law Review* 109: 1849–1910.

Hansen, Karen. 1992. *African Encounters with Domesticity*. New Brunswick, N.J.: Rutgers University Press.

Harvey, David. 2005. *A Brief History of Neoliberalism*. Oxford: Oxford University Press.

Harvey, Philip. 2004. "Aspirational Law." *Buffalo Law Review* 52: 701–26.

Hasso, Frances. 2009. "Empowering Governmentalities Rather Than Women: The *Arab Human Development Report 2005* and Western Development Logics." *International Journal of Middle East Studies* 41 (1): 63–82.

Hatem, Mervat F. 1992. "Economic and Political Liberation in Egypt and the Demise of State Feminism." *International Journal of Middle East Studies* 24 (2): 231–51.

———. 2006. "In the Eye of the Storm: Islamic Societies and Muslim Women in Globalization Discourses." *Comparative Studies of South Asia, Africa and the Middle East* 26 (1): 22–35.

Heilman, Jaymie. 2010. *Before the Shining Path: Politics in Rural Ayacucho, 1895–1980*. Stanford, Calif.: Stanford University Press.

Henry, Samantha. 2005. "Nowhere to Go." *North Jersey Herald News*, April 26, 2005.

———. 2006. "Controversy Surrounds Detainees." *North Jersey Herald News*, January 15, 2.

Herman, Judith Lewis. 2005. "Justice from the Victim's Perspective." *Violence Against Women* 11: 571–602.

Hernlund, Ylva and Bettina Shell-Duncan, eds. 2007. *Transcultural Bodies: Female Genital Cutting in Global Context*. New Brunswick, N.J.: Rutgers University Press.

Hesford, Wendy S. and Wendy Kozol, eds. 2005. *Just Advocacy? Women's Human Rights, Transnational Feminism, and the Politics of Representation*. New Brunswick, N.J.: Rutgers University Press.

Hider, James. 2009. "Names of Commanders to Be Kept Secret as Gaza Weapons Inquiry Begins." *TimesOnline*, January 22. www.timesonline.co.uk/tol/news/world/middle_east/article5563082.ece, accessed September 20.

Hine, Darlene Clark. 1989. "Rape and the Inner Lives of Black Women in the Middle West: Preliminary Thoughts on the Culture of Dissemblance." *Signs* 14: 912–20.

Hing, Bill Ong. 2006. *Deporting Our Souls: Values, Morality and Immigration Policy*. New York: Cambridge University Press.

Hirsch, Susan F. 1998. *Pronouncing and Persevering: Gender and the Discourses of Disputing in an African Islamic Court*. Chicago: University of Chicago Press.

Hodgson, Dorothy L. 1996. "'My Daughter . . . Belongs to the Government Now': Marriage, Maasai and the Tanzanian State." *Canadian Journal of African Studies/Revue Canadienne des Études Africaines* 30 (1): 106–23.

———. 1999. "Critical Interventions: Dilemmas of Accountability in Contemporary Ethnographic Research." *Identities: Global Studies in Culture and Power* 6 (2/3): 201–24.

———, ed. 2000. *Rethinking Pastoralism in Africa: Gender, Culture and the Myth of the Patriarchal Pastoralist.* Athens: Ohio University Press.

———. 2001a. *Once Intrepid Warriors: Gender, Ethnicity and the Cultural Politics of Maasai Development.* Bloomington: Indiana University Press.

———, ed. 2001b. *Gendered Modernities: Ethnographic Perspectives.* New York: Palgrave.

———. 2002a. "Women's Rights as Human Rights: Women in Law and Development in Africa." *Africa Today* 49 (2): 1–26.

———. 2002b. "Introduction: Comparative Perspectives on the Indigenous Rights Movement in Africa and the Americas." *American Anthropologist* 104(4): 1037–49.

———. 2002c. "Precarious Alliances: The Cultural Politics and Structural Predicaments of the Indigenous Rights Movement in Tanzania." *American Anthropologist* 104 (4):1086–97.

———. 2005. *The Church of Women: Gendered Encounters Between Maasai and Missionaries.* Bloomington: Indiana University Press.

———. 2008. "Cosmopolitics, Neoliberalism, and the State: The Indigenous Rights Movement in Africa." In Pnina Werbner, ed., *Anthropology and the New Cosmopolitanism: Rooted, Feminist and Vernacular Perspectives.* Oxford: Berg.

———. 2009. "Becoming Indigenous in Africa." *African Studies Review* 52 (3): 1–32.

———. 2011. *Being Maasai, Becoming Indigenous: Postcolonial Politics in a Neoliberal World.* Bloomington: Indiana University Press.

Hodgson, Dorothy L. and Ethel Brooks, eds. 2007. *Activisms.* Special issue of *Women's Studies Quarterly* 35 (3/4).

Hodgson, Dorothy L. and Sheryl McCurdy, eds. 2001. *"Wicked" Women and the Reconfiguration of Gender in Africa.* Social History of Africa Series. Portsmouth: Heinemann.

Hosken, Fran P. 1982. *The Hosken Report: Genital and Sexual Mutilation of Females.* Lexington, Mass.: Women's International Network News.

Human Rights Watch. 2006. *A Question of Security: Violence Against Palestinian Women and Girls.* http://www.hrw.org/en/reports/2006/11/06/question-security, accessed September 20, 2009.

———. 2009. *Forced Apart (By the Numbers).* http://www.hrw.org/en/reports/2009/04/15/forced-apart-numbers-0, accessed February 8, 2010.

Hunt, Lynn. 2007. *Inventing Human Rights: A History.* London: Norton.

Hunt, Nancy Rose. 2008. "An Acoustic Register, Tenacious Images, and Congolese Scenes of Rape and Repetition." *Cultural Anthropology* 23 (2): 220–53.

Ibhawoh, Bonny. 2007. "Restraining Universalism: Africanist Perspectives on Cultural Relativism in the Human Rights Discourse." In Rhonda L. Callaway and Julie Harreslon-Stephens, eds., *Exploring International Human Rights: Essential Readings.* Boulder, Colo.: Lynne Reinner.

Ignatieff, Michael. 1997. *The Warrior's Honor: Ethnic War and the Modern Conscience.* New York: Metropolitan

Incite-Critical Resistance and Julia Sudbury. 2005. "Gender Violence and the Prison Industrial Complex: Interpersonal and State Violence Against Women of Color." In Natalie J. Sokoloff and Christina Pratt, eds., *Domestic Violence at the Margins.* New Brunswick, N.J.: Rutgers University Press.

Ingrams, W. Harold. 2007 [1931]. *Zanzibar, Its History and Its People.* London: Stacey International.

Instituto Nacional de Estadística, Geografía e Informática (INEGI). 2006. *Estadísticas a propósito del día mundial de la población: datos de Oaxaca.* México, D.F.: Instituto Nacional de Estadística, Geografía e Informática. http://www.google.com/search?ie=UTF-8&oe=UTF-8&sourceid=navclient&gfns=1&q=poblacion+OAxaca+2006+INEGI, accessed January 26, 2009.

International Commission of Jurists (ICJ). 2009. *Assessing Damage, Urgent Action: Report of the Eminent Jurists Panel on Terrorism, Counter-terrorism and Human Rights.* Geneva: ICJ

International Work Group for Indigenous Affairs (IWGIA). 1998. "First African Indigenous Women's Conference: Sharing Knowledge, Experience and Strength." In *The Indigenous World 1997–1998.* Copenhagen: IWGIA.

———. 1999. "A New Millennium, A New Alliance: The African Indigenous Women's Organisation (AIWO)." In *The Indigenous World 1998–1999.* Copenhagen: IWGIA.

Jackson, Shelly, Lynette Feder, David R. Forde, Robert C. Davis, Christopher D. Maxwell, and Bruce G. Taylor. 2003. *Batterer Intervention Programs: Where Do We Go from Here?* Washington, D.C.: U.S. Department of Justice.

Jacobson, Robin Dale. 2008. *The New Nativism: Proposition 187 and the Debate over Immigration.* Minneapolis: University of Minnesota Press.

Jad, Islah. 2005. "Between Religion and Secularism: Islamist Women of Hamas." In Fereshteh Nouraie-Simone, ed., *On Shifting Ground: Muslim Women in the Global Era.* New York: Feminist Press at the City University of New York.

———. 2006. *Arab Human Development Report 2005: Towards the Rise of Women in the Arab World.* New York: UNDP.

———. 2008. "The Demobilization of the Palestinian Women's Movement in Palestine: From Empowered Active Militants to Powerless and Stateless 'Citizens.'" *MIT Electronic Journal of Middle East Studies* 8 (Spring): 94–111.

Jilani, Hina. 2008. Report of the Special Representative of the Secretary General on the situation of Human Rights Defenders, Human Rights Council 7th session, January 31, 2008. [A/HRC/7/28]

Johnson, Penny. 2008. "'Violence All Around Us': Dilemmas of Global and Local Agendas Addressing Violence Against Palestinian Women, an Initial Intervention." *Cultural Dynamics* 20 (2): 119–31.

Juma, Ali Shaaban. 2007. *Zanzibar Hadi Mwaka 2000.* Zanzibar: Rafiki Publishers.

Kahan, Dan M. 2000. "Gentle Nudges vs. Hard Shoves: Solving the Sticky Norms Problem." *University of Chicago Law Review* 67: 607–45.

Kandiyoti, Deniz. 1988. "Bargaining with Patriarchy." *Gender and Society* 2: 274–89.

———, ed. 1991. *Women, Islam and the State.* Philadelphia: Temple University Press.

———. 1997. "Beyond Beijing: Obstacles and Prospects for the Middle East." In Mahnaz Afkhani and Erika Friedl, eds., *Muslim Women and the Politics of Participation: Implementing the Beijing Platform.* Syracuse, N.Y.: Syracuse University Press.

Kanuha, Valli Kalei. 2005. "Compounding the Triple Jeopardy: Battering in Lesbian of Color Relationships." In Natalie J. Sokoloff and Christina Pratt, eds., *Domestic Violence at the Margins.* New Brunswick, N.J.: Rutgers University Press.

Kapur, Ratna. 2005. *Erotic Justice: Law and the New Politics of Postcolonialism.* New York: Routledge Cavendish.

Karam, Azza M. 1998. *Women, Islamisms, and the State: Contemporary Feminisms in Egypt.* London: Macmillan.

Kaushal, Neeraj, Robert Kaestner, and Cordelia Reimers. 2004. *Backlash: Effects of 9/11 on Muslims and Arabs Living in the U.S.* New York: Columbia School of Social Work.

Keller, Karen. 2006. "Protest Outside, 3 Arrests Inside Jail; Immigration Detention Stirs Strong Feelings." *Bergen County Record*, January 9, L1.

Kenyatta, Jomo. 1962. *Facing Mount Kenya.* New York: Vintage Books.

Kerber, Linda K. 1988. "Separate Spheres, Female Worlds, Woman's Place: The Rhetoric of Women's History." *Journal of American History* 75 (1): 9–37.

Khagram, Sanjeev and Peggy Levitt, eds. 2007. *The Transnational Studies Reader.* New York: Routledge.

Kimambo, N. Isaria and Temu J. Arnold, eds. 1969. *A History of Tanzania.* Nairobi: East African Publishing House

Kinsman, Margaret. 1983. "Beasts of Burden: The Subordination of Southern Tswana Women ca. 1800–1840." *Journal of Southern African Studies* 10 (1): 17–39.

Kipuri, Naomi. 2004. "Female Genital Mutilation." *Indigenous Affairs* 1–2: 22–27.

Klein, Martin and Richard Roberts. 2005. "Gender and Emancipation in French West Africa." In Pamela Scully and Diana Paton, eds., *Gender and Slave Emancipation in the Atlantic World.* Durham, N.C.: Duke University Press.

Knop, Karen. 1994. "Why Rethinking the Sovereign State Is Important for Women's International Human Rights Law." In Rebecca Cook, ed., *Human Rights of Women: National and International Perspectives.* Philadelphia: University of Philadelphia Press.

Kratz, Corinne. 2007. "Seeing Asylum, Debating Values, and Setting Precedents in the 1990s: The Cases of Kassindja and Abanakwah in the United States." In Ylva Hernlund and Bettina Shell-Duncan, eds., *Transcultural Bodies: Female Genital Cutting in Global Context.* New Brunswick, N.J.: Rutgers University Press.

Krieger, Linda Hamilton. 1995. "The Content of Our Categories: A Cognitive Bias Approach to Discrimination and Equal Employment Opportunity." *Stanford Law Review* 47: 1161–1248.

Lacey, Nicola. 2004. "Feminist Legal Theory and the Rights of Women." In Karen Knop, ed., *Gender and Human Rights.* Oxford: Oxford University Press.

Lalami, Laila. 2006. "The Missionary Position." *The Nation*, June 19. http://www.the nation.com/doc/20060619/lalami/, accessed September 20, 2009.

Larsen, Kjersti. 2004. "Change Continuity and Contestation: The Politics of Modern Identities in Zanzibar." In Pat Caplan and Farouk Topan, eds., *Swahili Modernities; Cultures, Politics and Identity on the East African Coast of Africa.* Trenton, N.J.: Africa World Press.

Latin American Studies Association 2007. *Violations Against Freedoms of Inquiry and Expression in Oaxaca de Juárez.* Report by the Fact-Finding Delegation of the Latin American Studies Association the Impact of the 2006 Social Conflict, August 1. Pittsburgh: LASA. http://lasa.international.pitt.edu/news/Documents/LASA-Oax acaDelegationReport.pdf, accessed January 26, 2009.

Latour, Bruno. 1999. "Circulating Reference." In *Pandora's Hope: Essays on the Reality of Science Studies.* Cambridge, Mass.: Harvard University Press.

Lauren, Paul Gordon. 1998. *The Evolution of International Human Rights: Visions Seen.* Philadelphia: University of Pennsylvania Press.

Law, Robin, ed. 1995. *From Slave Trade to Legitimate Commerce: The Commercial Transition in Nineteenth-Century West Africa.* Cambridge: Cambridge University Press.

Lesuuda, Margaret, Anne Resiano and Jecinta Silakan. 1998. "Violence Against the Laikipia Maasai Women." In Angeline Van Achterberg, ed., *Out of the Shadows: The First African Indigenous Women's Conference.* Amsterdam: Netherlands Centre for Indigenous Peoples.

Levitt, Peggy and Sally Engle Merry, eds. 2009a. "Vernacularization in Action: Using Global Women's Human Rights Locally." Special issue of *Global Networks* 9 (4).

———. 2009b. "Vernacularization on the Ground: Local Uses of Global Women's Rights in Peru, China, India and the United States." *Global Networks* 9 (4): 441–61.

Leyva, Solano, Xochitl. 2009. "Nuevos procesos sociales y políticos en América Latina." In Raphael Hoetmer (coordinador), *Repensar la política desde América Latina: política, cultura, democracia radical y mvimientos sociales.* Lima: Programa Democracia y Transformación Global.

Liebst, Flo. 1992. *Zanzibar: History of the Ruins in Mbweni.* Zanzibar: Out of Africa.

Lihamba, Amandina, L. Fulata Moyo, M. M. Mulokozi, L. Naomi Shitemi, and Saida Yahya-Othman, eds. 2007. *Women Writing Africa.* Vol. 3, *The Eastern Region.* Women Writing Africa Project. New York: Feminist Press.

Little, Shannon. 2008. "Challenging Changing Legal Definitions of Family in Same-Sex Domestic Violence." *Hastings Women's Law Journal* 19: 259–79.

Llorente, Elizabeth and Miguel Perez. 2005. "Immigration Crackdown Nets Laborers, Not Terrorists; Meant to Combat Al-Qaida, Raids Snare Latinos Instead." *Bergen County Record*, March 6.

Lockwood, Bert B., ed. 2006. *Women's Rights: A Human Rights Quarterly Reader*. Baltimore: Johns Hopkins University Press.

Lofchie, Michael and Rhys Payne. 1999. "Zanzibar: The Politics of Polarization." Online research paper, Department of Political Science, University of California.

Loimeier, Roman. 2009. *Between Social Skills and Marketable Skills: The Politics of Islamic Education in 20th Century Zanzibar*. Leiden: Brill.

Lutz, Catherine. 2001. *Homefront: A Military City and the American Twentieth Century*. Boston: Beacon Press.

Maasai Women Development Organization (MWEDO). nd. 1 page glossy brochure describing "programs and activities."

———. 2005. "Five Year Strategic Plan 2005–2009." Copy in author's possession.

———. 2006. "Baseline Survey on Pastoralists Education in 3 Districts of Monduli, Kiteto and Simanjiro." Prepared by FAIDA BDS Co. Photocopy in author's possession.

Maathai, Wangari. 2006. *Unbowed: A Memoir*. New York: Knopf.

MacKinnon, Catharine A. 1989. *Toward a Feminist Theory of the State*. Cambridge, Mass.: Harvard University Press.

———. 2000. "Disputing Male Sovereignty: On *United States v. Morrison*." *Harvard Law Review* 114: 135–77.

Magaña, Maurice. 2008. "Articulating Social Networks in a Mexican Social Movement: The Case of the Asamblea Popular de los Pueblos de Oaxaca (APPO) in Oaxaca." Master's paper, Department of Anthropology, University of Oregon, June.

Mahmood, Saba. 2006. "Secularism, Hermeneutics and Empire: The Politics of Islamic Reformation." *Public Culture* 18 (2): 323–47.

———. 2008. "Feminism, Democracy, and Empire: Islam and the War on Terror." In Joan Wallach Scott, ed., *Women's Studies on the Edge*. Durham, N.C.: Duke University Press.

Mahoney, Martha. 1991. "Legal Images of Battered Women: Redefining the Issue of Separation." *Michigan Law Review* 90: 1–94.

Marshall, Sandra. 1997. "Feminists and the State: A Theoretical Exploration." In Cynthia R. Daniels, ed., *Feminists Negotiate the State: The Politics of Domestic Violence*. Lanham, Md.: University Press of America.

Martin, Pamela and Franke Wilme. 2006. "The Movement for Indigenous Rights: Transnational Norms, Networks, and Domestic Politics." Paper presented at the International Studies Association Annual Meeting, San Diego, March 22–25. http://www.allacademic.com//meta/p_mla_apa_research_citation/0/9/8/2/3/pages98236/p98236–1.php, accessed December 14, 2009.

May, Ann. 2002. "Unexpected Migrations: Urban Labor Migration of Rural Youth and Maasai Pastoralists in Tanzania." Ph.D. dissertation, Department of Anthropology, University of Colorado.

May, Ann and Frances Ndipapa Ole Ikayo. 2007. "Wearing Ilkarash: Narratives of Image, Identity and Change Among Maasai Labour Migrants in Tanzania." *Development and Change* 38 (2): 275–98.

McClain, Linda. 2006. *The Place of Families: Fostering Capacity, Equality, and Responsibility.* Cambridge, Mass.: Harvard University Press.

McCormack, Carol. 1980. "Proto-Social to Adult: A Sherbro Transformation." In Carol McCormack and Marilyn Strathern, eds., *Nature, Culture, and Gender.* Cambridge: Cambridge University Press.

McKinley, Michelle A. 2009. "Cultural Culprits." *Berkeley Journal of Gender, Law, and Justice* 24 (2).

Meintjes, Sheila, Anu Pillay, and Meredeth Turshen. 2002. *The Aftermath: Women in Post-Conflict Transformation.* London: Zed Books.

Mernissi, Fatima. 1975. *Beyond the Veil: Male and Female Dynamics in a Modern Muslim Society.* New York: Wiley.

———. 2005. "The Satellite, the Prince, and Scheherazade: Women as Communicators in Digital Islam." In Fereshteh Nouraie-Simone, ed., *On Shifting Ground: Muslim Women in the Global Era.* New York: Feminist Press at the City University of New York.

Merry, Sally Engle. 1995. "Resistance and the Cultural Power of Law." *Law and Society Review* 29: 11–26.

———. 1998. "Law, Culture and Cultural Appropriation." *Yale Journal of Law and Humanities* 10: 575–603.

———. 2006. *Human Rights and Gender Violence: Translating International Law into Local Justice.* Chicago: University of Chicago Press.

Mezey, Naomi. 2001. "Law as Culture." *Yale Journal of Law and Humanities* 13: 35–67.

Miccio, G. Kristian. 2005. "A House Divided: Mandatory Arrest, Domestic Violence, and the Conservatization of the Battered Women's Movement." *Houston Law Review* 42: 237–323.

Middleton, John. 1961. *Land Tenure in Zanzibar.* Colonial Research Studies 33. London: H.M.S.O.

Midgley, Clare. 1992. *Women Against Slavery: The British Campaigns 1780–1870.* London: Routledge.

Mikell, Gwendolyn. 1997. *African Feminism: The Politics of Survival in Sub-Saharan Africa.* Philadelphia: University of Pennsylvania Press.

Miller, Geoffrey. 2002. "Circumcision: A Legal-Cultural Analysis." *Virginia Journal of Social Policy and the Law* 9: 498–585.

Mills, Linda G. 2003. *Insult to Injury: Rethinking Our Responses to Intimate Abuse.* Princeton, N.J.: Princeton University Press.

Minde, Henry. 1996. "The Making of an International Movement of Indigenous Peoples." *Scandinavian Journal of History* 21: 221–46.

Minow, Martha. 1987. "Interpreting Rights: An Essay for Robert Cover." *Yale Law Journal* 96: 1860–1915.

Mirza, Sara and Strobel, Margaret. 1989. *Three Swahili Women: Life Histories from Mombasa, Kenya.* Bloomington: Indiana University Press.

Mitchell, William P. 1991. *Peasants on the Edge: Crop, Cult and Crisis in the Andes.* Berkeley: University of California Press.

——. 2006. *Voices from the Global Margin: Confronting Poverty and Inventing New Lives in the Andes*. Austin: University of Texas Press.

Moghadam, Valentine M. 2005. *Globalizing Women: Transnational Feminist Networks*. Baltimore: Johns Hopkins University Press.

Moll, Yasmin. 2004. "Iman Bibars: Feminist, Founder of ADEW." *Egypt Today*, September. http://www.egypttoday.com/article.aspx?ArticleID-2274, accessed January 26, 2009.

Moran, Mary H. 1989. "Collective Action and the 'Representation' of African Women: A Liberian Case Study." *Feminist Studies* 15 (3): 443–60.

Morgan, Jennifer. 2004. *Laboring Women: Reproduction and Gender in New World Slavery*. Philadelphia: University of Pennsylvania Press.

Moustafa, Tamir. 2000. "Conflict and Cooperation Between the State and Religious Institutions in Contemporary Egypt." *International Journal of Middle East Studies* 32 (1): 3–22.

Movimiento Flora Tristán. 2003. *Violencia familiar y sexual: diagnóstico sobre servicios de atenección*. Lima: Movimiento Flora Tristán.

Mulenkei, Lucy. 1999a. "The African Indigenous Women's Organisation." *Indigenous Affairs* 2: 42–43.

——. 1999b. "A Voice at Last for the African Indigenous Women." *Indigenous Affairs* 2: 10–11.

Mutua, Makau. 2002. *Human Rights: A Political and Cultural Critique*. Philadelphia: University of Pennsylvania Press.

Mvungi, Sengodo. 2005. "Constitutional Development in Tanzania in 2002." In Fredrick W. Juuko, ed., *Constitutionalism in East Africa: Progress, Challenges and Prospects in 2002*. Kituo cha Katiba: East African Centre for Constitutional Development; Kampala: Fountain Publishers.

Najmabadi, Afsaneh 1998. "Crafting an Educated Housewife in Iran." In Lila Abu-Lughod, ed., *Remaking Women: Feminism and Modernity in the Middle East*. Princeton, N.J.: Princeton University Press.

Napoli, Fatma Jiddawi and Mohammed Ahmed Saleh. 2005. "The Role of Sexual Violence Against Zanzibari Women in the Human Rights Conflict with Tanzania over Sovereignty." In Faye V. Harrison, ed., *Resisting Racism and Xenophobia: Global Perspectives on Race, Gender and Human Rights*. Lanham, Md.: Alta Mira Press.

Narayan, Uma. 1997. *Dislocating Cultures: Identities, Traditions and Third World Feminisms*. New York: Routledge.

National Network for Immigrant and Refugee Rights (NNIRR). 2008. "Guilty by Immigration Status: A Report on U.S. Violations of the Rights of Immigrant Families, Workers and Communities in 2008." http://www.nnirr.org/hurricane/Guiltyby ImmigrationStatus2008.pdf/, accessed December 21, 2009.

Nedelsky, Jennifer. 1989. "Reconceiving Autonomy: Sources, Thoughts and Possibilities." *Yale Journal of Law and Feminism* 1: 7–36.

Nelson, Cynthia. 1996. *Doria Shafik, Egyptian Feminist: A Woman Apart*. Cairo: American University in Cairo Press.

Nelson, Diane. 2009. "Horror's Special Effects." *Reckoning: The Ends of War in Guatemala*. Durham, N.C.: Duke University Press.

New Jersey Civil Rights Defense Committee (NJCRDC). 2004. *Detainee Newsletter: Inside the Jails*, October 7. http://www.nj-civilrights.org/detaineenews/Vol1Issue1. pdf, accessed February 8, 2010.

———. 2006. *Thirty Five Passaic County Immigration Detainees Demand to be Released, not Transferred*. http://www.nj-civilrights.org/index.php?content=statements, accessed February 8, 2010.

———. 2007. *Voices of the Disappeared: An Investigative Report of New Jersey Immigrant Detention*. http://www.nj-civilrights.org/, accessed February 4, 2010.

Newton, Linda. 2008. *Illegal, Alien or Immigrant: The Politics of Immigration Reform*. New York: New York University Press.

Nnaemeka, Obioma. 2005. "African Women, Colonial Discourses, and Imperialist Interventions: Female Circumcision as Impetus." In Obioma Nnaemeka, ed., *Female Circumcision and the Politics of Knowledge*. Westport, Conn.: Praeger.

"No More Jail Time for Zanzibar's Young Mothers." 2005. *Sapa-AFP*, January 26. 05:03 available at http://home.globalfrontiers.com/Zanzibar/zanzibar_news.htm, February 9, 2005.

Nopper, Tamara K. 2008. "What Black Immigrants Matter: Refocusing the Discussion on Racism and Immigration Enforcement." In David C. Brotherton and Philip Kretsedemas, eds., *Keeping Out the Other: A Critical Introduction to Immigration Enforcement Today*. New York: Columbia University Press.

Nouraie-Simone, Fereshteh, ed. 2005. *On Shifting Ground: Muslim Women in the Global Era*. New York: Feminist Press at the City University of New York.

Nussbaum, Martha. 2000. *Women and Human Development: The Capabilities Approach*. Cambridge: Cambridge University Press.

Obiora, L. Amede. 1997. "Little Foxes That Spoil the Vine: Revisiting the Feminist Critique of Female Circumcision." *Canadian Journal of Women and the Law* 9 (1): 46–73.

Office of the High Commissioner on Human Rights (OHCHR). 2004. Fact Sheet 29: Protecting the Right to Defend Human Rights. Geneva: OHCHR

Office of the Inspector General, Department of Homeland Security. 2006. "Treatment of Immigration Detainees Housed at Immigration and Customs Enforcement Facilities." OIG-07–01. http://www.dhs.gov/xoig/index.shtm/, accessed December 21, 2009.

Okome, Mojubaolu Olufunke. 2003. "What Women, Whose Development? A Critical Analysis of Reformist Evangelism." In Oyeronke Oyewumi, ed., *African Women & Feminism*. Trenton, N.J.: Africa World Press.

Olekina, Ledama. 2005. "Maasai Women Speak Out. FGM: Why International Attempts to Stop Female Circumcision Are Putting Maasai Women at Even Greater Risk." *Cultural Survival Quarterly* (Winter): 21–23.

Oloka-Onyango, J. Olaka. 2002. "Modern-Day Missionaries or Misguided Miscreants? NGOs, the Women's Movement and the Promotion of Human Rights in Africa." In Wolfgang Benedek, Esther M. Kisaakye and Gerd Oblerleitner, eds., *Human Rights of Women: International Instruments and African Experiences*. London: Zed Books.

Oyewumi, Oyeronke. 2002. "Conceptualizing Gender: The Eurocentric Foundations of Feminist Concepts and The Challenge Of African Epistemologies." *Jenda: A Journal of Culture and African Women Studies* 2 (1). http://www.jendajournal.com/vol2.1/oyewumi.html

———. 2003. "The White Woman's Burden: African Women in Western Discourse." In Oyeronke Oyewumi, ed., *African Women & Feminism*. Trenton, N.J.: Africa World Press.

Páez, Ángel 2006 "Elections-Peru: Voting for the Accused." Inter Press Service News Agency http://ipsnews.net/print.asp?idnews=33347, accessed December 5, 2009.

Parkipuny, Moringe. 1989. "The Human Rights Situation of Indigenous Peoples in Africa." Address to the Sixth Session of the UN Working Group on Indigenous Populations. Geneva, August 3. Full text: http://www.cwis.org/fwj/22/hra.htm, accessed October 19, 2001.

Parrenas, Rachel S. 2003. "The Care Crisis in the Philippines: Children and Transnational Families in the New Global Economy." In Barbara Ehrenreich and Arlie Russell Hochschild, eds., *Global Woman: Nannies, Maids, and Sex Workers in the New Economy*. New York: Henry Holt.

Paton, Diana. 2004. *No Bond But the Law: Punishment, Race, and Gender in Jamaican State Formation, 1780–1870*. Durham, N.C.: Duke University Press.

Paton, Diana and Pamela Scully, 2005. "Introduction." In Pamela Scully and Diana Paton, eds., *Gender and Slave Emancipation in the Atlantic World*. Durham, N.C.: Duke University Press.

Pearce, Francis Barrow. 1967 [1921]. *Zanzibar, the Island Metropolis of Eastern Africa*. London: Frank Cass.

Peters, Julie and Andrea Wolper, eds. 1995. *Women's Rights, Human Rights: International Feminist Perspectives*. New York: Routledge.

Pickthall, Mohammed Marmaduke, trans. 1973. *The Meaning of the Glorious Qur'an*. Cairo: Dar al Kitab al Masri.

Poole, Deborah. 2004. "Between Threat and Guarantee: Justice and Community on the Margins of the Peruvian State." In Deborah Poole and Veena Das, eds., *Anthropology in the Margins of the State*. Santa Fe, N.M.: School of American Research.

———. 2007a. "Political Autonomy and Cultural Diversity in the Oaxaca Rebellion." *Anthropology News* 48 (3): 10–11.

———. 2007b. "The Right to Be Heard." *Socialism and Democracy* 21 (2): 1113–16.

Poole, Deborah and Gerardo Rénique. 1992. *Peru: Time of Fear*. London: Latin American Bureau.

Post, Robert. 2003. "Law and Cultural Conflict." *Chicago-Kent Law Review* 78: 485–508.

Postero, Nancy. 2006. *Now We Are Citizens: Indigenous Politics in Postmulticultural Bolivia*. Stanford, Calif.: Stanford University Press.

Ptacek, James. 1999. *Battered Women in the Courtroom*. Boston: Northeastern University Press.

Rajupt, Nazlin Omar. 2004–5. *Nur* 1, 1 (December–March): 6, chap 9.

Ramos, Maria D. and Michael W. Runner. 1999. *Cultural Considerations in Domestic Violence Cases: A National Judges Benchbook*. San Francisco: Family Violence Prevention Fund.

Raphael, Jody. 2003. "Battering Through the Lens of Class." *American University Journal of Gender, Social Policy and the Law* 11: 367–75.

Razack, Sherene. 2007. "'Sharia Law Debate' in Ontario: The Modernity/Premodernity Distinction in Legal Efforts to Protect Women from Culture." *Feminist Legal Studies* 15 (1): 3–32.

Real, Mary Jane N. and Michael Chai, eds. 2006. *Resource Book on the International Consultation of Women Human Rights Defenders*. Chiangmai: APWLD

Redfield, Peter. 2006. "A Less Modest Witness: Collective Advocacy and Motivated Truth in a Medical Humanitarian Movement" *American Ethnologist* 33 (1): 3–26.

Reinelt, Claire. 1995. "Moving onto the Terrain of the State: The Battered Women's Movement and the Politics of Engagement." In Myra Marx Ferree and Patricia Yancey Martin, eds., *Feminist Organizations: Harvest of the New Women's Movement*. Philadelphia: Temple University Press.

Rénique, Gerardo. 2007. "Subaltern Political Formation and the Struggle for Autonomy in Oaxaca" *Socialism and Democracy* 21 (2): 62–73.

Reute, Emily. 1998. *Memoirs of an Arabian Princess from Zanzibar*. Zanzibar: Gallery Publications

Reynaga, Gumercinda. 1996. "Cambios en las relaciones familiares campesinas a partir de la violencia politica y el nuevo rol de la mujer." Documento de Trabajo 75, Serie Talleres 3. Lima: Instituto de Estudios Peruanos.

Rhode, Deborah L. and Carol Sanger, eds. 2005. *Gender and Rights*. Hants: Ashgate.

Risse, Thomas, Stephen C. Ropp and Kathryn Sikkink, eds. 1999. *The Power of Human Rights: International Norms and Domestic Change*. Cambridge: Cambridge University Press.

Rivera, Jenny. 1998. "Intimate Partner Violence Strategies: Models for Community Participation." *Maine Law Review* 50: 283–306.

Roberts, Dorothy E. 1991. "Punishing Drug Addicts Who Have Babies: Women of Color, Equality, and the Right of Privacy." *Harvard Law Review* 104: 1419–82.

———. 1999. "Why Culture Matters to Law: The Difference Politics Makes." In Austin Sarat and Thomas R. Kearns, eds., *Cultural Pluralism, Identity Politics, and the Law*. Ann Arbor: University of Michigan Press.

Roberts, Richard. 2005. *Litigants and Households: African Disputes and Colonial Courts in the French Soudan, 1895–1912*. Portsmouth: Heinemann.

Robertson, Claire and Martin Klein, eds. 1983. *Women and Slavery in Africa*. Madison: University of Wisconsin Press.

Robertson, Geoffrey. 2006. *Crimes Against Humanity: The Struggle for Global Justice*. 3rd ed. London: Penguin.

Römkens, Renée. 2001. "Law as a Trojan Horse: Unintended Consequences of Rights-Based Interventions to Support Battered Women." *Yale Journal of Law and Feminism* 13: 265–90.

Rosen, Lawrence. 2006. *Law as Culture*. Princeton, N.J.: Princeton University Press.

Rubin, Jeffrey. 1997. *Decentering the Regime: Ethnicity, Radicalism, and Democracy in Juchitán, Mexico*. Durham, N.C.: Duke University Press.

Russell-Brown, Sherrie L. 2003. "Rape as an Act of Genocide." *Berkeley Journal of International Law* 21(2): 350–74.

Saibull, Agnes Sestha. 1998. "Violence Against Women by the Larusa-Maasai." In Angeline Van Achterberg, ed., *Out of the Shadows: The First African Indigenous Women's Conference*. Amsterdam: Netherlands Centre for Indigenous Peoples.

Sakr, Naomi. 2004. "Friend or Foe? Dependency Theory and Women's Media Activism in the Arab Middle East." *Critique: Critical Middle Eastern Studies* 13 (2): 153–74.

Salvatore, Armando. 1999. "Global Influences and Discontinuities in a Religious Tradition: Public Islam and the 'New' Shari'a." In Katja Füllberg-Stolberg, Petra Heidrich, and Ellinor Schöne, eds., *Dissociation and Appropriation Responses to Globalization in Asia and Africa*. Berlin: Arabische Buch.

Sangtin Collective. 2006. *Playing with Fire: Feminist Thought and Activism Through Seven Lives in India*. Minneapolis: University of Minnesota Press.

Saperstein, Pamela. 2005. "Teen Dating Violence: Eliminating Statutory Barriers to Civil Protection Orders." *Family Law Quarterly* 39: 181–96.

Sarat, Austin D. 2000. "Redirecting Legal Scholarship in Law Schools." *Yale Journal of Law and Humanities* 12: 129–50.

Saugestad, Sidsel. 2001. *The Inconvenient Indigenous: Remote Area Development in Botswana, Donor Assistance, and the First People of the Kalahari*. Uppsala: Nordic Africa Institute.

Schafran, Lynn Hecht. 1990. "Overwhelming Evidence: Reports on Gender Bias in the Courts. *Trial* 26 (February): 28–35.

——. 1995. "There's No Accounting for Judges." *Albany Law Review* 58: 1063–85.

Schechter, Susan. 1982. *Women and Male Violence*. Boston: South End Press.

Schmidt, Elizabeth. 1992. *Peasants, Traders and Wives: Shona Women in the History of Zimbabwe, 1870–1939*. Portsmouth: Heinemann.

Schmidt, Janell D. and Lawrence W. Sherman. 1996. "Does Arrest Deter Domestic Violence?" In Eve S. Buzawa and Carl G. Buzawa, eds., *Do Arrests and Restraining Orders Work?* Thousand Oaks, Calif.: Sage.

Schneider, Elizabeth M. 2000. *Battered Women and Feminist Lawmaking*. New Haven, Conn.: Yale University Press.

——. 2004. "Transnational Law as a Domestic Resource: Thoughts on the Case of Women's Rights." *New England Law Review* 38: 689–723.

Schneider, Leander. 2006. "The Maasai's New Clothes: A Developmentalist Modernity and its Exclusions." *Africa Today* 53 (1): 100–131.

Schuler, Margaret, ed. 1995. *From Basic Needs to Basic Rights: Women's Claim to Human Rights*. Washington, D.C.: Women, Law and Development International.

Schulz, Dorothea. 2005. "Promises of (Im)mediate Salvation: Islam, Broadcast Media, and the Remaking of Religious Experience in Mali." *American Ethnologist* 33 (2): 210–29.

Schumer, Tanja. 2008. *New Humanitarianism: Britain and Sierra Leone, 1997–2003*. Houndsmill: Palgrave Macmillan.

Scully, Pamela. 1997. *Liberating the Family? Gender and British Slave Emancipation in the Rural Western Cape, South Africa, 1823–1853*. Portsmouth: Heinemann.

———. 2009a. "Vulnerable Women: A Critical Reflection on Human Rights Discourse and Sexual Violence." *Emory International Law Review* 23 (1): 112–24.

———. 2009b. "Gender Based Violence and the Vulnerable Woman." Paper delivered at Conference on Violence and Vulnerability, Emory University, November.

Scully, Pamela and Erin McCandless, eds. 2010. *Gender Violence and Gender Justice*. Special Issue, *Journal of Peacebuilding and Development* 5 (3).

Sekaggya, Margaret. 2009. Report of the Special Rapporteur on the situation of human rights defenders, Human Rights Council 10th session, March 4, 2009. [A/HRC/10/12/Add.1]

Shalhoub-Kevorkian, Nadera. 2004a. "Conceptualizing Voices of the Oppressed in Conflict Areas." In Khawla Abu-Baker, ed., *Women, Armed Conflict and Loss: The Mental Health of Palestinian Women in the Occupied Territories*. Jerusalem: Women's Studies Centre.

———. 2004b. "The Hidden Casualties of War: Palestinian Women and the Second Intifada." *Indigenous People's Journal of Law, Culture, and Resistance* 1 (1): 67–82.

———. 2005a. "Counter-Spaces as Resistance in Conflict Zones: Palestinian Women Recreating a Home." *Journal of Feminist Family Therapy* 17 (3/4): 109–41.

———. 2005b. "Voice Therapy for Women Aligned with Political Prisoners: A Case Study of Trauma Among Palestinian Women in the Second Intifada." *Social Service Review* 79 (2): 322–43.

———. 2009. *Militarization and Violence Against Women in Conflict Zones in the Middle East: A Palestinian Case-Study*. New York: Cambridge University Press.

Sharma, Maya. 2006. *Loving Women: Being Lesbian in Unprivileged India*. New Delhi: Yoda Press.

Shaw, Rosalind. 2005. *Rethinking Truth and Reconciliation Commissions: Lessons from Sierra Leone*. Washington, D.C.: U.S. Institute of Peace.

Shehabuddin, Elora. 2008. *Reshaping the Holy: Democracy, Development, and Muslim Women in Bangladesh*. New York: Columbia University Press.

Sheikh, Irum. 2008. "Racializing, Criminalizing, and Silencing 9/11 Deportees." In David C. Brotherton and Philip Kretsedemas, eds., *Keeping Out the Other: A Criti-*

cal Introduction to Immigration Enforcement Today. New York: Columbia University Press.

Shell-Duncan, Bettina. 2001. "The Medicalization of Female 'Circumcision': Harm Reduction or Promotion of a Dangerous Practice?" *Social Science and Medicine* 52: 1013–28.

———. 2008. "From Health to Human Rights: Female Genital Cutting and the Politics of Intervention." *American Anthropologist* 110 (2): 225–36.

Shell-Duncan, Bettina and Ylva Hernlund, eds. 2000. *Female "Circumcision" in Africa: Culture, Controversy, and Change.* Boulder, Colo.: Lynn Rienner.

Shivji, Issa G. 1989. *The Concept of Human Rights in Africa.* London: Codesria Book Series.

———. 1990. *The Legal Foundations of the Union of Tanganyika and Zanzibari.* Dar es Salaam: Dar es Salaam University Press

Siegel, Reva B. 1996. "'The Rule of Love': Wife Beating as Prerogative and Privacy." *Yale Law Journal* 105: 2117–2207.

Sikar, Ndinini Kimesera and Dorothy L. Hodgson. 2006. "In the Shadow of the MDGs: Pastoralist Women and Children in Tanzania." In *Africa and the Millennium Development Goals*, Special issue, *Indigenous Affairs* 1 (6): 30–37.

Silbey, Susan S. 1992. "Making a Place for Cultural Analyses of Law." *Law and Social Inquiry* 17: 39–48.

Silverblatt, Irene. 1987. *Moon, Sun, and Witches: Gender Ideologies and Class in Inca and Colonial Peru.* Princeton, N.J.: Princeton University Press.

Simanjiro District Report. 2005. Photocopy of sections in author's possession.

Simat, Mary. 1999. "The Situation of the Maasai Women." *Indigenous Affairs* 2: 38–39.

Singerman, Diane. 2005. "Rewriting Divorce in Egypt: Reclaiming Islam, Legal Activism, and Coalition Politics." In Robert W. Hefner, ed., *Remaking Muslim Politics: Pluralism, Contestation, Democratization.* Princeton, N.J.: Princeton University Press.

Sjorslev, Inger. 1998. "Epilogue: Women, Gender Studies and the International Indigenous Movement." In Diana Vinding, ed., *Indigenous Women: The Right to a Voice.* Copenhagen: International Work Group on Indigenous Affairs.

Skalli, Loubna. 2006. "Communicating Gender in the Public Sphere: Women and Information Technologies in the MENA Region." *Journal of Middle East Women's Studies* 2 (2): 35–59.

Sklar, Katherine Kish, and James Brewer Stewart, eds. 2007. *Women's Rights and Transatlantic Antislavery in the Era of Emancipation.* New Haven, Conn.: Yale University Press.

Slyomovics, Susan. 2005. *The Performance of Human Rights in Morocco.* Philadelphia: University of Pennsylvania Press.

Smith, Michael L. 1992. *Entre dos fuegos: ONG, desarrollo rural y violencia política.* Lima: Instituto de Estudios Peruanos.

Snow, Keith Harmon. 2007. "Three Cheers for Eve Ensler?" www.zmag.org http://www

.allthingspass.com/uploads/html-230THREE%20CHEERS%20for%20Eve%20
ENSLER%5B8%5D.htm, October 4, accessed December 8, 2009.

Sokoloff, Natalie J., and Christina Pratt, eds. 2005. *Domestic Violence at the Margins.*
New Brunswick, N.J: Rutgers University Press.

Speed, Shannon. 2005. "Dangerous Discourses: Human Rights and Multiculturalism in
Neoliberal Mexico." *Political and Legal Anthropology Review* 28 (1): 29–50.

———. 2007. "Exercising rights and reconfiguring resistance in the Zapatista Juntas
de Buen Gobierno." In Mark Goodale and Sally Engle Merry, eds., *The Practice of
Human Rights: Tracking Law Between the Global and the Local.* Cambridge: Cambridge University Press.

Speed, Shannon and Jane Collier. 2000. "Limiting Indigenous Autonomy in Chiapas,
Mexico: The State Government's Use of Human Rights." *Human Rights Quarterly*
22: 877–905.

Spencer, Robert, and Phyllis Chesler. 2007. *The Violent Oppression of Women in Islam.*
Los Angeles: David Horowitz Freedom Center.

Spivak, Gayatri Chakravorty. 1988. "Can the Subaltern Speak?" In Cary Nelson and
Lawrence Grossberg, eds., *Marxism and the Interpretation of Culture.* Urbana: University of Illinois Press.

Stark, Evan. 2007. *Coercive Control: The Entrapment of Women in Personal Life.* Oxford:
Oxford University Press.

Starn, Orin. 1995. "Maoism in the Andes: The Communist Party of Peru-Shining Path
and the Refusal of History." *Journal of Latin American Studies* 27 (2): 399–421.

———. 1998. "Villagers at Arms: War and Counterrevolution in the Central-South
Andes." In Steve J. Stern, ed., *Shining and Other Paths: War and Society in Peru,
1980–1995.* Durham, N.C.: Duke University Press.

———. 1999. *Nightwatch: The Politics of Protest in the Andes.* Durham, N.C.: Duke University Press.

Stavenhagen, Rodolfo. 1995. "Indigenous Peoples: Emerging Actors in Latin America."
In Ralph Esbach, ed., *Ethnic Conflict and Governance in Comparative Perspective.*
Washington, D.C.: Woodrow Wilson International Center for Scholars.

Steans, Jill. 2007. "Debating women's human rights as a universal feminist project: defending women's human rights as a political tool." *Review of International Studies*
33 (1): 11–27.

Stephen, Lynn. 2002. *Zapata Lives! Histories and Cultural Politics in Southern Mexico.*
Berkeley: University of California Press.

———. 2007. "'We are brown, we are short, we are fat . . . We are the face of Oaxaca':
Women Leaders in the Oaxaca Rebellion." *Socialism and Democracy* 21 (2): 97–112.

Stiglmeyer, Alexander. 1994. *Mass Rape: The War on Women in Bosnia-Herzegovina.*
Lincoln: University of Nebraska Press.

Strathern, Marilyn. 1988. *The Gender of the Gift: Problems with Women and Problems with
Society in Melanesia.* Berkeley: University of California Press.

Strobel, Margaret. 1979. *Muslim Women in Mombasa 1890–1975*. New Haven, Conn.:
  Yale University Press.
——. 1989. *Three Swahili Women*. Bloomington: Indiana University Press.
Suk, Jeannie. 2006. "Criminal Law Comes Home." *Yale Law Journal* 116: 2–70.
Sussman, Erika A. 2006. "The Civil Protection Order as a Tool for Economic Justice."
  Advocate's Quarterly 3: 1–7.
Swyngedouw, Erik. 1997. "Neither Global Nor Local: 'Glocalization" and the Politics of
  Scale." In Kevin Cox, ed., *Spaces of Globalization*. New York: Guilford.
Sylvain, Renée. 2002. "'Land, Water and Truth': San Identity and Global Indigenism."
  American Anthropologist 104 (4): 1074–85.
Theidon, Kimberly. 1999. "Domesticando la violencia: el alcohol y las secuelas de la
  guerra." *Ideele* 120 (July).
——. 2003. "Disarming the Subject: Remembering War and Imagining Citizenship in
  Peru." *Cultural Critique* 54: 67–87.
Thomas, Chris. 2006. *Oaxaca: The Beating Heart in Mexico's Crises of Legitimacy*. San
  Cristóbal de las Casas: Chiapas Peace House. http://www.chiapaspeacehouse.org/
  node/323, accessed November 9, 2008.
Thomas, Lynn. 1998. "Imperial Concerns and Women's Affairs: State Efforts to Regulate
  Clitoridectomy and Eradicate Abortion in Meru Kenya, 1910–1950." *Journal of Af-
  rican History* 39 (1): 121–45.
——. 2003. *The Politics of the Womb: Women, Reproduction and the State in Kenya*.
  Berkeley: University of California Press.
Thurner, Mark. 1997. *From Two Republics to One Divided: Contradictions of Postcolonial
  Nationmaking in Andean Peru*. Durham, N.C.: Duke University Press.
Topan, Farouk. 2004. "From Mwana Kupona to Mwamvita: Representations of Female Status
  in Swahili Literature" In Pat Caplan and Farouk Topin, eds., *Swahili Modernities: Cultures,
  Politics and Identity on the East African Coast of Africa*. London: Africa World Press.
Tracy, Carol, Terry Fromson, and Dabney Miller. 2006. "Justice in the Domestic Rela-
  tions Division of Philadelphia Family Court: A Report to the Community." In Joan
  Zorza, ed., *Violence Against Women*. Kingston, N.J.: Civic Research Institute.
United Nations Egypt (UN/E). 2006. "United Nations Development Assistance Frame-
  work 2007–2011 Egypt"; "Moving in the Spirit of the Millennium Declaration:
  The DNA of Progress." March 28. http://planipolis.iiep.unesco.org/upload/Egypt/
  Egypt%20UNDAF%202007–2011.pdf, accessed May 21.
UN Human Rights Council. 2009. "Human Rights in Palestine and Other Occupied
  Arab Territories: Report of the United Nations Fact Finding Mission on the Gaza
  Conflict." http://www2.ohchr.org/english/bodies/hrcouncil/specialsession/9/docs/
  UNFFMGC_Report.pdf, accessed September 27.
United Republic of Tanzania (URT). 2006. Millennium Development Goals, United Re-
  public of Tanzania. Progress Report 2006. Ministry of Planning, Economy and Em-
  powerment. Available online at http://www.tz.undp.org/docs/MDGprogressreport
  .pdf, accessed February 14, 2007.

Van Achterberg, Angeline, ed. 1998. *Out of the Shadows: The First African Indigenous Women's Conference*. Amsterdam: Netherlands Centre for Indigenous Peoples.

Van Wolputte, Steven. 2004. "Hang on to Your Self: Of Bodies, Embodiment and Selves." *Annual Review of Anthropology* 33: 251–269.

Voices of Women Organizing Project and Human Rights Project of the Urban Justice Center. 2008. *Justice Denied: How Family Courts in NYC Endanger Battered Women and Children*. Brooklyn, N.Y.: Battered Women's Resource Center.

Volpp, Leti. 2001. "Feminism Versus Multiculturalism." *Columbia Law Review* 101: 1181–1218.

———. 2003. "On Culture, Difference, and Domestic Violence." *American University Journal of Gender, Social Policy and the Law* 11: 393–99.

Wadud, Amina. 1999. *Qur'an and Woman: Rereading the Scared Texts from a Woman's Perspective*. Oxford: Oxford University Press.

Walker, Cherryl, ed. 1990. *Women and Gender in Southern Africa to 1945*. Cape Town: David Philip.

Walker, Lenore E. 1979. *The Battered Woman*. New York: Harper & Row.

———. 1984. *The Battered Woman Syndrome*. New York: Springer.

Wallace-Sanders, Kimberly. 2008. *Mammy: A Century of Race, Gender, and Southern Memory*. Ann Arbor: University of Michigan Press.

Walley, Christine J. 1997. "Searching for 'Voices': Feminism, Anthropology, and the Global Debate over Female Genital Operations." *Cultural Anthropology* 12 (3): 405–38.

———. n.d. "What We Women Want: An Ethnography of Transnational Feminism." Manuscript.

Warsame, Aamina, Sadiya Ahmed, and Aud Talle. 1985. "Social and Cultural Aspects of Female Circumcision and Infibulation: A Preliminary Report." Somali Academy of Sciences and Arts and Swedish Agency for Research Cooperation with Developing Countries.

Waslin, Michele. 2003. *Counterterrorism and the Latino Community Since September 11*. Washington, D.C.: National Council of La Raza.

Williams, Patricia J. 1991. *The Alchemy of Race and Rights*. Cambridge, Mass.: Harvard University Press.

Wilson, Richard Ashby. 1996. "Introduction: Human Rights, Culture and Context." In Richard A. Wilson, ed., *Human Rights, Culture and Context: Anthropological Perspectives*. London: Pluto Press.

———. 2006. Afterword to "Anthropology and Human Rights in a New Key." *American Anthropologist* 108 (1): 77–83.

———. 2007. "Tyrannosaurus Lex: The Anthropology of Human Rights and Transnational Law." In Mark Goodale and Sally Engle Merry, eds., *The Practice of Human Rights: Tracking Law Between the Global and the Local*. Cambridge: Cambridge University Press.

Wiseman, Sue. 2004. "Abolishing Romance: Representing Rape in Oroonoko." In Bryccan Carey, Markman Ellis, and Sarah Salih, eds., *Discourses of Slavery and Abolition: Britain and Its Colonies, 1760–1838*. Houndsmills: Palgrave Macmillan

Women Living Under Muslim Laws (WLUML). 2007. The Global Campaign "Stop Stoning and Killing Women!" Concept paper. http://wluml.org/english/news/stop_stoning_and_killing_women%20_concept_paper.pdf, accessed September 24, 2009.

Wriggins, Jennifer. 2001. "Domestic Violence Torts." *Southern California Law Review* 75: 121–84.

Yezer, Caroline. 2005. "Patriotic Peasants and Narco-Terrorists: Legacies of Peru's Dirty War in the War on Drugs." *Anthropology Newsletter* (March): 37–38.

———. 2007. *Anxious Citizenship: Insecurity, Apocalypse and War Memories in Peru's Andes*. Ph.D. Dissertation, Department of Cultural Anthropology, Duke University.

———. 2008. "Who Wants to Know? Rumors, Suspicions, and Opposition to Truth-Telling in Ayacucho." *Latin American and Caribbean Ethnic Studies* 3 (3): 271–89.

Yoshioka, Marianne R. and Deborah Y. Choi. 2005. "Culture and Interpersonal Violence Research." *Journal of Interpersonal Violence* 20: 513–19.

Youngers, Coletta. 2003. *Violencia política y sociedad civil en el Perú: historia de la Coordinadora Nacional de Derechos Humanos*. Lima: Instituto de Estudios Peruanos.

"Zanzibar Minister to Press for Repeal of Repressive Law." 2003. *The Guardian*, Friday, September 12.

Zeghal, Malika. 1999. "Religion and Politics in Egypt: The Ulema of Al-Azhar, Radical Islam, and the State (1952–94)." *International Journal of Middle East Studies* 31 (3): 371–99.

Zinsser, Judith. 2002. "From Mexico, to Copenhagen, to Nairobi: The United Nations Decade for Women, 1975 to 1985." *Journal of World History* 13: 139–68.

Contributors

Lila Abu-Lughod is Joseph L. Buttenwieser Professor of Social Science in the Department of Anthropology and Institute for Research on Women and Gender at Columbia University. She is a former director of IRWAG and now co-directs the Center for the Critical Analysis of Social Difference. An anthropologist who has done extensive fieldwork in Egypt over the past thirty years on women, gender politics, and expressive culture (from poetry to television dramas), she is the author of three award-winning ethnographies: *Veiled Sentiments: Honor and Poetry in a Bedouin Society, Writing Women's Worlds: Bedouin Stories*, and *Dramas of Nationhood: The Politics of Television in Egypt*. She has edited or coedited several important collections including *Language and the Politics of Emotion, Remaking Women: Feminism and Modernity in the Middle East, Media Worlds: Anthropology on New Terrain*, and *Nakba: Palestine, 1948, and the Claims of Memory*. She is completing a book called *Do Muslim Women Need Saving?* that examines the politics and ethics of the transnational circulation of discourses on Muslim women's rights, having carried out the research as a Carnegie Scholar in 2007–2009, with support from ACLS.

Ousseina D. Alidou is Director of the Center for African Studies and Associate Professor in the Department of African, Middle Eastern, and South Asian Languages and Literatures and in the Program in Comparative Literature at Rutgers University, where she is also a graduate faculty affiliate in the Department of Anthropology and Women's and Gender Studies. She is current Chair of the Association of African Studies Programs. She holds a Ph.D. in theoretical linguistics from Indiana University (Bloomington). Her research focuses mainly on the study of women's discourses and literacy practices in Afro-Islamic societies; African (Muslim) women's agency; African women's literatures; and gendered discourses of identity and the politics of cultural production in Francophone African countries. Her current project is on

Kenya Muslim women's discourses on citizenship and human rights. She is
the author of *Engaging Modernity: Muslim Women and the Politics of Agency
in Postcolonial Niger*, a runner-up for the ASA 2007 Women Caucus Ama
Ato Aidoo-Margaret Snyder Book Prize, among other publications.

Sally F. Goldfarb is Professor at Rutgers University School of Law, Camden, where she has received several teaching awards. She has also taught at
Harvard Law School, New York University School of Law, and University
of Pennsylvania Law School. She is a graduate of Yale College and Yale Law
School. Before joining the Rutgers faculty, she was a senior staff attorney at
the NOW Legal Defense and Education Fund (now known as Legal Momentum), where she directed the organization's Family Law Project. While in that
position, she founded and chaired the National Task Force on the Violence
Against Women Act and was instrumental in the drafting and enactment of
the federal Violence Against Women Act of 1994. She is the author of articles
and book chapters on violence against women, family law, and other topics. She has served on state, national and international boards and commissions, including the New Jersey Supreme Court Committee on Women in
the Courts, the Board of Advisers for the American Law Institute Principles
of the Law of Family Dissolution, and the United Nations Division for the
Advancement of Women Expert Group on Violence Against Women.

Dorothy L. Hodgson is Professor and Chair of the Department of Anthropology and former Director of the Institute for Research on Women at Rutgers
University. She is current President of the Association for Feminist Anthropology. As a historical anthropologist, she has worked in Tanzania for over
twenty-five years on such topics as gender, ethnicity, cultural politics, colonialism, nationalism, modernity, the missionary encounter, transnational
organizing, and the indigenous rights movement. She is the author of *Being
Maasai, Becoming Indigenous: Postcolonial Politics in a Neoliberal World*, *The
Church of Women: Gendered Encounters Between Maasai and Missionaries*,
and *Once Intrepid Warriors: Gender, Ethnicity and the Cultural Politics of
Maasai Development*; editor of *Gendered Modernities: Ethnographic Perspectives* and *Rethinking Pastoralism in Africa: Gender, Culture and the Myth of
the Patriarchal Pastoralist*; and coeditor of *Activisms* and *"Wicked" Women
and the Reconfiguration of Gender in Africa*. She is currently completing an
anthrohistorical study of gender justice and collective action in Tanzania and
a book of essays on the ethics and politics of contemporary ethnographic

research. Her work has been supported by awards from the National Endowment for the Humanities, John Simon Guggenheim Memorial Foundation, Fulbright-Hays, American Council for Learned Societies, National Science Foundation, American Philosophical Society, Wenner-Gren Foundation, Social Science Research Council, and Center for Advanced Study in the Behavioral Sciences.

Peggy Levitt is a Professor of Sociology at Wellesley College and a Research Fellow at the Weatherhead Center for International Affairs and the Hauser Center for Nonprofit Organizations at Harvard University where she co-directs the Transnational Studies Initiative. She was Willy Brandt Guest Professor at Malmö University in Spring 2009, a visiting lecturer at the University of Limerick in Fall 2008, and a visiting professor at the University of Bologna during summer 2008. In 2010-2011, she is visiting Fellow at the Vrije University in Amsterdam. She is author of *God Needs No Passport: Immigrants and the Changing American Religious Landscape*, *The Transnational Villagers* and *The Changing Face of Home: The Transnational Lives of the Second Generation* and coeditor (with Sanjeev Khagram) of *The Transnational Studies Reader*. She coordinates the Social Science Research Council working group on religion and globalization and is Co-Principal Investigator on a National Science Foundation project about how global ideas about women's rights are translated in local contexts.

Salma Maoulidi is Executive Director of Sahiba☆Sisters Foundation, a women's development and advocacy network with members in 13 regions of Tanzania concerned with the impact of cultural and religious discourses on women. She received an LLM from Georgetown University with a focus on Human Rights and Women's Law, and has published widely on legal and development issues from an African woman's feminist activist perspective. Her current research interest is documenting the history of women in Zanzibar, with a focus on women's legal, education, and political status over time.

Sally Engle Merry is Professor of Anthropology at New York University. Her work explores the role of law in urban life in the U.S., the colonizing process, and contemporary transnationalism. Her recent books are *Law and Empire in the Pacific: Hawai'i and Fiji* (co-edited with Donald Brenneis), *The Possibility of Popular Justice: A Case Study of American Community Mediation* (co-edited with Neal Milner), *Getting Justice and Getting Even: Legal Consciousness*

Among Working Class Americans, Urban Danger: Life in a Neighborhood of Strangers, Colonizing Hawai'i: The Cultural Power of Law (which received the 2001 J. Willard Hurst Prize from the Law and Society Association), *Human Rights and Gender Violence: Translating International Law into Local Justice, The Practice of Human Rights: Tracking Law Between the Local and the Global* (co-edited with Mark Goodale), and *Gender Violence: A Cultural Perspective.* She is past president of the Law and Society Association and the Association for Political and Legal Anthropology. In 2007 she received the Kalven Prize of the Law and Society Association, an award that recognizes a significant body of scholarship in the field. In 2010, she was awarded the J. I. Staley Prize from the School of Advanced Research for *Human Rights and Gender Violence*, an award "for a book that exemplifies outstanding scholarship and writing in anthropology." She is president-elect of the American Ethnological Society.

Mary Jane N. Real is Coordinator of the International Campaign on Women Human Rights Defenders and a Visiting Global Associate at the Center for Women's Global Leadership at Rutgers University. She has drawn on her training as a lawyer and her master's degree in development studies to work as an international advocate and activist for women's rights for the Asia Pacific Forum on Women, Law and Development (APWLD), Southeast Asia Watch, and the Center for Women and Gender Initiatives, among other organizations. She has also written widely about women's human rights in newspapers, legal briefs, and policy papers.

Robyn M. Rodriguez is Assistant Professor of Sociology and an affiliated faculty member of the Department of Women and Gender Studies at Rutgers University. Her book *Migrants for Export: How the Philippine State Brokers Labor to the World* examines how the neoliberal Philippine state has emerged as a "labor brokerage state" that has reconfigured notions of national belonging and citizenship and developed a transnational bureaucratic apparatus to normalize and facilitate the outmigration of workers and profit from migrants' remittances. She is also interested in Philippine migrant workers' transnational activism. Her work has appeared in academic journals including *Citizenship Studies, Signs, Sociological Forum, Peace Review*, and *Philippine Sociological Review.* She is currently working on a project that examines the local politics of race, immigration, rights, and belonging in New Jersey after 9/11. In addition to her academic work, she has worked actively in the immigrant rights movement in the United States. In 2003, she helped found

FOCUS (Filipino Community Support), a community-based organization serving Filipino immigrant workers in San Jose, California. After moving to the New Jersey/New York area, she served on the board of the Philippine Forum, a community-based organization for Filipino immigrants in Queens, and on the national board of the National Alliance for Filipino Concerns (NAFCON). She also provides support to the New Jersey Civil Rights Defense Committee against the detentions of immigrants in New Jersey's county jails.

Pamela Scully is chair of the Department of Women's Studies and Professor of Women's Studies and African Studies at Emory University. She has published widely on race, gender, and slave emancipation, and more recently on the relevance of history to understanding contemporary international projects to end gender-based violence in post-conflict societies. Her first book was *Liberating the Family? Gender and British Slave Emancipation in the Rural Western Cape South Africa, 1823–1853*. Her most recent book is *Sara Baartman and the Hottentot Venus: A Ghost Story and a Biography* (co-authored with Clifton Crais). She is deputy editor of *Women's History Review*, serves on the boards of *Journal of British Studies*, *Social Dynamics* and *Journal of Women's History*, and works closely with the Institute of Developing Nations, a collaborative research institute between the Carter Center and Emory University. She teaches courses on women's international human rights, feminist theory, and gender, genocide, and justice. Her current project examines international interventions around rape in wartime in the 1990s, and analyzes contemporary government initiatives and international and local development projects to end gender-based violence in conflict and post-conflict societies in Africa.

Lynn Stephen is Distinguished Professor of Anthropology and Ethnic Studies at the University of Oregon. Her work has centered on the intersection of culture and politics. Born in Chicago, she has a particular interest in the ways political identities articulate with ethnicity, gender, class, and nationalism in relation to local, regional, and national histories, cultural politics, and systems of governance in Latin America. During the past ten years she has added the dimension of migration to her research. In May 2009 she launched a digital ethnography, "Making Rights a Reality: the Oaxaca Social Movement, 2006–Present," http://www.mraroaxaca.uoregon.edu/. Her books include *Dissident Women: Gender and Cultural Politics in Chiapas* (co-edited with Aida Hernández Castillo and Shannon Speed), *Zapotec Women: Gen-*

der, Class, and Ethnicity in Globalized Oaxaca, Zapata Lives! Histories and Cultural Politics in Southern Mexico, Perspectives on las Américas: A Reader in Culture, History, and Representation (co-edited with Matt Gutmann, Felix Matos Rodríguez, and Pat Zavella), and *Transborder Lives: Indigenous Oaxacans in Mexico, California, and Oregon.* She is recipient of fellowships from the National Endowment for Humanities, Center for U.S.-Mexican Studies, Radcliffe Institute for Advanced Studies at Harvard University and research grants from the National Science Foundation, Wenner-Gren Foundation, and Inter-American Foundation. Her most recent research focuses on identity formation and political and civic participation among Mexican immigrant youth.

Caroline Yezer teaches anthropology at the College of the Holy Cross in Worcester, Massachusetts, where she teaches on indigenous rights, citizenship, and post-conflict justice. She began her ethnographic fieldwork on war history and village reconciliation in Peru's Ayacucho highlands in 1999. Her research examines indigenous peasants' demands for reparations and security in an era of emerging unfamiliar forms of transnational governance and clandestine drug war violence. She has published on Peru's Truth and Reconciliation Commission and village struggles to control the memory of the dirty war in the *Journal of Latin American and Caribbean Ethnic Studies*, and has received research awards from the Harry Frank Guggenheim Foundation, Wenner-Gren Foundation and U.S. Institute of Peace. Her current research is on the rise of indigenous cultural politics and born-again Christianity among Peru's coca farmers.

Index

Acknowledgments

Most of the chapters in this book were originally presented as part of a weekly seminar or three day symposium on "The Culture of Rights/The Rights of Culture" organized by the Institute for Research on Women (IRW) at Rutgers University in 2008–9, of which I had the tremendous pleasure to serve as director in 2007–10. We are very grateful to the Institute for supporting our work and to the funders who sustain the Institute—the School of Arts and Sciences, the Office of the Executive Vice President, and, for the symposium, the Committee to Advance our Common Purposes. Beth Hutchison (then Associate Director of the IRW) and Marlene Importico (Office Manager) facilitated the work of the seminar and logistics of the symposium with their usual grace, hard work and good humor. All of us also benefited tremendously from the insightful and provocative comments of the symposium discussants, Daniel Goldstein, Mary Hawkesworth, and Indrani Chatterjee; symposium keynote speaker and rapporteur Sally Engle Merry; and participants in the seminar and symposium.